React Native for Mobile Development

Creating Stunning Cross-Platform Mobile Applications with React Native

Third Edition

Abhishek Nalwaya
Akshat Paul

Apress®

React Native for Mobile Development: Creating Stunning Cross-Platform Mobile Applications with React Native, Third Edition

Abhishek Nalwaya
Jaipur, Rajasthan, India

Akshat Paul
Gurugram, Haryana, India

ISBN-13 (pbk): 979-8-8688-2976-5
ISBN-13 (electronic): 979-8-8688-2977-2
https://doi.org/10.1007/979-8-8688-2977-2

Managing Director, Apress Media LLC: Welmoed Spahr
Acquisitions Editor: Miriam Haidara
Coordinating Editor: Marina Engler

Cover image by Rawpixel.com

Distributed to the book trade worldwide by Springer Science+Business Media New York, 1 New York Plaza, New York, NY 10004. Phone 1-800-SPRINGER, fax (201) 348-4505, e-mail orders-ny@springer-sbm.com, or visit www.springeronline.com. Apress Media, LLC is a Delaware LLC and the sole member (owner) is Springer Science + Business Media Finance Inc (SSBM Finance Inc). SSBM Finance Inc is a **Delaware** corporation.

For information on translations, please e-mail booktranslations@springernature.com; for reprint, paperback, or audio rights, please e-mail bookpermissions@springernature.com.

Apress titles may be purchased in bulk for academic, corporate, or promotional use. eBook versions and licenses are also available for most titles. For more information, reference our Print and eBook Bulk Sales web page at http://www.apress.com/bulk-sales.

Any source code or other supplementary material referenced by the author in this book is available to readers on GitHub (https://github.com/Apress). For more detailed information, please visit https://www.apress.com/gp/services/source-code.

If disposing of this product, please recycle the paper

Table of Contents

About the Authors

Abhishek Nalwaya is a technology leader, digital transformation expert, and author of many books on modern engineering and innovation. He serves as Director of Engineering and Head of the Digital Hub for one of the largest retailers in the Middle East, where he drives large-scale digital platforms and customer-centric solutions across markets. Previously, Abhishek was with McKinsey & Company, where he partnered with CXOs across multiple countries to deliver high-impact digital transformation initiatives. His expertise spans customer experience, AI, microservices architecture, DevOps, and data-driven engineering.

A passionate practitioner and educator, he speaks regularly at conferences and conducts workshops on emerging technologies, helping organizations adopt modern architectures and build future-ready solutions.

Akshat Paul is a serial entrepreneur, technology leader, and the author of five books on React Native, AWS Amplify, and Ruby programming. A former consultant at McKinsey & Company, he brings together deep technical expertise and strategic thinking to build enterprise and consumer applications.

Akshat is a frequent speaker at globally recognized tech conferences, including React Universe Conf, React Native EU, DevOps@Scale Amsterdam, and Cross Platform Mobile Summit. He has also delivered keynote talks at technology leadership events across Asia.

Outside of work, he enjoys spending time with his family, reading, and maintaining a healthy lifestyle. Learn more at `www.akshatpaul.com`.

About the Technical Reviewer

Mahesh Haldar is a software architect specializing in distributed systems and AI-native platforms and co-author of *Serverless Web Applications with AWS Amplify* (Apress). With over a decade of experience, he has taken products from zero to scale. As a founding engineer, he helped build Jago, a fully regulated digital bank, and he has architected ecommerce systems at Carrefour, serving tens of millions of requests a day. Earlier in his career, he built banking applications for McKinsey & Company clients across Japan, Mauritius, and South Africa.

Mahesh is now a Software Architect at AVAYL, building an AI-native platform for the medical affairs industry, spanning vision-model pipelines, document tooling, and event-driven back ends. Mahesh is also a technical writer whose articles on API design and web technologies have reached hundreds of thousands of readers, an open-source contributor, and a conference speaker with talks in Bangalore, Johannesburg, and Singapore. He lives in Berlin, Germany.

Acknowledgments

To my family—**Rajendra Nalwaya**, **Saroj Nalwaya**, **Shruti Bolia**, and **Apeksha Nalwaya**—thank you for your constant encouragement, patience, and unwavering faith in me. Your support has been the foundation of every milestone in my journey.

To my son, **Shiven Nalwaya**—may you always embrace curiosity, never stop learning, and pursue your dreams with courage.

To my colleagues and mentors—thank you for challenging me, inspiring me, and making me a better engineer and leader every day.

—Abhishek Nalwaya

I would like to express my heartfelt gratitude to my parents, **Shakuntala Paul** and **Anup Paul**, for their unwavering love, encouragement, and belief in me. Your support has been the foundation of everything I have achieved.

To my wife, **Anu Sharma**—thank you for your endless patience, understanding, and constant encouragement. Over the years, you've supported me through multiple books, projects, and countless late nights of writing and building. This book would not have been possible without you by my side.

Finally, thank you to everyone who has been a part of my journey and contributed, directly or indirectly, to making this book a reality.

—Akshat Paul

We would both like to sincerely thank the Apress team—**Miriam Haidara**, **Nirmal Selvaraj**, and **Jessica Vakili**—for their guidance, professionalism, and support throughout the publication process. It has been a pleasure working with all of you.

CHAPTER 1

Learning the Basics: A Whistle-Stop Tour of React

Before diving into React Native, it's important to understand the core technology it builds upon—React (also known as ReactJS or React.js). React Native is a powerful framework that extends React's capabilities to mobile development, enabling you to build cross-platform apps for iOS, Android, and more from a single code base.

This chapter is your starting point, offering a concise yet solid introduction to the fundamental concepts of React. These principles are vital, as React Native shares the same mental model and architectural patterns as React for the web.

In this chapter, we'll briefly explore

- What React is and why it matters-Declarative vs. Imperative React Paradigms
- The concept of one-way data flow and how it simplifies UI logic
- How to install and set up a React environment
- Creating your first React application
- Understanding components—the core building blocks of React
- An introduction to hooks
- How to share data between components

A. Nalwaya and A. Paul, *React Native for Mobile Development*, https://doi.org/10.1007/979-8-8688-2977-2_1

React takes a distinctive approach to building user interfaces, especially when compared to traditional libraries like jQuery, AngularJS, or Backbone. While those tools often rely on directly manipulating the DOM or managing complex two-way data bindings, React introduces a new mindset—often called the **React way**—where the UI is a direct result of state and components serve as reusable, composable units.

If you're coming from a background in conventional web development, React's model may initially seem unfamiliar. However, this shift in thinking is what gives React its strength—especially when building scalable applications that can run across multiple platforms.

1.1. The Philosophy Behind React

You may have heard the phrase "*Write once, run everywhere*"—a common (but often elusive) goal in software development. In contrast, React offers a more realistic and practical philosophy: "*Learn once, write anywhere*." This means once you're familiar with the React paradigm, you can apply it across different platforms—the web with React and mobile apps with React Native.

React is not a framework—it's a *JavaScript library for building user interfaces*. Developed and open-sourced by Meta (formerly known as Facebook), it was first deployed in Facebook's news feed in 2011. After the acquisition of Instagram in 2012, the need to share this technology across teams accelerated is refinement. React was officially open-sourced in May 2013, and since then, it has grown rapidly in popularity and adoption, becoming a central part of modern front-end development.

Interestingly, React focuses solely on the *"view" layer* of an application—the *V* in *MVC (Model-View-Controller)*. This gives you the freedom to pair it with any other library or framework of your choice for routing, state management, or back-end interactions. Whether you want to convert part of an existing app to React or build something entirely new, React is flexible enough to support incremental adoption.

1.2. Declarative vs. Imperative React Paradigms

In React, understanding the shift from Imperative to Declarative programming is often the "lightbulb moment" for developers. It's the difference between telling the browser how to do something step-by-step vs. telling React what you want the end result to look like. React adopts a declarative paradigm, where you instead describe what the UI should look like for any given state, rather than how to change it. You define a blueprint—for instance, specifying that a button should be gray and disabled if a loading variable is true. When that state changes, React's reconciliation engine handles the heavy lifting of updating the browser to match your description. This turns the UI into a predictable function of your data.

1.3. Why React?

In a world overflowing with JavaScript libraries and frameworks—where it feels like a new one emerges almost every month—it's fair to ask: Do we really need another one?

The answer lies not in the sheer existence of React, but in the problem it was designed to solve. React wasn't created to follow the trend of new libraries or to offer yet another flavor of MVC. It was born out of a real engineering challenge at Facebook: how to build large-scale applications where the user interface (UI) needs to update frequently and efficiently as data changes.

This is a common scenario in modern apps—from social media feeds to ecommerce dashboards—where managing dynamic UI becomes incredibly complex and error-prone. Many popular frameworks at the time followed the traditional MVC (Model-View-Controller) or MV (Model-View-whatever) architecture. While those architectures have their strengths, they began to show cracks when scaling applications with frequent and unpredictable UI updates.

React approached the problem differently—not as a framework, but as a library focused purely on building composable, state-driven user interfaces.

React is fundamentally different from many other UI libraries in a few key ways:

- **Component-Based Architecture**: React promotes the idea of building your UI as a collection of small, reusable components. Each component encapsulates its structure, behavior, and styling—making code more modular, maintainable, and scalable.

- **Full Power of JavaScript**: React doesn't rely on HTML templates or string-based markup languages. Instead, it treats UI as a function of state and leverages JavaScript (and JSX—JavaScript XML) to define views. This gives developers the full expressive power of a programming language while constructing interfaces.

- **Virtual DOM for Performance (Only in Web)**: One of React's standout innovations is the **Virtual DOM**—an in-memory representation of the real DOM. When a component's state changes, React computes the minimal set of changes needed using a *diffing algorithm* and then updates only the necessary parts of the real DOM. This leads to **highly efficient rendering** and a snappy user experience.
- **One-Way Data Flow**: Many earlier libraries embraced **two-way data binding**, where changes in the UI could automatically update the data model, and vice versa. While convenient at first, this often led to unpredictable data mutations and complex debugging. React simplifies this with **unidirectional (one-way) data flow**—making it clear where and how data changes, leading to code that's easier to debug, test, and reason about.

To truly master React (and by extension, React Native), it's essential to build a solid understanding of these foundational principles. In the next section, we will set up React.

1.4. Installation and Setup

Before diving into practical React.js examples, it's essential to set up a proper development environment. React is a JavaScript library that runs in the browser, but during development, we use a powerful toolchain to write modular code, manage dependencies, transpile modern JavaScript (and JSX), and refactor code.

1.4.1. Prerequisite: Install Node.js

The first and most critical prerequisite is installing Node.js, a JavaScript runtime that allows you to run JavaScript code outside the browser. Node.js also includes npm (Node Package Manager), which is used to install React and related libraries.

We recommend installing the LTS (Long-Term Support) version of Node.js for better stability and compatibility with most tools in the React ecosystem.

Download Node.js from the official website: `https://nodejs.org/`.

Once installed, verify the installation using your terminal or command prompt:

```
node -v     # Checks the installed Node.js version
npm -v      # Checks the installed npm version
```

Note This approach allows you to install only a single version of Node.js. If you need to work with multiple Node.js versions, it's recommended to use NVM (Node Version Manager) instead. For Windows, you can use nvm-windows.

This foundational setup is essential because

- React projects rely on package managers to install dependencies like react, react-dom, and build tools like webpack or vite.
- Node.js provides the environment for running build tools and development servers.
- Without this setup, you won't be able to initialize or run modern React applications locally.

1.4.2. React Setup

React, at its core, is simply a JavaScript library distributed as a Node module. This simplicity and modularity make it highly flexible—allowing developers to integrate React into a wide range of projects in different ways.

If you're working on an existing project, adding React is as straightforward as installing it via package managers like npm or yarn. You can begin enhancing parts of your front end incrementally by using React components alongside your existing code base.

However, if you're starting a new React project from scratch, the ecosystem offers several well-maintained frameworks that streamline development and enforce best practices out of the box. These frameworks not only provide powerful abstractions over the React core but also handle complex configurations related to routing, bundling, SSR/SSG, and performance optimizations.

Some of the most recommended frameworks include

- **Next.js**: Ideal for both SSR (Server-Side Rendering) and SSG (Static Site Generation)
- **Remix**: Focuses on nested routing and modern web performance
- **Gatsby**: Great for static sites and content-rich applications
- **Vite with React**: Lightweight and fast for CSR (Client-Side Rendering)–focused apps

All of these frameworks inherently support key React patterns such as

- **Client-Side Rendering (CSR)**: Content is rendered in the browser, providing a highly interactive experience.
- **Single-Page Applications (SPA)**: The application runs on a single HTML page and updates the view dynamically without full page reloads.
- **Static Site Generation (SSG)**: HTML pages are pre-built during the build process, resulting in faster load times and better SEO.
- **React Server Components (RSC)**: Components that render exclusively on the server, reducing client-side JavaScript and improving performance.

Alternative Ways	Tool/Framework	Rendering Supported	Use Case
Add to existing app	npm/yarn	CSR	Incremental adoption
New SPA	Create React App (deprecated), create-react-router	SPA, CSR	Quick setup, learning React
Modern build tool	Vite	SPA, CSR, SSG, SSR	Fast dev, modern features
Advanced frameworks	Next.js, Astro	SPA, CSR, SSG, SSR, RSC	SEO, hybrid rendering, flexibility

> React doesn't prescribe how you build your app—it gives you the tools and leaves the architecture to you. Frameworks help you set up that architecture.

We'll be using Vite as our build tool to set up and run a React.js project. Vite is a next-generation front-end build tool for the web that significantly improves the development experience compared to older tools like Webpack or Parcel. It's designed to be lightweight, lightning-fast, and developer-friendly—perfect for modern JavaScript frameworks like React.

Now that your development environment is ready, it's time to create your first React project using Vite.

We'll be building a simple *To-Do List* app to understand the fundamentals of React.

1. Use *Terminal* (macOS/Linux) or *Command Prompt/PowerShell* (Windows). Navigate to the folder where you want your project to be created.

   ```
   npm create vite@latest to-do-list -- --template react
   ```

   Let's break this down:

   - `npm create vite@latest`: This fetches the latest version of the Vite project initializer.
   - `to-do-list`: The name of your new project folder.
   - `-- --template` react: Specifies that the React template should be used (including JSX support and the React runtime). If you're comfortable, you can also choose the TypeScript template—it's one of the best ways to write more structured and maintainable JavaScript code.

   If you run this command without the parameters, Vite will prompt you with a few questions, such as project name and framework. Since we specified the template, most of it will be pre-filled.

2. Navigate into the project folder:

   ```
   cd to-do-list
   ```

3. Install all project dependencies:

```
npm install
```

This will install all the required packages listed in the package.json file. These include

- react and react-dom (the core libraries)
- vite (for development server and build process)
- Any additional tools required by the React template

4. Start the development server using the following commands:

```
npm run dev
```

```
VITE vX.X.X  ready in Yms

  ➜  Local:   http://localhost:5173/
  ➜  Network: use --host to expose
```

Click or copy the **Local URL** (usually http://localhost:5173) into your browser to view your running React app.

5. You're up and running!

Congratulations—you now have a fully functional React project set up using Vite! You can start editing the App.jsx file for any changes.

Next, we'll look at the folder structure and then start writing our first component!

1.5. Building a To-Do App with React

> "React is best learned by doing. A hands-on approach helps you understand not just the 'how' but the 'why' behind the code."

Now that we've successfully set up our React project using Vite, it's time to start building a simple yet powerful application: a `To-Do List`.

The `To-Do` app is one of the most popular beginner-friendly projects—and for good reason. It allows you to learn and apply core React concepts in a practical and intuitive way.

The simplicity of a `To-Do` list makes it a perfect playground for learning React. Despite being a basic app, it covers all the essential concepts you'll need to build real-world applications:

- **Components**: Break UI into small, reusable pieces.
- **Event Handling**: Handle user interactions like clicks and form submissions.
- **State Management**: Track tasks, completion status, and user input.
- **Hooks**: Use `useState`, `useEffect`, and `useContext` for dynamic behavior.
- **Context**: Sharing data across components.

1.5.1. Introduction to Components

Components are the most fundamental units in React application development. They serve as the building blocks for constructing user interfaces in a React app. Much like widgets in other frameworks, React components are modular, encapsulated pieces of UI that can be plugged together to create complex applications. Their encapsulated nature makes them easy to test, reuse, and maintain. These components define how DOM elements are created and how users can interact with them. Let's create your first component.

Open App.jsx and update the following code:

```
import './App.css';
function App() {
  return (
    <div>
      <h1>To Do App</h1>
      <p>This is a simple To Do app.</p>
    </div>
  )
}

export default App
```

And open App.css and update the following CSS:

```
#root {
  font-family: system-ui, Avenir, Helvetica, Arial, sans-serif;
  line-height: 1.5;
  font-weight: 400;
  max-width: 1280px;
  padding: 2rem;
}

body {
  margin: 20px;
  display: flex;
  min-width: 320px;
  min-height: 100vh;
}
```

```
h1 {
  font-size: 2.2em;
  line-height: 1.1;
}
```

Now, run the application. If it's already running, it will automatically perform hot-reloading `npm run dev` and open the browser:

Now let's understand our component. This code defines a component (a JavaScript function) named App that returns a small block of HTML-like code (JSX). `JSX` allows developers to write markup directly within JavaScript, making it easier to visualize and manage UI structure

Now let's understand our App component; the "App" function is a **functional component,** the modern and recommended way to write a React component. It returns JSX markup that describes what the UI should look like. Functional components should be **pure functions:** given the same props and state, they should always return the same output without side effects. It's like a single frame in a movie, as it represents the UI at a certain point in time. Updating the props or state returns a new JSX markup. We are also importing `CSS` in the App component. Build tool like `Vite` or `Webpack`, which takes care of importing `CSS` in the final bundle.

To build meaningful components, keep these key principles in mind:

- **Encapsulation:** Each component should manage its own structure and behavior, making it self-contained and easy to reuse.
- **Reusability:** Design components so they can be reused across the application, minimizing code duplication and improving consistency.
- **Isolation:** Components should function independently. Changes in one component shouldn't impact others unless they're explicitly connected.
- **Separation of Concerns:** Breaking the UI into smaller, focused components allows developers to concentrate on specific features or sections without needing to understand the entire application at once.

These principles become even more important in React Native, where components must work across iOS and Android platforms while maintaining consistent behavior.

State Management and Hooks

State management is a fundamental concept in React that deals with handling dynamic data within an application. It ensures that components display the most up-to-date information by triggering re-renders whenever the underlying data changes. React introduces Hooks as a modern way to manage state and side effects in functional components. The `useState` hook allows developers to add local state to components, while `useEffect` handles side effects such as data fetching or updating the DOM. Hooks like `useContext`, `useReducer`, and `useRef` offer additional capabilities for managing shared state, complex logic, and persistent values. By using Hooks, developers can write cleaner, modular code without relying on class components. For applications that require global state management, tools like the `Context API`, `Redux`, or `Zustand` can be integrated.

To understand this concept better, we will update our `ToDo` app by creating a list and managing its state.

Let's create a file `ToDoList.jsx` and add the following code:

```
import React, { useState, useEffect } from 'react';
import './TodoList.css'; //  Importing the CSS file to style the component

function TodoList() {
  // State to store all tasks
  const [tasks, setTasks] = useState([]);

  // State to track the current input value
  const [input, setInput] = useState('');

  // State to hold a dynamic message (e.g., number of tasks in this case)
  const [message, setMessage] = useState('');

  // Function to add a new task to the task list
  const addTask = () => {
    // Only add non-empty (non-whitespace) tasks
    if (input.trim()) {
      setTasks([...tasks, input.trim()]); // Add the new task to the list
      setInput(''); // Clear the input field
    }
  };

  // Function to remove a task from the list by its index
  const removeTask = (index) => {
    // Keep all tasks except the one at the given index
    setTasks(tasks.filter((_, i) => i !== index));
  };

  // This useEffect updates the message whenever the `tasks` array changes
  useEffect(() => {
    setMessage(`You have ${tasks.length} task(s).`);
  }, [tasks]); // Dependency array ensures this runs only when `tasks` changes

  return (
    <div className="todo-container">

      {/* Input section with text input and add button */}
      <div className="todo-input-wrapper">
```

```
        <input
          value={input}
          onChange={e => setInput(e.target.value)} // Update `input` state
          as user types
          placeholder="Enter a task"
        />
        <button onClick={addTask}>Add Task</button>
      </div>

      {/* Display message about number of tasks */}
      <p>{message}</p>

      {/* Render list of tasks */}
      <ul>
        {tasks.map((task, index) => (
          <li key={index}>
            {/* Task text */}
            {task}
            {/* Delete button */}
            <button onClick={() => removeTask(index)}>delete</button>
          </li>
        ))}
      </ul>
    </div>
  );
}

export default TodoList; // Exporting the component for use in App.js or
elsewhere
```

And then create `TodoList.css` in the same folder:

```
/* Container styles */
.todo-container {
  top: 0;
  left: 0;
  width: 60vw;
  height: 100vh;
```

```
  margin: 0;
  padding: 25px;
  border-radius: 0;
  background-color: #f9f9f9;
  box-shadow: none;
  font-family: 'Segoe UI', sans-serif;
  display: flex;
  flex-direction: column;

}

/* Title */
.todo-container h2 {
  text-align: center;
  margin-bottom: 20px;
  color: #333;
}

/* Input and button wrapper */
.todo-input-wrapper {
  display: flex;
  gap: 10px;
  margin-bottom: 15px;
}

/* Input styling */
.todo-container input {
  flex: 1;
  padding: 10px;
  border: 1px solid #ccc;
  border-radius: 8px;
  font-size: 16px;
}

/* Add Task button */
.todo-container button {
  padding: 10px 15px;
```

```
  background-color: #4caf50;
  color: white;
  border: none;
  border-radius: 8px;
  cursor: pointer;
  font-size: 16px;
}

.todo-container button:hover {
  background-color: #45a049;
}

/* Task message */
.todo-container p {
  color: #555;
  font-size: 14px;
  margin-bottom: 10px;
}

/* Task list */
.todo-container ul {
  list-style-type: none;
  padding: 0;
}

.todo-container li {
  background: #fff;
  padding: 10px;
  margin-bottom: 8px;
  border-radius: 6px;
  display: flex;
  justify-content: space-between;
  align-items: center;
  border: 1px solid #eee;
}
```

```
/* Remove button */
.todo-container li button {
  background-color: transparent;
  color: red;
  font-size: 18px;
  border: none;
  cursor: pointer;
}

.todo-container li button:hover {
  color: darkred;
}
```

Now, finally, we need to link the `ToDoList.jsx` component in `App.jsx`:

```
import './App.css';
import TodoList from './ToDoList';

function App() {
  return (
    <div>
      <h1>To Do App</h1>
      <TodoList />
    </div>
  )
}

export default App
```

Run up the terminal and check the app, and add a few to-do tasks.

Now, let's deep dive and understand the code.

Hooks are functions that let you "hook into" React features like state, lifecycle, and context in functional components.

Before Hooks, these features were only available in class components. Now, you can write cleaner and more powerful logic using function components.

TodoList component uses two React hooks:

- `useState`
- `useEffect`

Let's go over each one in the context of our code.

useState: For Managing State

The `useState` hook allows you to add state to functional components in React. It returns a state variable and a function to update that variable. When the state changes, React re-renders the component to reflect the new data.

In our To Do app, hook is used to handle state and track changing values in the component like

- The list of tasks (`tasks`)
- The input field value (`input`)

- The message shown to the user (`message`)

```
const [tasks, setTasks] = useState([]);
const [input, setInput] = useState('');
const [message, setMessage] = useState('');
```

`useState(initialValue)` returns a state variable and a setter function. Example: `tasks` is the current value and `setTasks` is the function to update it. And the initial value of tasks is an empty array [].

Whenever you call `setTasks`, the component re-renders with the new state.

It's like a memory slot in your component where you can store and change data as users interact.

useEffect: For Side Effects

The useEffect hook lets you perform side effects in React functional components such as fetching data and setting up subscriptions. It runs after the component renders, and you can control when it runs by passing a dependency array. Without dependencies, it runs after every render; with an empty array, it runs only once. In our example:

```
useEffect(() => {
  setMessage(`You have ${tasks.length} task(s).`);
}, [tasks]);
```

This `useEffect` runs every time the value of the "tasks" variable changes and then updates the `message` to show the current task count. The useEffect takes two arguments:

- **First argument**: A function with the logic you want to run.
- **Second argument**: A dependency array. If any value inside changes, the effect runs.

When a task is added or removed → `tasks` changes → `useEffect` runs → `message` updates. React Re-render Cycle in This Component

- User types a `task` → input state updates.
- User clicks `Add Task` → tasks state updates.
- React re-renders the component.

- `useEffect` sees that tasks changed → updates the `message` state.
- Component re-renders again with updated `message`.

This is a summary of what we learned:

Hook	Purpose	Our Use Case
`useState`	Store data that changes	`tasks, input, message`
`useEffect`	Run code when state changes	Update `message` when `tasks` change

1.6. Context

When we create a simple to-do example, we often write all the code in a single file. While this approach works for small projects, it becomes difficult to manage as your application grows. To make the code more organized and maintainable, it's better to break it down into smaller components.

However, splitting your app into smaller components introduces a new challenge: sharing state or data between multiple components. Passing data through props at every level can become cumbersome and messy, especially as the component tree grows deeper. To solve this problem, React provides the concept of Context.

Context in React is a feature that lets you share data (such as state, functions, or values) across your component tree without having to pass props manually at every level. This is especially useful for sharing global data like authentication status, theme, or user information with deeply nested components that need access to the same data.

When to Use Context

- Theme data (dark/light mode)
- Authentication state
- Localization/language settings
- Data needed by many components at different nesting levels

When NOT to Use Context

- Data only needed by one or two closely related components (use props)
- Frequently changing data that affects many components (consider state management libraries like Zustand or Redux for better performance)

Context triggers re-renders in all consuming components when its value changes, which can impact performance if overused.

We will refactor the same ToDo app to make it cleaner and more modular by breaking it into smaller components. The `TaskInput` component will handle the input field and adding new tasks, while the `TaskList` component will be responsible for displaying the list of tasks. We'll also use `TaskContext` to manage and share the application's state across these components.

Component	Responsibility
`TaskInput`	Manages the input field and adds new tasks
`TaskList`	Displays the list of tasks
`TaskContext`	Shares and manages the state across components

Let's open the ToDo app and create `TaskContext.jsx`:

```
// Importing necessary hooks and utilities from React
import  { createContext, useState, useContext } from 'react';

// 1. Create the context
// This creates a new context for tasks that will be used to share state
across components
const TaskContext = createContext();

// 2. Create the provider component
// This component will wrap the parts of the app that need access to
task state
export function TaskProvider({ children }) {
  // State to hold the list of tasks
  const [tasks, setTasks] = useState([]);
```

```
  // State to hold the current input value for a new task
  const [task, setTask] = useState('');

  // Function to add a task to the list
  const addTask = () => {
    // Only add the task if it's not just empty spaces
    if (task.trim()) {
      // Add the new task to the existing tasks array
      setTasks([...tasks, task]);
      // Clear the input after adding
      setTask('');
    }
  };

  // Function to remove a task by its index
  const removeTask = (index) => {
    // Create a new array without the task at the specified index
    setTasks(tasks.filter((_, i) => i !== index));
  };

  // The provider shares tasks state and related functions with any
  children components
  return (
    <TaskContextvalue={{ tasks, task, setTask, addTask, removeTask }}>
      {children}
    </TaskContext>
  );
}

// 3. Export a custom hook to use the context more easily
// This allows other components to use task-related state and functions
export const useTasks = () => useContext(TaskContext);
```

We have created a new context object called TaskContext. This is like creating a "box" where you can store state and functions (tasks, addTask, etc.), and any component can access this box—if it is inside the Provider.

A Provider is a component that makes the context's value available to all children components inside it.

Let's now take the next step by creating a new file named `TaskInput.jsx`.

```
// Importing the custom hook 'useTasks' from TaskContext
// This hook provides shared task state and functions like setTask
and addTask
import { useTasks } from './TaskContext';

// Functional component for the task input area
function TaskInput() {
  // Destructure task state and handler functions from the custom hook
  const { task, setTask, addTask } = useTasks();

  return (
    <div className="todo-input-wrapper">
      <input
        type="text"
        value={task}
        onChange={(e) => setTask(e.target.value)}
        placeholder="Enter a task"
      />
      <button onClick={addTask}>Add</button>
    </div>
  );
}

// Exporting the TaskInput component
export default TaskInput;
```

Create a new file `TaskList.jsx` and update the following code:

```
import  { useState, useEffect } from 'react';
import { useTasks } from './TaskContext';

function TaskList() {
  // Get tasks and removeTask function from context
  const { tasks, removeTask } = useTasks();
  // State to hold the message about the number of tasks
  const [message, setMessage] = useState('');
```

```
  // Update the message whenever the tasks array changes
  useEffect(() => {
    setMessage(`You have ${tasks.length} task(s).`);
  }, [tasks]);

  return (
    <div>
      <p>{message}</p>
      <ul>
        {tasks.map((t, index) => (
          <li key={index}>
            {t}
            <button onClick={() => removeTask(index)}>delete</button>
          </li>
        ))}
      </ul>
    </div>
  );
}

export default TaskList;
```

And now update `ToDoList.jsx`:

```
import { TaskProvider } from './TaskContext';
import TaskInput from './TaskInput';
import TaskList from './TaskList';
import './TodoList.css';

function TodoList() {
  return (
    <div className="todo-container">

      {/* Wrapping components with TaskProvider so they can access shared
      task state */}
      <TaskProvider>
        {/* Component to input a new task */}
        <TaskInput />
```

```
        {/* Component to display the list of tasks */}
        <TaskList />
      </TaskProvider>

    </div>
  );
}
export default TodoList;
```

After this change, you can run the application. Visually, the screen will look the same, but behind the scenes, our code base has been refactored to follow a cleaner and more modular structure. By breaking the application into smaller, focused components, we've improved its readability, maintainability, and scalability.

Now that our structure is cleaner, we're in a great position to dive deeper into how state is shared across components. In the next section, we'll explore the Provider concept in React and understand how it enables different components to access and share state using the Context API—all by looking at our updated code.

In this example:

- `TaskProvider` wraps the part of your app that needs access to the tasks.
- Inside it, you manage the state (`useState`) and functions (`addTask`, `removeTask`).
- It uses `<TaskContext>` to pass that state and logic to all its children.

Any component wrapped inside `<TaskProvider>` can now **access the context**. How this works:

```
App
└── <TaskProvider>               ← Provides tasks state to children
      └── <ChildComponentA>      ← Uses useTasks() to access and
                                   update tasks
      └── <ChildComponentB>      ← Also uses useTasks()
```

1.7. Summary

This chapter provided a quick tour of React. Before we move on to the next chapter, let's take a moment to reflect on and consolidate what you've learned so far. From understanding React's component-based architecture to exploring key concepts like JSX, state, and hooks—you now have a solid foundation. These principles are essential, as they form the core building blocks of any React or React Native application. With this knowledge in place, you're well-prepared to dive deeper into more advanced topics in the chapters ahead. This is a quick recap of what you have learned so far.

Concept	Description	Purpose/Usage
Component	The basic building block of a React UI. In modern React, these are typically JavaScript functions'.	Encapsulates UI, logic, and state. Used to build reusable UI elements.
Hooks	Special functions (e.g., `useState,useEffect,useContext`) for using state and other React features in function components.	Allows functional components to manage state, side effects, context, etc., without writing classes.
Context	A way to share data (state, functions, values) across the component tree without prop drilling.	Provides a global value accessible by any nested component, avoiding manual prop passing at every level.
Provider	A component included in the context object that supplies the context value to all descendants.	Wraps part of the component tree and provides a value to all consuming components inside it via `thevalueprop`.

In the upcoming chapter, your journey truly begins as we transition from the world of web development with React to building native mobile applications using React Native. With the core concepts already in your toolkit—like components, state, props, and hooks—you'll find yourself well-prepared to understand and adapt to the mobile-first mindset. Get ready to bring your ideas to life on real devices!

CHAPTER 2

The Simplest Program: Hello World with React Native

In the last chapter, you got a good overview of the React ecosystem. Now it's time to get your hands dirty with React Native. In this chapter, you will set up your development environment by installing the prerequisites, and then you will create your first React Native application.

The best way to learn is through practical examples. We continue this theme throughout the book, as you will follow simple examples to learn React Native by programming yourself to understand the key concepts.

This chapter explores the following topics:

- An introduction to React Native
- The essentials of React Native
- The installation of React Native
- Your first application
- The anatomy of a React Native application
- How to debug your application

2.1. An Introduction to React Native

React Native is an open-source framework developed primarily by a team at Meta (formerly Facebook) designed for building fully native mobile applications using web technologies such as JavaScript (JSX) and styling systems that resemble CSS

A. Nalwaya and A. Paul, *React Native for Mobile Development*, https://doi.org/10.1007/979-8-8688-2977-2_2

(via StyleSheet API). React Native style is not CSS; it's JavaScript objects with camelCase properties. What sets React Native apart is its ability to deliver performance apps that feel truly native—similar in responsiveness and smoothness to those developed using traditional native development languages like Swift or Kotlin.

Unlike many hybrid frameworks that render apps through web views (often compromising on speed and user experience), React Native uses a bridge architecture to render actual native UI components. This results in a look and feel that is indistinguishable from apps built with traditional native languages.

Some modern "hybrid" competitors (e.g., Flutter with Impeller) are very close or occasionally better in specific cases (animations, consistent FPS). Flutter apps are written in the Dart language, and hence, React Native provides the lowest barrier to entry for JavaScript developers, offering access to a massive npm ecosystem and native platform components.

One of React Native's core philosophies is derived from React itself: *Learn once, write anywhere.* This means that many components written for the web in React can often be reused in mobile apps with minimal or no changes. The framework adopts a declarative and component-driven approach to UI development, which is a significant departure from the imperative style traditionally used in native mobile development.

While Meta originally initiated the development of React Native, its governance evolved significantly in October 2025, when React, React Native, and JSX were contributed to the React Foundation under the Linux Foundation. This transition reflects a shift toward a more open, community-driven ecosystem with broader industry participation.

Today, React Native continues to receive strong support and contributions from Meta, Microsoft, Expo, Callstack, and Software Mansion, along with a vibrant global developer community. Developers worldwide actively contribute to its evolution, and its source code remains publicly accessible:

`https://github.com/facebook/react-native`

2.2. The Essentials of React Native

React Native allows you to build native mobile applications using JavaScript—combining the best of React (web UI) with native platform capabilities. Under the hood, it bridges your JavaScript code with native components for iOS and Android. Because of this hybrid nature, setting up React Native requires a mix of JavaScript tools and native development environments.

Let's walk through everything you need to do, step-by-step.

2.2.1. Install Node.js and npm (JavaScript Runtime)

The first and most critical prerequisite is installing Node.js, a JavaScript runtime that allows you to run JavaScript code outside the browser. Node.js also includes npm (Node Package Manager), which is used to install React and related libraries.

We recommend installing the LTS (Long-Term Support) version of Node.js for better stability and compatibility with most tools in the React ecosystem.

Download Node.js from the official website: `https://nodejs.org/`. Once installed, verify the installation using your terminal or command prompt:

```
node -v     # Checks the installed Node.js version
npm -v      # Checks the installed npm version
```

Note For Windows, you can use nvm-windows. This approach installs only a single version of Node.js on your system. If you need to work with multiple Node.js versions, it's recommended to use Node Version Manager (NVM). On macOS, NVM allows you to easily switch between different Node.js versions, while on Windows, you can use nvm-windows for similar functionality.

2.2.2. Install Xcode (for iOS Development: macOS Only)

To build iOS applications using React Native, it is essential to have Xcode installed on your macOS system. Xcode provides the necessary tools, libraries, and emulators required to compile and run iOS apps. You can download Xcode directly from the Mac App Store. Once installed, you should also install the **Command-Line Tools**, which are required for building and managing iOS projects via the terminal. This can be done by running the command `xcode-select --install` in your terminal. After installation, it's important to open Xcode at least once to accept the license agreement, which is a mandatory step before the build tools can function properly with React Native. Skipping this may result in permission or build errors later during project setup.

2.2.3. Set Up Android Studio (for Android Development)

Since your app needs to run on Android, you need Android Studio with the SDK and emulator tools.

1. Download and install Android Studio from: `https://developer.android.com/studio`.
2. During installation, make sure to install
   - Android SDK
   - Android SDK Platform
   - Android Virtual Device (AVD)
   - Android Emulator
   - Android Platform Tools
3. Open `Android Studio` → `Settings` → `SDK Manager` → `Install` recommended tools.
4. Update the env file Environment Variables `.bashrc` or `.zshrc`:

```
export ANDROID_HOME=$HOME/Library/Android/sdk
export PATH=$PATH:$ANDROID_HOME/emulator
export PATH=$PATH:$ANDROID_HOME/platform-tools
```

On Windows, you don't use .bashrc or .zshrc. Instead, environment variables are configured through the System Environment Variables settings.

2.3. The Installation of React Native

There are several ways to set up React Native, each suited to different levels of expertise and project needs.

The simplest method is using Expo CLI, which provides a managed environment that allows developers to quickly build and test apps without dealing with native code. This is ideal for beginners and rapid prototyping.

For more advanced use cases, especially when native modules or deeper customization is required, the React Native CLI setup is preferred. This method gives full control over native Android and iOS code, making it suitable for complex apps.

```
npm install -g create-expo-app
```

Alternate Approach: You don't need to globally install Expo CLI anymore. Instead, you can use NPX, which comes bundled with Node.js, to run the latest version of the tool directly.

```
npx create-expo-app <Application Name>
```

This will

- Download and execute the latest version of Create Expo App
- Set up a new React Native project using Expo
- Install all required dependencies automatically

2.4. Your First React Native App

Now that you are all charged up about React Native and have your system set up, it's time to create your first application. To keep things simple, in the beginning, just follow along. Sometimes, you might feel disconnected by monotonously typing in the code, but following along is enough for now. Remember that mimicry is a powerful form of learning; it's how we learned most of our skills, such as talking, reading, and writing, and it's how you will learn to program with React Native. As you proceed, this method will help you understand thoroughly why you authored certain pieces of code.

Throughout this book, you'll build a single application from scratch—evolving it from a simple View screen to a fully functional, distribution-ready mobile app. This structured, hands-on approach will help you gradually understand and apply React Native concepts in real-world scenarios. While the main focus will remain on this core app, there will be occasional diversions where we explore specific concepts in isolation for clarity.

The app you'll be developing is called ExpenseTracker, a simple yet practical personal finance tracker. It will start with basic features such as adding and managing expenses and assets, viewing summaries, and organizing your financial records. As we progress through each chapter, new features and improvements will be introduced. This approach will help you see how React Native components, APIs, and design principles naturally fit together to build a modern mobile application. By the end of the journey, you'll not only have a working app but also a solid understanding of how to develop and scale cross-platform mobile apps using React Native.

2.4.1. Create a Basic Skeleton

Let's begin by setting up the foundational structure for your React Native project. Open your terminal and run the command below to create a new project. This will initialize the necessary files and directories.

```
create-expo-app ExpenseTracker --template blank
```

This command is used to create a new React Native project using **Expo**, which simplifies development and testing across Android, iOS, and web platforms.

- `create-expo-app`: A command-line utility that bootstraps a new Expo-managed React Native project.
- `ExpenseTracker`: This is the name of the new project directory that will be created. Your app's files will be inside this folder.
- `--template` blank: Specifies that the app should use the basic blank template, which sets up a minimal starting point with just the essentials (no navigation, no additional screens, etc.).

To test your React Native applications locally, you need to set up simulators for both iOS and Android. For iOS, install Xcode on macOS, which includes the iOS Simulator by default. For Android, install Android Studio, which provides the Android Emulator along with the required SDK tools. After installation, configure virtual devices (AVDs) using Android Studio and ensure environment variables are properly set so your system can access the emulator tools seamlessly.

Once the installation completes successfully, navigate into your newly created project directory.

```
cd ExpenseTracker
```

Starts the development server so you can open your React Native app:

```
npm run ios
  (Mac only, requires Xcode)
```

Starts the development server and loads your app in an iOS simulator:

```
npm run android
  (Requires Android build tools)
```

After running, it will give the following output and open the simulator:

```
$ expo start --ios
Starting project at /Users/abhishek/Documents/React Native Book/FinalCode/
chapter2/ExpenseTracker
› Port 8081 is being used by another process
✔ Use port 8082 instead? … yes
Starting Metro Bundler
› Opening exp://192.168.68.105:8082 on iPhone 15 Pro
```

```
› Metro waiting on exp://192.168.68.105:8082
› Scan the QR code above with Expo Go (Android) or the Camera app (iOS)
```

```
› Using Expo Go
› Press s │ switch to development build

› Press a │ open Android
› Press i │ open iOS simulator
› Press w │ open web

› Press j │ open debugger
› Press r │ reload app
› Press m │ toggle menu
› shift+m │ more tools
› Press o │ open project code in your editor

› Press ? │ show all commands

Logs for your project will appear below. Press Ctrl+C to exit.
```

To run and test your app on a physical device, simply download the **Expo Go** app from the App Store (iOS) or Google Play Store (Android). Open Expo Go on your phone and scan the QR code displayed in your terminal when you start the app using Expo. Within seconds, your application will automatically load on your device.

It feels like magic—and in many ways, it is! You can instantly see your changes reflected on the app in real time, allowing you to live debug and interact with your React Native application directly on your mobile device during development.

As you've seen earlier, we've used Expo a few times—but what exactly is it? Expo is an open-source platform and toolchain built around React Native, designed to simplify the process of developing, building, and testing mobile apps for iOS and Android. It is one of the fastest and most beginner-friendly ways to get started with React Native.

Expo eliminates the need for complex native setup (like Xcode or Android Studio) by providing a pre-configured environment that works out of the box. This means you can begin building mobile apps immediately without configuring native build tools on your system. All you need to do is install the Expo CLI and start developing.

Thanks to a single command, the basic structure of your project is in place, and your application is loaded in the device. Also note that the terminal always needs to be open. This is the Node package manager for React Native. If you kill this, the app will stop working.

The terminal is opened to start the React Native Packager and a server to handle the preceding request. The React Native Packager is responsible for reading and building the JSX (you'll look at this later) and JavaScript code.

Set up your project in any editor you prefer. React Native does not force you to use nor does it have a preference for any specific editor, so you can continue to use your favorites.

In your project directory, locate the App.js file in the root folder. This is the entry point of your application. Open it in your editor—you'll see some boilerplate code. Replace all the existing code with the following:

```
import { StatusBar } from 'expo-status-bar';
import { StyleSheet, Text, View } from 'react-native';
export default function App() {
  return (
    <View style={styles.container}>
      <Text>Hello World !!</Text>
      <Text> This is my First React Native App</Text>
      <StatusBar style="auto" />
    </View>
  );
}
```

```
const styles = StyleSheet.create({
  container: {
    flex: 1,
    backgroundColor: '#fff',
    alignItems: 'center',
    justifyContent: 'center',
  },
});
```

Simply save the file, and the Expo app on your device or simulator will automatically reload, displaying the screen as shown in the figure.

That was quick! In a fraction of a second, you can see the changes you applied. You don't need to compile the code and restart the simulator for React Native changes. If you have done any native iOS app development before, pressing Refresh to see the changes might seem like a miracle.

Now, let's understand the code. At the top of the file are the following lines:

```
import { StatusBar } from 'expo-status-bar';
import { StyleSheet, Text, View } from 'react-native';
```

This loads the React module and assigns it to a React variable that can be used in your code. React Native uses the same module-loading technology as Node.js; this is roughly equivalent to linking and importing libraries in Swift.

You are assigning multiple object properties to a single variable; this is called destructuring the assignment. This cool feature is in there in versions of JavaScript after ES6. Although it is optional, it's very beneficial; otherwise, every time you use a component in your code, you would have to use a fully qualified name for it, such as `React.Stylesheet`, and so on. This saves quite a bit of time.

Next, you create a view:

```
export default function App() {
  return (
    <View style={styles.container}>
      <Text>Hello World !!</Text>
      <Text> This is my First React Native App</Text>
      <StatusBar style="auto" />
    </View>
  );
}
```

This defines the **main component** of your React Native application. In React Native, everything starts from a component—and the default exported one (App) is the entry point. When the app runs, this is the first screen the user will see.

View tag is a container component, similar to a `<div>` in HTML. It acts as a layout wrapper to hold other UI elements like text, buttons, or images. Here, it's styled with `styles.container` (which would typically be defined below using `StyleSheet.create()`).

Text is React Native way of displaying text. Unlike web development where you might use `<p>` or `<span>`, in React Native, all text must be wrapped in a `<Text>` component. The two lines here display a greeting and a description.

Stylesheet.create() method is used to define and organize styles in React Native. It ensures better performance by optimizing style objects, and it also improves code readability.

Now you define the styling of your app. Here you will use Flexbox; it is similar to what CSS is to HTML. For now, you can type this code. We explain styling in the next chapter.

2.4.2. Learn How to Perform Basic Debugging Effectively

"Debugging is twice as hard as writing the code in the first place."

—Brian Kernighan

As you build more complex applications in React Native, debugging and inspecting your app's components, state, and layout becomes essential. That's where `React Native DevTools` comes into play—a powerful set of tools that help developers understand, inspect, and troubleshoot React Native applications in real time.

Enable Developer Menu

- **iOS Simulator**: Press `Cmd + D`.
- **Android Emulator**: Press `Cmd + M` (Mac) or `Ctrl + M` (Windows).
- **Physical Device**: Shake the device or tap with four fingers (for newer iOS versions).

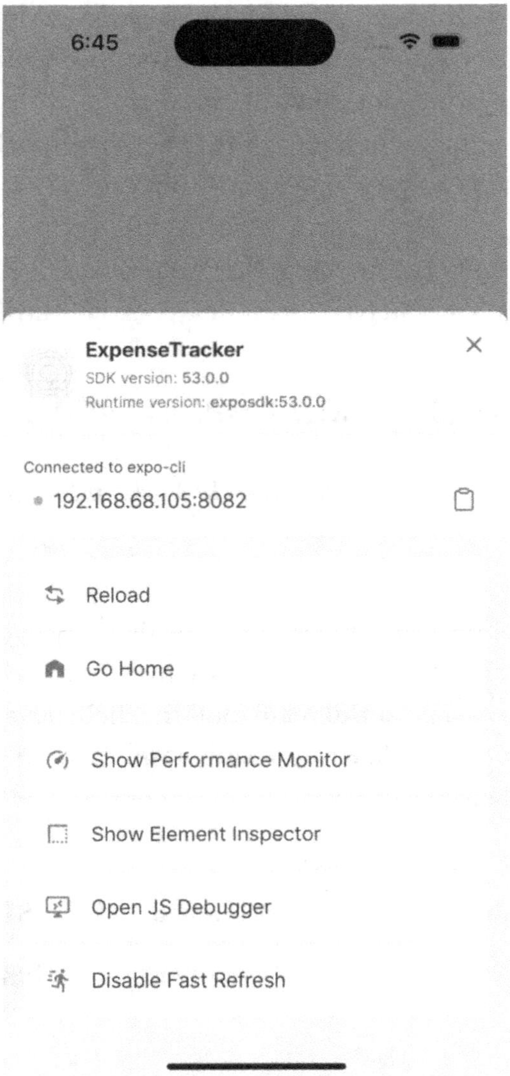

Click Open JS Debugger.

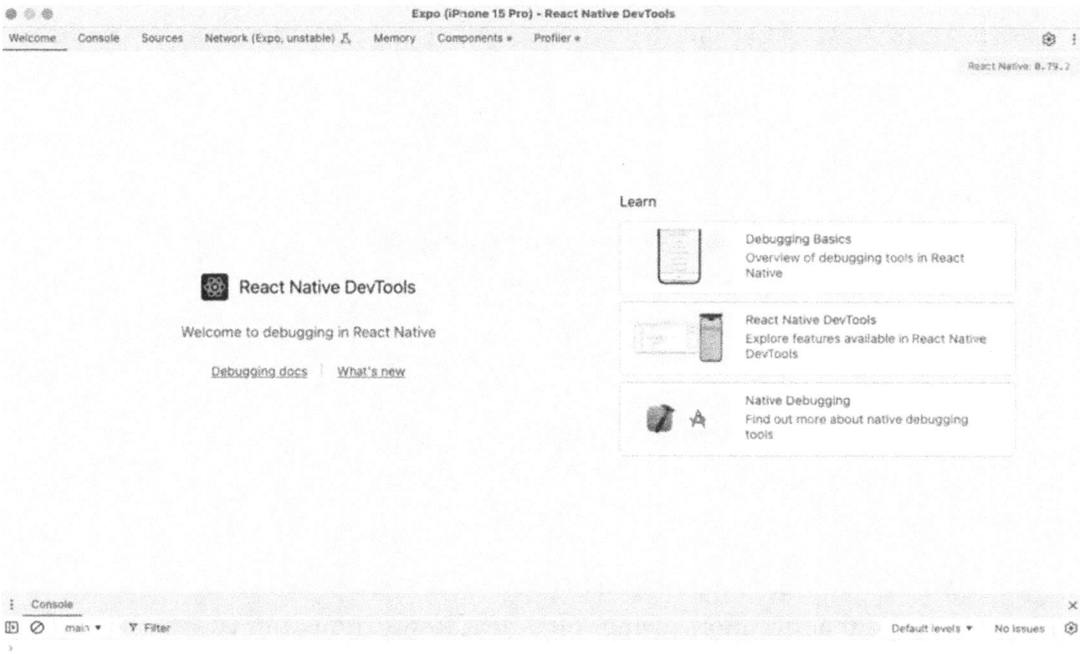

`React Native DevTools` is a desktop application or browser-based extension that allows you to

- Inspect the component tree of your app
- View and modify component props and state
- Monitor render cycles
- Profile performance
- Debug styles and layout

Click the Components tab to navigate and view the complete hierarchy of all components in your application.

`React Native DevTools` allows you to visualize the complete hierarchy of components in your application, giving you a clear view of how your UI is structured. It lets you inspect the props and state of each component in real time, making it easier to understand how data flows through your app. When you click on any component in the tree, the corresponding element is automatically highlighted on the screen, helping you identify its visual location within the interface. Additionally, you can view and even manually update the current values of state and props, which is particularly useful for testing UI changes on the fly without modifying your code.

Behind every bug lies a story waiting to be uncovered—and `React Native DevTools` helps you reveal it faster. Mastering these tools is essential if you want to debug efficiently and develop like a pro.

2.5. Summary

This chapter provides a comprehensive foundation for getting started with React Native. It begins with an introduction to React Native, explaining what it is and how it enables building mobile applications using JavaScript and React. You learned how to set up the React Native development environment, and the installation section guides you through setting up the development environment using either Expo.

Once set up, you'll create your first application, gaining hands-on experience with running and testing a basic app. Finally, it introduces basic debugging techniques and tools to help you identify and fix issues efficiently during development.

You are now all set to explore a UI with React Native.

CHAPTER 3

Structuring Screens: Tabs, Stacks, and Beyond

In Chapter 2, you were introduced to the fundamentals of React Native and successfully created your first basic application. With the core project structure now in place, you're ready to start building a more interactive and multi-screen experience.

In this chapter, we'll dive into React Navigation, a powerful library that enables seamless navigation between different screens in a React Native app. You'll learn how to create new pages (also known as screens), manage navigation stacks, and implement various methods to move between pages—such as button-based navigation, tab bars, and drawer menus.

By the end of this chapter, you'll have a clear understanding of how navigation works in React Native, and you'll be able to build apps that offer a smooth and user-friendly experience across multiple screens.

3.1. Navigating Within the Application

Navigation is a core concept in mobile app development, allowing users to move between different screens and workflows. In React Native, navigation is not built-in but is enabled through various libraries and patterns. Below is an in-depth exploration of the main types of navigation in React Native, including their conceptual models, practical use cases, and architectural implications.

A. Nalwaya and A. Paul, *React Native for Mobile Development*, https://doi.org/10.1007/979-8-8688-2977-2_3

3.1.1. Introduction to React Navigation

React Navigation is a JavaScript-based navigation library used to handle navigation in React Native applications. Navigation is the backbone of any mobile application, determining how users move between screens and interact with content. Poor navigation can make even the most feature-rich app feel clunky and confusing. React Navigation addresses this challenge by providing

- Cross-platform consistency across iOS and Android
- JavaScript-based implementation for faster development cycles
- Extensive customization options for unique user experiences
- Strong TypeScript support for a better development experience
- Comprehensive documentation with practical examples

While React Navigation dominates the React Native navigation landscape, alternatives exist:

- **React Native Navigation (Wix):** Native navigation with JavaScript bridge
- **Expo Router:** File-based routing similar to Next.js
- **React Navigation:** Latest version with static API improvements

Each approach has trade-offs in performance, complexity, and feature set.

3.1.2. Different Type of React Navigations

React Navigation provides multiple navigation patterns to suit various app structures and user experiences. Understanding these options is essential to designing a smooth and intuitive app flow. The primary navigation types in React Native include

- **Stack Navigation**: Works like a stack of pages, allowing users to push and pop screens. Ideal for workflows where screens follow one another, like product details or checkout flows.
- **Tab Navigation**: Displays a tab bar (typically at the bottom) to switch between key sections of the app such as Home, Profile, or Cart. Each tab can maintain its own navigation history.

- **Drawer Navigation**: Offers a side menu that slides in from the edge of the screen, commonly used for global navigation links or settings.
- **Modal Navigation**: Displays screens in a modal style, typically over the current screen. It's useful for tasks like user input, alerts, or short workflows. Modal is not a separate navigator—it's a presentation option within the Stack Navigator.

These navigation types can be combined and nested within each other to support complex app architectures. Selecting the right type depends on the intended user flow, the depth of content, and the platform's user interface conventions.

Stack Navigation

React Native Stack Navigation is a navigation method that allows users to move between screens in a structured, linear way, similar to stacking cards. Each new screen is added (or "pushed") onto the navigation stack, and going back removes (or "pops") the top screen, returning to the previous one. This behavior closely resembles native iOS and Android navigation patterns, providing a familiar user experience. It is best suited for flows that move step by step, such as login processes, onboarding, or navigating from a list to a detailed view. Stack Navigation automatically handles screen transitions, headers, and gestures like swipe-to-go-back on iOS. It supports passing data between screens and can be customized with animations or modal-style presentations. This form of navigation is highly flexible and forms the backbone of most navigation systems in React Native apps, often used alongside tabs or drawers for more complex flows.

Note Stack Navigation is modelled after the classic stack data structure (Last-In-First-Out, or LIFO). Each time a user navigates to a new screen, that screen is "pushed" onto the top of the stack. When the user goes back, the top screen is "popped" off, revealing the previous screen.

Key Stack Navigation Features

These are key concepts and important points in Stack Navigations:

- **Push**: Adds a new screen to the top of the stack
- **Pop**: Removes the top screen, returning to the previous one

- **PopToTop**: Removes all screens above the root, returning to the first screen in the stack
- **Replace**: Substitutes the current screen with a new one without altering the rest of the stack
- **Parameters**: Parameter passing between screens
- **Configurable**: Configurable headers with titles, buttons, and styling
- **Swipe Back**: Gesture navigation supporting swipe-back on iOS

Best Use Cases for Stack Navigation

Stack Navigation is ideal for workflows where users move through a sequence of screens and may need to return to previous ones. It mirrors the forward-backward navigation behavior of web browsers. Common scenarios include

- Navigating from a Home screen to a Details screen, then to a Profile, and back by popping screens
- Multi-step processes like onboarding flows, form submissions, or content detail views

This pattern ensures a clear navigation history and is perfect when screen transitions follow a linear or hierarchical path.

Libraries

```
@react-navigation/stack
@react-navigation/native-stack
```

Tab Navigation

Tab navigation in React Native is a widely used pattern that enables users to switch between different screens or sections of an app using a tab bar, typically located at the bottom or top of the interface. Each tab represents a distinct route or feature, such as Home, Profile, or Settings, and users can move seamlessly between them with a single tap. This navigation style is particularly effective for apps with multiple independent sections, as it allows users to quickly access primary functionalities without losing the state of inactive screens—meaning each tab preserves its own navigation history and data until revisited.

Tab navigation allows users to switch between top-level screens using tabs, usually displayed at the bottom (or top) of the screen.

Key Tab Navigation Features

- **Tab Bar:** UI component displaying the available tabs.
- **Tab Switching:** Instantly switches context without losing the state of inactive tabs.
- **Nested Navigation**: Each tab can have its own stack or nested navigator for deeper navigation within that section.
- Custom icons that change based on active state.
- Badge notifications for unread content.
- Custom tab bar styling and positioning.
- Dynamic tab visibility based on user state.

Best Use Cases for Tab Navigation

Tab Navigation is best suited for apps with multiple core sections that users switch between frequently. Each tab typically represents an independent feature or module of the app, allowing for quick and consistent access. Common use cases include

- Apps with **multiple independent sections** like Home, Profile, and Settings
- When users need to **quickly switch between main features** without losing context
- **Social media apps** with tabs for **Feed**, **Search**, **Notifications**, and **Profile**

This navigation pattern enhances usability by keeping primary app areas easily accessible with a single tap.

Libraries

```
@react-navigation/bottom-tabs
@react-navigation/material-top-tabs
```

Drawer Navigation

Drawer navigation in React Native is a popular navigation pattern that provides users with access to multiple screens or sections of an app through a side panel, commonly called a *drawer*. This drawer remains hidden by default and can be revealed by swiping from the edge of the screen or tapping a menu icon. When opened, the drawer slides in from the left (or right, depending on configuration) and displays a list of navigation options or custom content, such as user profiles or settings. Drawer navigation is especially useful in apps with many sections or features, as it helps declutter the main interface while still offering quick access to different parts of the app.

Drawer navigation uses a sliding panel (drawer) that appears from the side of the screen, typically triggered by a menu button or a swipe gesture.

The drawer contains navigation links to different screens or sections of the app.

Key Drawer Navigation Features

- **Drawer**: Hidden panel that slides in and out
- **Menu Items:** Links to various screens or routes
- **Custom Content:** Can include user info, settings, or other interactive elements

Best Use Cases for Drawer

Drawer Navigation is ideal for apps with a large number of sections or settings that don't require constant visibility. It provides a hidden side menu that users can open when needed, making it useful for decluttering the main UI. Common use cases include

- Apps with many sections, like email clients or productivity tools, where the drawer can organize access to folders, labels, or settings
- When you need to offer secondary navigation options without crowding the screen
- Complex menus that benefit from vertical space and structured grouping

Best practices when using drawer navigation:

- Organize menu items logically into groups.
- Use icons and typography to establish visual hierarchy.
- Ensure accessibility by labelling drawer controls properly.
- Lazy load content inside the drawer for better performance.

Drawer navigation helps maintain a clean UI while still offering deep navigational control.

Libraries

```
@react-navigation/drawer
```

Modal Navigation

Modal Navigation presents screens as overlays or pop-ups, often used for transient tasks like editing or confirmation dialogs.

Modals can be stacked, but they are visually and behaviorally distinct from standard stack navigation.

Key Modal Navigation Features

- **Overlay**: The modal appears above the current screen.
- **Dismissal**: Modals are typically dismissed by user action or programmatically.

Best Use Cases for Modal Navigation

Modal Navigation is perfect for short, focused tasks that require user attention without navigating away from the current screen. Modals appear as overlays, helping maintain context while prompting users to take quick actions. This navigation style is best suited for

- **Editing a profile** or updating user-specific details
- **Confirming an action**, such as deletions or submissions
- **Displaying alerts** or system messages that require acknowledgment or a decision

By design, modals are lightweight and interrupt-driven, making them ideal for workflows that demand immediate user focus without a full-screen transition.

In the latest versions of React Navigation, modals are not created using a separate navigator or the old mode: `'modal'` option. Instead, modal behavior is configured directly in the Stack Navigator using the presentation property.

To use Modal Navigation, configure your Stack Navigator and set presentation: 'modal' for the relevant screen.

```
import { createNativeStackNavigator } from '@react-navigation/
native-stack';

const Stack = createNativeStackNavigator();

function AppStack() {
  return (
    <Stack.Navigator>
      <Stack.Screen name="Home" component={HomeScreen} />

      <Stack.Screen
        name="MyModal"
        component={ModalScreen}
        options={{
          presentation: 'modal',
        }}
      />
    </Stack.Navigator>
  );
}
```

The real power of React Navigation emerges when combining different navigator types. A typical app might use

- Drawer navigator as the root for main sections
- Tab navigator within drawer sections for sub-categories
- Stack navigator within tabs for detailed views

This creates a hierarchy where each navigator manages its own screen stack while participating in the larger navigation structure.

3.2. Example: Building an Expense Tracker App with Tab and Stack Navigation

Now that we've explored the different types of navigation in React Native, it's time to put that knowledge into practice. In this hands-on example, we'll build an Expense Tracker App that combines both Tab Navigation and Stack Navigation—a common pattern in real-world applications.

We'll continue using the project folder set up in the previous chapter to maintain continuity.

This section will walk you through the practical implementation, demonstrating how to use

- **Tab Navigation** to switch between core sections of the app
- **Stack Navigation** to manage deeper flows like adding new entries or viewing transaction details

This example not only helps reinforce the navigation concepts but also provides a solid foundation for building scalable and intuitive mobile apps.

Installation and Setup

Before diving into implementation, you need to install React Navigation and its dependencies. The installation process varies depending on whether you're using Expo:

For Expo projects:

```
npm install @react-navigation/native @react-navigation/native-stack @react-navigation/bottom-tabs
```

3.2.1. Tab Navigation

We'll begin by implementing Tab Navigation and creating the following screens as individual tabs in our app:

- **Home**: Displays a dashboard with the current balance and a summary of recent financial activity
- **Add Assets**: Allows users to add new income sources or assets
- **Transactions**: Enables users to view, filter, and manage all transactions
- **Stats**: Visualizes income and expenses through charts and trends

To get started, open App.js, and replace its content with the following code:

```
// App.js
// Main entry point for the Expense Tracker React Native app
// Sets up bottom tab navigation for transactions

import React from 'react';
import { NavigationContainer } from '@react-navigation/native'; // Provides
navigation context
import { createBottomTabNavigator } from '@react-navigation/bottom-tabs';
// For bottom tab navigation

// Import screen components (each displays its own screen name)
import HomeScreen from './screens/HomeScreen';
import AddAssetsScreen from './screens/AddAssetsScreen';
import TransactionScreen from './screens/TransactionScreen';
import StatsScreen from './screens/StatsScreen';

// Create navigators
const Tab = createBottomTabNavigator();

export default function App() {
  return (
    <NavigationContainer>
      <Tab.Navigator>
        <Tab.Screen name="Home" component={HomeScreen} />
        <Tab.Screen name="Add Assets" component={AddAssetsScreen} />
        <Tab.Screen name="Transaction" component={TransactionScreen} />
        <Tab.Screen name="Stats" component={StatsScreen} />
      </Tab.Navigator>
    </NavigationContainer>
  );
}
```

This code sets up the main navigation structure of the app using React Navigation's Tab Navigator wrapped inside a `NavigationContainer`, which is essential for managing navigation state in a React Native app. Inside the `NavigationContainer`, the `Tab.Navigator` component defines a bottom tab navigation system. Each `Tab.Screen` represents a separate tab in the app's interface, linked to a specific component or screen.

For example, the Home tab displays the HomeScreen component, while the Add Assets, Transaction, and Stats tabs link to their respective components (AddAssetsScreen, TransactionScreen, and StatsScreen). This setup allows users to easily switch between key sections of the app through a persistent tab bar at the bottom of the screen.

To keep your project well-organized and maintainable, we'll create a separate folder to hold all the screen components used in our Tab Navigation. Inside your project's root directory, create a new folder named screens. This folder will contain all the individual screen files linked to each tab in the Tab Navigator. Now, inside the screens folder, create a new file named HomeScreen.js:

```
import React from 'react';
import { View, Text, StyleSheet } from 'react-native';

const HomeScreen = () => (
  <View style={styles.container}>
    <Text style={styles.text}>HomeScreen</Text>
  </View>
);

const styles = StyleSheet.create({
  container: {
    flex: 1,
    justifyContent: 'center',
    alignItems: 'center',
  },
});

export default HomeScreen;
```

This component uses basic React Native elements to render a Tab Name as a message. As the app evolves, this screen will be expanded to dynamically show user data.

Create AddAssetsScreen.js and add the following code:

```
import React from 'react';
import { View, Text, StyleSheet } from 'react-native';

const AddAssetsScreen = () => (
   <View style={styles.container}>
        <Text>AddAssetsScreen</Text>
```

```
  </View>
);

const styles = StyleSheet.create({
  container: {
    flex: 1,
    justifyContent: 'center',
    alignItems: 'center',
  }
});

export default AddAssetsScreen;
```

Create `StatsScreen.js`:

```
import React from 'react';
import { View, Text, StyleSheet } from 'react-native';

const StatsScreen = () => (
  <View style={styles.container}>
    <Text>StatsScreen</Text>
  </View>
);

const styles = StyleSheet.create({
  container: {
    flex: 1,
    justifyContent: 'center',
    alignItems: 'center',
  },
});

export default StatsScreen;
```

Create `TransactionScreen.js` and add the following code:

```
import React from 'react';
import { View, Text, StyleSheet} from 'react-native';
```

```
const TransactionScreen = () => (
  <View style={styles.container}>
    <Text>TransactionScreen</Text>
  </View>
);

const styles = StyleSheet.create({
  container: {
    flex: 1,
    justifyContent: 'center',
    alignItems: 'center',
  },
});

export default TransactionScreen;
```

Now that we've set up the Tab Navigator and created four tabs, it's time to run the application and see the navigation in action.

To start the app, open your terminal and run the following command from your project root:

```
npm run ios
```

Once the app launches in your emulator or physical device, you'll see a bottom tab bar with multiple tabs—Home, Add Assets, Transaction, and Stats. Each tab is interactive and allows you to switch between different sections of the app. Right now, the tabs display the basic screens we've set up. As you tap on each tab, the corresponding screen component will be rendered, providing a smooth and intuitive navigation experience.

This setup mimics the structure of real-world mobile apps, where core features are grouped into tabs for quick and easy access. In the upcoming sections, we'll continue enhancing these screens and add more functionality.

3.3. Integrating Stack Navigation Within Tabs

In this step, we'll enhance our navigation setup by adding Stack Navigation inside each Tab—a common and highly effective approach used in complex applications.

Using a Stack Navigator inside each tab allows individual tabs to manage their own navigation flows independently. This means that each tab can navigate to deeper screens without affecting the global tab structure. Users can explore additional features or details within a section while still being anchored to the active tab. This provides a seamless and familiar experience that mirrors how most production-grade mobile apps behave.

3.3.1. Use Case Example: Stack Navigation in the Transactions Tab

Let's implement this pattern in the `Transactions` tab. We'll

1. Wrap the `Transactions` tab in a `Stack Navigator`.
2. Create an additional screen named `TransactionDetailScreen.js`.
3. Add a button on the main Transactions screen to navigate to the details screen using the stack.

This setup will allow the user to view a list of transactions and tap to view detailed information on a new screen—without leaving the Transactions tab.

This approach maintains a clean separation of concerns:

- **Tab Navigation** handles high-level app sections.
- **Stack Navigation** manages screen transitions within a specific section.

Now we will walk through the code to set this up, beginning with creating the `TransactionDetailScreen.js` screen and configuring the Stack Navigator inside the Transactions tab.

Step 1: Wrap the Transactions tab in a Stack Navigator; update the bold code in `App.js`:

```
// Main entry point for the Expense Tracker React Native app
// Sets up bottom tab navigation and stack navigation for transactions

import React from 'react';
import { NavigationContainer } from '@react-navigation/native'; // Provides
navigation context
import { createBottomTabNavigator } from '@react-navigation/bottom-tabs';
// For bottom tab navigation
import { createNativeStackNavigator } from '@react-navigation/native-
stack'; // For stack navigation within tabs

// Import screen components (each displays its own screen name)
import HomeScreen from './screens/HomeScreen';
import AddAssetsScreen from './screens/AddAssetsScreen';
import TransactionScreen from './screens/TransactionScreen';
import StatsScreen from './screens/StatsScreen';
import TransactionDetailScreen from './screens/TransactionDetailScreen';

// Create navigators
const Tab = createBottomTabNavigator();
const Stack = createNativeStackNavigator();

//Stack navigator for the Transaction tab
// Allows navigation from the transaction list to transaction details
function TransactionStack() {
   return (
    <Stack.Navigator>
      <Stack.Screen name="Transactions" component={TransactionScreen} />
      <Stack.Screen name="TransactionDetail" component={TransactionDetail
      Screen} />
    </Stack.Navigator>
  );
}
```

```
export default function App() {
  return (
    <NavigationContainer>
      <Tab.Navigator>
        <Tab.Screen name="Home" component={HomeScreen} />
        <Tab.Screen name="Add Assets" component={AddAssetsScreen} />
        <Tab.Screen name="Transaction" component={TransactionStack} />
        <Tab.Screen name="Stats" component={StatsScreen} />
      </Tab.Navigator>
    </NavigationContainer>
  );
}
```

Step 2: Create an additional screen named `TransactionDetailScreen.js`:

```
import React from 'react';
import { View, Text, StyleSheet } from 'react-native';

const TransactionDetailScreen = ({ route }) => {
  const { id } = route.params;

  return (
    <View style={styles.container}>
      <Text style={styles.text}>TransactionDetailScreen for {id}</Text>
    </View>
  );
};

const styles = StyleSheet.create({
  container: {
    flex: 1,
    justifyContent: 'center',
    alignItems: 'center',
  },
  text: {
    fontSize: 24,
```

```
    fontWeight: 'bold',
  },
});

export default TransactionDetailScreen;
```

Step 3: Add a button on the main Transactions screen to navigate to the details screen using the stack. Update TransactionScreen.js file and a

```
const TransactionScreen = ({navigation}) => (
  <View style={styles.container}>
    <Text>TransactionScreen</Text>
        <Button
        title="View Transaction Detail"
        onPress={() => navigation.navigate('TransactionDetail', { id: 1 })}
      />
  </View>
);
```

This React Native code renders a button labeled "View Transaction Detail". When the button is pressed, it triggers the onPress function. This function uses React Navigation's navigate method to move to the TransactionDetail screen. It also passes an object { id: 1 } as a parameter to that screen, though here we have hard-coded the id as 1, but in production apps, this id would come from a list item. On the target screen, this id can be accessed using route.params.id. This is useful for displaying details related to a specific transaction.

And now run the application and go to the Transactions tab:

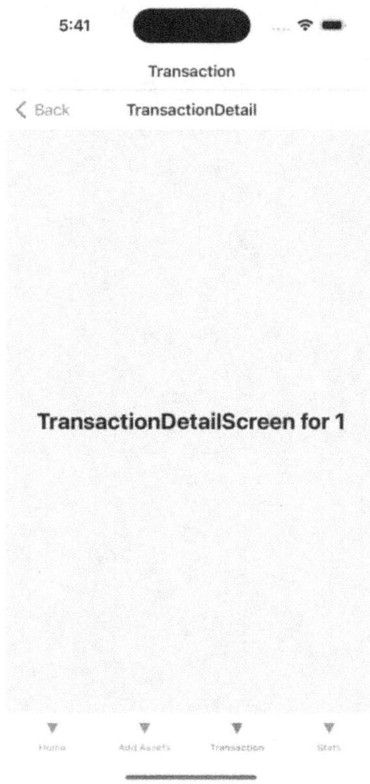

Now that we've added Stack Navigation inside the Transactions tab, you'll notice that the navigation flow has become more dynamic. From the main `TransactionScreen`, users can tap a button to navigate to the `TransactionDetailsScreen`, which is pushed onto the stack. This means users can move between these screens using the *Back button*, just like in a typical mobile app navigation experience.

However, you might also observe that multiple headers are appearing—one from the Tab Navigator and another from the Stack Navigator. This can make the UI look cluttered or inconsistent, especially if both headers display similar titles or navigation controls.

To improve the user experience and maintain a clean interface, we need to hide the default header from one of the navigators. In most cases, it's ideal to disable the Tab Navigator's header and rely on the Stack Navigator's header for better control and consistency across screen transitions.

To hide the redundant headers and customize the navigation bar to better match the app's design, update `app.js` with the following code, and it will remove multiple headers:

```
<Tab.Screen name="Transaction" component={TransactionStack}
options={{ headerShown: false }} />
```

Now, go ahead and run the app again 🚀. You'll notice that the interface looks much cleaner—with only one header visible at the top. This confirms that our Stack Navigator is correctly handling the screen transitions within the Transactions tab, and the redundant headers have been removed.

3.4. Summary: Mastering React Navigation

In this chapter, we explored the foundational and advanced concepts of React Navigation, one of the most essential libraries for handling navigation in React Native applications.

We began by understanding the different types of navigation—including Stack Navigation, Tab Navigation, Drawer Navigation, and Modal Navigation—along with their best use cases. Through hands-on implementation, we built a practical `Expense Tracker App`, combining both **Tab and Stack Navigation**, a structure commonly seen in real-world mobile apps.

This table presents a comprehensive overview.

Table 3-1. *Different ways of Navigation in React Native*

	Stack Navigation	**Tab Navigation**	**Drawer Navigation**	**Modal Navigation**
Conceptual Model	Stack (LIFO)	Tabbed interface	Sliding side panel	Overlay/modal presentation
Feature	Push/pop screens, back navigation, replace, popToTop	Persistent state per tab, quick switching, tab bar UI	Hidden drawer, menu links, custom content	Overlay screens, dismissible, transient tasks
Pros	Simple, intuitive, mirrors mobile/web navigation	Easy access to main features, state preserved	Declutters UI, flexible, custom content	Focused user tasks, visually distinct
Cons	Limited for multi-section apps	Not ideal for deep or complex flows	Can hide important navigation, less discoverable	Not for main navigation, can disrupt flow
Use Cases	Linear flows, forms, detail pages	Social, shopping, dashboard apps	Email, productivity, apps with many sections	Editing, confirmation, alerts
Libraries	@react-navigation/stack, native-stack	@react-navigation/bottom-tabs	@react-navigation/drawer	Stack with mode: 'modal'

CHAPTER 4

Canvas, Brush, and Paint: Working with Styling and Layout

In Chapter 3, we examined React Native Navigation in detail and implemented an application that incorporated multiple forms of navigation. Having established a functional project skeleton, the next logical step is to enrich it with a well-designed and aesthetically pleasing user interface.

- **Styling**: Controls the visual appearance of components (colors, fonts, spacing, borders) using JavaScript style objects. It ensures the app looks consistent and visually appealing.
- **Flexbox**: The layout system in React Native that arranges components responsively.

> *Styling defines how your app looks, while Flexbox defines how your app's components are arranged.*

It is widely acknowledged within the field of software engineering that the success of an application is determined not solely by its functional reliability but also by its visual presentation. A carefully designed user interface not only enhances usability but can also contribute substantially to the adoption and overall success of an application.

A. Nalwaya and A. Paul, *React Native for Mobile Development*, https://doi.org/10.1007/979-8-8688-2977-2_4

4.1. Styling in React Native

Styling is what transforms bare UI components into beautiful, usable, and consistent designs. In React Native, styling works differently than in traditional web development, but the underlying concepts are familiar if you know CSS. Instead of writing separate CSS files, styles in React Native are written in JavaScript objects and applied directly to components. Understanding React Native styling is critical for creating professional apps that look and feel natural on both iOS and Android.

Unlike the web, React Native does not use CSS selectors or stylesheets. Instead, it uses a `StyleSheet` API and inline style objects. Let's start with the primary way to style your components in React Native that is `StyleSheet` API.

4.1.1. The StyleSheet API

The `StyleSheet` API is the recommended way to style React Native components, offering a structured and efficient method for defining an app's appearance. It's a JavaScript-based approach that mimics the function of a CSS stylesheet. The `StyleSheet.create()` method is a key part of this API. It takes a plain JavaScript object as input, where each key represents a named style, and its corresponding value is an object containing various style properties (e.g., `color, fontSize`).

Using `StyleSheet.create()` offers several benefits:

- **Readability**: By separating your styles into a dedicated `StyleSheet` object, you create a clear distinction between the component's structure (JSX) and its visual presentation. This separation makes your code easier to read and maintain, as you can quickly find and modify styles without cluttering the component's logic.

Let's understand this with code:

```
import { StyleSheet } from 'react-native';

const styles = StyleSheet.create({
  container: {
    backgroundColor: 'lightblue',
    padding: 20,
    margin: 10,
  },
```

```
  title: {
    fontSize: 24,
    color: 'darkblue',
    fontWeight: 'bold',
  },
});
```

We have created a StyleSheet object with styles, and now to apply the styles you've created, you use the style prop on your components. This prop accepts an object of style properties or, more commonly, a reference to a style object created with StyleSheet.

```
import React from 'react'
import { View, Text, StyleSheet } from 'react-native';

const MyComponent = () => {
  return (
    <View style={styles.container}>
      <Text style={styles.title}>Hello, React Native!</Text>
    </View>
  );
};

export default MyComponent;
```

4.1.2. Inline Styling

Inline styling in React Native allows you to apply styles directly to a component using a plain JavaScript object. This approach is similar to inline CSS on the web. You pass the style object to the style prop, and because it's a JavaScript object, you use double curly braces: one for the JSX expression and the other to define the object itself.

```
<Text style={{ fontSize: 18, color: 'red' }}>  Inline </Text>
```

Here, style directly sets the font size and color of the text. This method is useful for quick, simple style adjustments or when a style value needs to be dynamically calculated based on a component's state or props.

While convenient, inline styling comes with notable drawbacks, which is why it's recommended to use it sparingly in production applications. React Native must re-create the style object on every single render. This constant re-creation is inefficient and can impact performance, especially in components that re-render frequently.

Unlike styles created with `StyleSheet.create()`, inline styles are not validated by React Native, so typos in property names or invalid values may not be flagged with a helpful warning, leading to silent failures.

4.1.3. Style Properties

React Native style properties are similar to CSS, but with some key differences. All property names are camel-cased, and most don't have hyphens. For example, `font-size` in CSS becomes `fontSize` in React Native.

We will not cover every style property here; you will naturally encounter and learn them as you build real-world applications. Below is a breakdown of the most commonly used style properties:

- **Layout Properties**: `width, height, margin, padding`. These are fundamental for spacing and sizing.
- **Color and Background**: `backgroundColor, color`. Colors can be specified using hex codes, RGB, RGBA, or color names.
- **Border Properties**: `borderWidth, borderColor, borderStyle, borderRadius`. You can also style individual sides like `borderTopWidth`.
- **Typography**: `fontSize`, `fontWeight`, `fontStyle`, `textAlign`, `lineHeight`, etc.
- **Shadows**: `shadowColor, shadowOffset, shadowOpacity, shadowRadius`. Note that these properties only work on iOS. For Android, you use elevation.

Styling with Platform Differences

React Native allows developers to apply platform-specific styles so that apps feel native on both iOS and Android. This is achieved using the Platform API or conditional logic, enabling adjustments such as different colors, shadows, or spacing depending on the operating system.

```
import { Platform } from "react-native";
const styles = StyleSheet.create({
  button: {
    padding: 10,
    backgroundColor: Platform.OS === "ios" ? "blue" : "green",
  },
});
```

4.1.4. Combining and Overriding Styles

React Native allows you to combine multiple style objects by passing them in an array to the `style` prop. The styles are applied in the order they appear, with later styles overriding earlier ones if there are conflicting properties.

```
import React from 'react'
import { View, Text, StyleSheet } from 'react-native';

const MyButton = ({ isPrimary }) => {
  const buttonStyles = [styles.button];

  if (isPrimary) {
    buttonStyles.push(styles.primaryButton);
  }

  return (
    <View style={buttonStyles}>
      <Text style={styles.buttonText}>Click Me</Text>
    </View>
  );
};
```

```
const styles = StyleSheet.create({
  button: {
    padding: 10,
    borderWidth: 1,
    borderColor: '#ccc',
    borderRadius: 5,
  },
  primaryButton: {
    backgroundColor: 'blue',
    borderColor: 'darkblue',
  },
  buttonText: {
    color: 'black',
  }
});
```

In this example, if `isPrimary` is true, the `backgroundColor` and `borderColor` from `primaryButton` will override the default button styles.

4.1.5. Dimension API

To create responsive layouts that adapt to different screen sizes, you can use the Dimensions API. This API provides the width and height of the device screen.

```
import { Dimensions } from 'react-native';

const screenWidth = Dimensions.get('window').width;

const styles = StyleSheet.create({
  fullWidthImage: {
    width: screenWidth,
    height: screenWidth * 0.5, // Maintain aspect ratio
  },
});
```

Using `Dimensions` helps in creating fluid layouts that aren't tied to fixed pixel values.

4.2. Creating Layout with Flexbox

In creating the layout in the previous example, you must have seen the flex property mentioned in the styles. This appears because React Native apps use the Flexbox layout model.

The React Native Flexbox layout model is inspired by the `CSS Flex Box` layout from `CSS3`. The React Native team has rewritten this feature specifically for Mobile devices. The main idea behind Flexbox is being able to create a layout without worrying about different screen sizes or device orientation. A flex container expands items to fill available free space or shrinks them to prevent overflow. Let's get some basic knowledge of Flexbox to expedite our layout development.

Flexbox is the cornerstone of React Native layout design—a powerful, flexible system that transforms how we think about arranging components on screen. Unlike traditional layout systems that rely on absolute positioning or complex calculations, Flexbox provides an intuitive, mathematical approach to distributing space and aligning elements. This comprehensive guide will take you from basic concepts to advanced techniques, ensuring you can build any layout with confidence.

4.2.1. Understanding the Flexbox Model

Every `Flexbox` layout starts with a **flex container** (parent) that holds **flex items** (children). When you set a View's style to include any flex property, it becomes a flex container, and all its direct children automatically become flex items that participate in the flex layout algorithm.

```
// Container becomes a flex container
<View style={{ flex: 1, flexDirection: 'row' }}>
  {/* These are flex items */}
  <View style={{ flex: 1 }}>Item 1</View>
  <View style={{ flex: 2 }}>Item 2</View>
  <View style={{ flex: 1 }}>Item 3</View>
</View>
```

The relationship is hierarchical: a flex item can also be a flex container for its own children, enabling complex nested layouts that maintain flexibility and responsiveness.

Main Axis vs. Cross Axis: The Foundation of Alignment

Understanding axes is crucial to mastering Flexbox. Every flex container has two perpendicular axes that determine how items are arranged and aligned:

- **Main Axis:** The primary direction of layout, controlled by `flexDirection`
- **Cross Axis**: Always perpendicular to the main axis

When `flexDirection` is column (React Native's default), the main axis runs vertically and the cross axis horizontally. When `flexDirection` is row, the main axis runs horizontally and the cross axis vertically.

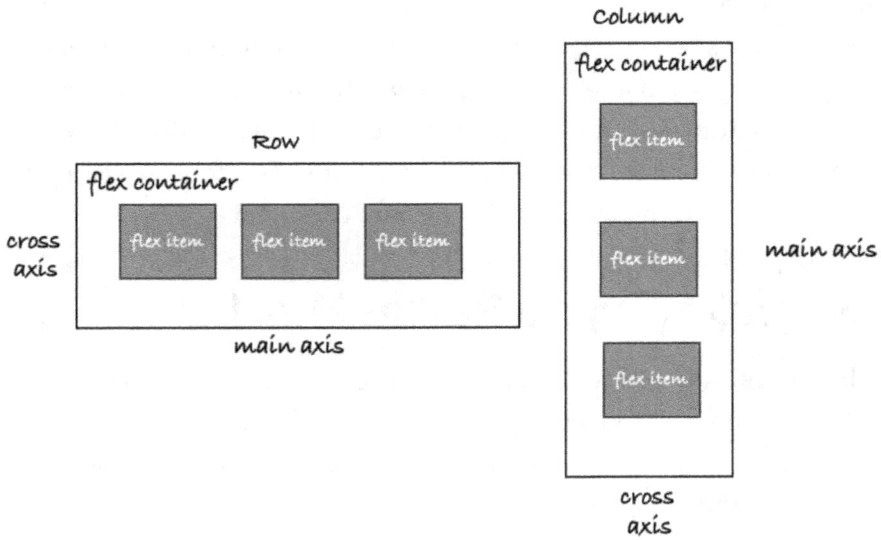

Fundamental Properties of a Flex Container

To make an element a flex container, you need to apply the flex property to it. Here are some fundamental properties that you can apply to the flex container:

- **flexDirection**: This property determines the main axis direction, allowing you to set the flow of flex items as either rows or columns.
- **justifyContent:** It controls the alignment of flex items along the main axis. You can set them to be distributed at the start, end, center, or spaced evenly.

- **alignItems:** This property aligns flex items along the cross axis. It can be used to center or align them to the start or end of the container.
- **alignContent**: When you have multiple rows or columns of flex items, this property defines how **they** are aligned in the cross axis.

Let's dive deeper into this.

1. flexDirection: Defining Your Layout's Main Axis

The *flexDirection* property is your layout's compass—it determines the primary direction in which child components flow within their container. This fundamental property establishes what developers call the "main axis," which becomes the reference point for all other flex properties.

The flex Direction property establishes the main axis which in turn determines how the flex items are placed within the container.

Available values and their behavior:

- `column (default):` Arranges children from top to bottom vertically. This differs from CSS web development, where row is the default.
- `row`: Arranges children from left to right horizontally.
- `column-reverse`: Arranges children from bottom to top.
- `row-reverse`: Aligns children from right to left.

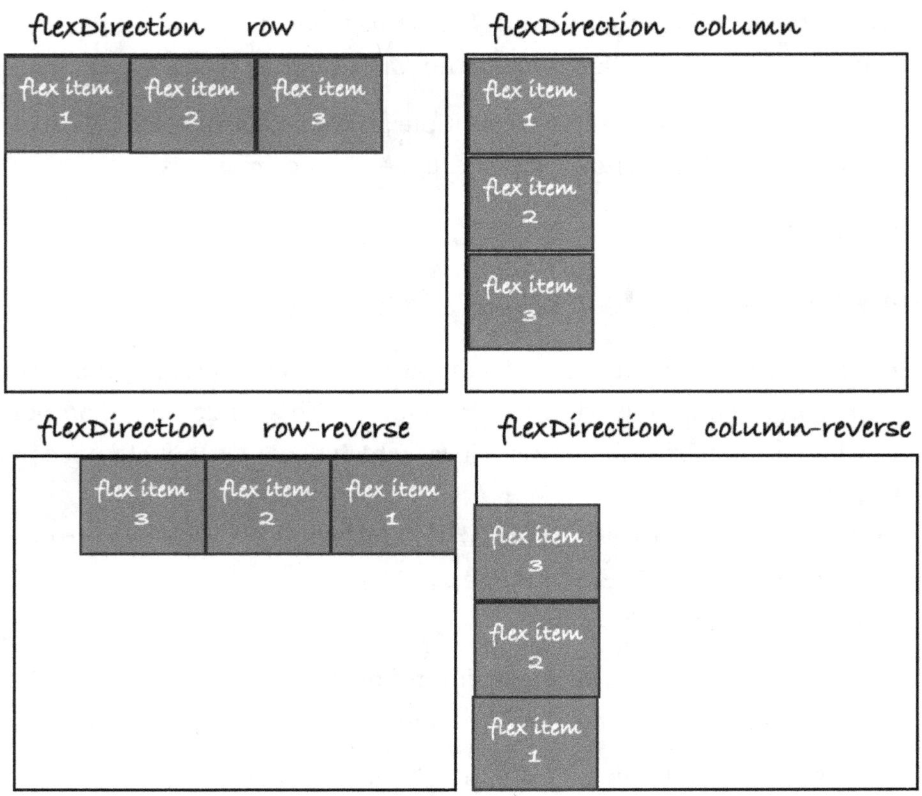

Practical Example

```
import { View, Text, StyleSheet } from 'react-native';

const FlexExample = () => {
  return (
      <View style={styles.columnBox}>
        <View style={styles.box} >
          <Text>flex item 1 </Text>
     </View>
        <View style={styles.box} >
          <Text> flex item 2 </Text
     </View>
        <View style={styles.box} >
          <Text>flex item 3</Text>
     </View>
```

```
    </View>
  );
};

const styles = StyleSheet.create({

  columnBox: {
    flexDirection: 'row-reverse',
  },
  box: {
    width: 50,
    height: 50,
    backgroundColor: 'lightblue',
  }
});

export default FlexExample;
```

- A crucial point to remember: when you change flexDirection, you're also changing which axis is considered "main" and which is "cross." This affects how justifyContent and alignItems behave.

2. justifyContent: Distributing Space Along the Main Axis

The *justifyContent* property controls how flex items are distributed along the main axis—the direction you've established with flexDirection. Think of it as the property that answers "How should I space out my components along the primary flow?"

Available Values

- **flex-start (Default)**: Items align at the beginning of the main axis.
- **flex-end**: Items align at the end of the main axis.
- **center**: Items center along the main axis.
- **space-between**: Items spread evenly with the first item at the start, last at the end.

- **space-around**: Items spread evenly with equal space around each item.
- **space-evenly**: Items distributed with equal space between all items and edges.

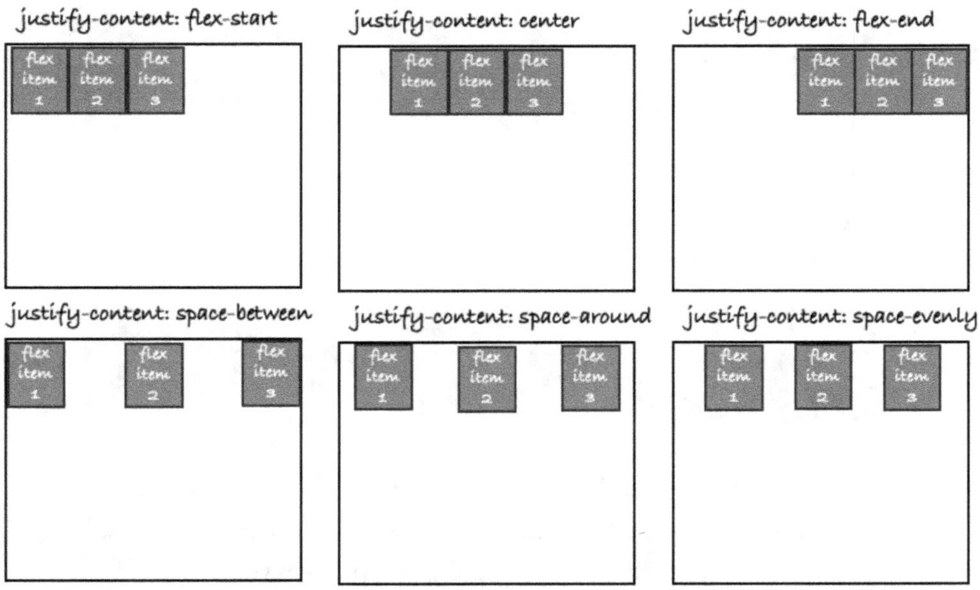

"The justify content property defines the alignment along the main axis."

Practical Example

```
import React from 'react';
import { View, Text, StyleSheet } from 'react-native';

const FlexExample = () => {
  return (
      <View style={styles.columnBox}>
        <View style={styles.box} >
              <Text>flex item 1</Text>
          </View>
        <View style={styles.box} >
              <Text>flex item 2</Text>
          </View>
```

```
      <View style={styles.box} >
            <Text>flex item 3 </Text>
        </View>
    </View>
  );
};

const styles = StyleSheet.create({

  columnBox: {
    flexDirection: 'row',
    justifyContent: 'space-around',
  },
  box: {
    width: 50,
    height: 50,
    backgroundColor: 'lightblue',
  }
});

export default FlexExample;
```

An important behavior to understand: `justifyContent` always works along the main axis. If your `flexDirection` is row, then `justifyContent` controls horizontal distribution. If it's column, then it controls vertical distribution.

3. alignItems: Positioning Items Along the Cross Axis

While `justifyContent` handles the main axis, `alignItems` manages the cross axis—the direction perpendicular to your main axis. This property determines how items align when they don't fill the entire cross-axis space.

Available Values

- **stretch (Default)**: Items stretch to fill the container's cross-axis.
- **flex-start**: Items align to the start of the cross-axis.
- **flex-end**: Items align to the end of the cross-axis.
- **center**: Items center along the cross-axis.
- **baseline**: Items align along their text baseline.

"alignItems describes how to align children along the cross axis of their container. Align items is very similar to justifyContent, but instead of applying to the main axis, alignItems applies to the cross axis."

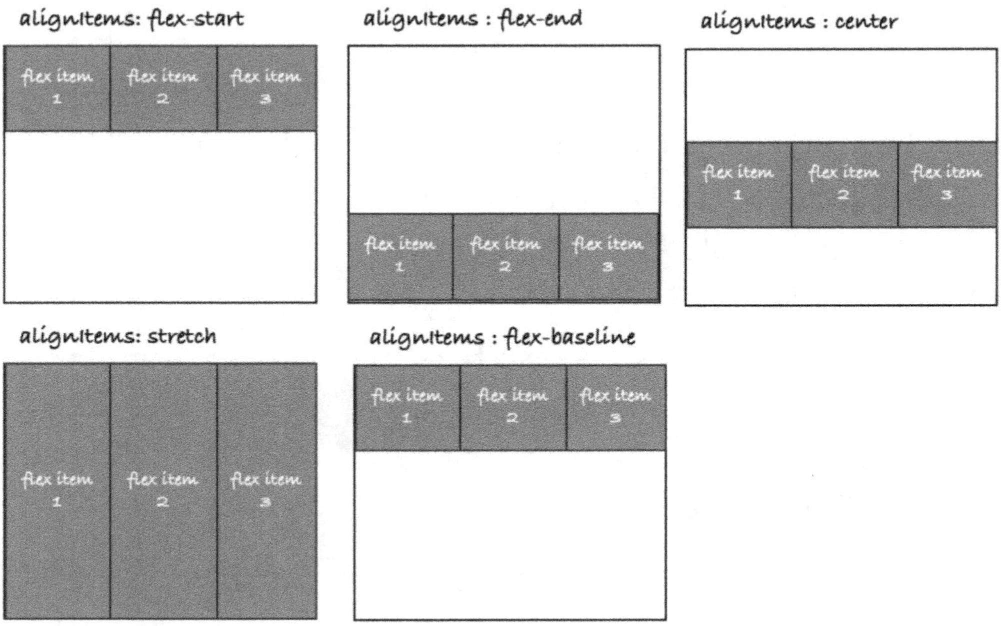

Practical Example

```
// Centering items vertically in a row layout
<View style={{
  flexDirection: 'row',
  alignItems: 'center',
  height: 100
}}>
  <View style={{ width: 50, height: 30, backgroundColor: 'red' }} />
  <View style={{ width: 50, height: 60, backgroundColor: 'blue' }} />
  <View style={{ width: 50, height: 40, backgroundColor: 'green' }} />
</View>

// Stretching items to fill height in column layout
<View style={{
  flexDirection: 'column',
```

```
  alignItems: 'stretch',
  height: 200
}}>
  <View style={{ height: 50, backgroundColor: 'red' }} />
  <View style={{ height: 50, backgroundColor: 'blue' }} />
</View>
```

"The default value of alignItems is 'stretch.'"

A key insight from experienced developers: "One common pitfall when starting with Flexbox is misunderstanding the flexDirection property in React Native. Always consider the cross axis. Use alignItems to control alignment along the cross axis and remember that the cross axis is perpendicular to the main axis defined by flexDirection."

4. alignContent: Managing Multiple Lines of Content

The alignContent property becomes essential when you're working with wrapped content—multiple lines or columns of flex items. Unlike alignItems, which aligns individual items within a single line, alignContent aligns the lines themselves.

Key requirement: This property only works when flexWrap: 'wrap' is enabled and you have multiple lines of content.

Available Values

- **flex-start (Default)**: Lines align at the start of the cross-axis.
- **flex-end**: Lines align at the end of the cross-axis.
- **center**: Lines center along the cross-axis.
- **stretch**: Lines stretch to fill the container.
- **space-between**: Lines distribute evenly with equal space between them.
- **space-around**: Lines distribute with equal space around each line.

"The Align content property aligns lines of content along the cross axis. However, a very important condition is that multiple columns or rows must exist within the container."

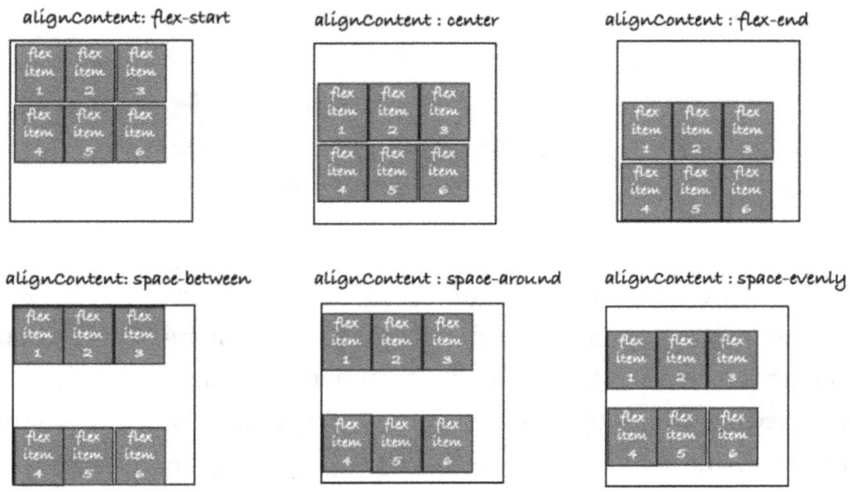

Practical Example

```
import React from 'react';
import { View, StyleSheet, Text } from 'react-native';

const AlignContentExample = () => {
  return (
    <View style={styles.container}>
          <View style={styles.box}><Text>flex item 1 </Text></View>
          <View style={styles.box}><Text>flex item 2 </Text></View>
           <View style={styles.box}><Text>flex item 3 </Text></View>
          <View style={styles.box}><Text>flex item 4 </Text></View>
          <View style={styles.box}><Text>flex item 5 </Text></View>
          <View style={styles.box}><Text>flex item 6 </Text></View>

    </View>
  );
};

const styles = StyleSheet.create({
  container: {
    flexDirection: 'row',
    flexWrap: 'wrap',
```

```
    alignContent: 'space-evenly', // Try changing this to 'flex-start',
    'flex-end', 'space-between', etc.
    height: 300,
    width: 300,
  },
  box: {
    backgroundColor: 'lightblue',
    margin: 5,
    justifyContent: 'center',
    alignItems: 'center',
  },
});

export default AlignContentExample;
```

The distinction between alignItems and alignContent is crucial: "The main difference between alignContent and alignItems lies in their scope and the alignment they control along the cross axis. alignContent controls the alignment of all the lines of content (the overall layout of multiple rows or columns) along the cross axis relative to the parent container. alignItems controls the alignment of individual items within a single line along the cross axis."

Property	Possible Values	Description
flexDirection	'row', 'column', 'row-reverse', 'column-reverse'	Sets the main axis direction
justifyContent	'flex-start', 'flex-end', 'center', 'space-between', 'space-around', 'space-evenly'	Aligns children **along main axis**
alignItems	'flex-start', 'flex-end', 'center', 'stretch', 'baseline'	Aligns children **along cross axis**
alignContent	'flex-start', 'flex-end', 'center', 'stretch', 'space-between', 'space-around'	Aligns **multiple lines** if wrapping
flexWrap	'nowrap', 'wrap', 'wrap-reverse'	Allows items to wrap to the next line

Row Gap, Column Gap, and Gap (React Native 0.71+)

With React Native 0.71 and later, layout styling became more intuitive with the introduction of `rowGap`, `columnGap`, and `gap`—properties long familiar to web developers using Flexbox and CSS Grid. These additions significantly simplify spacing between elements without requiring manual margins on child components.

Before these properties, developers typically added spacing using margin on individual child elements. This often led to

- Inconsistent spacing
- Extra logic for first/last elements
- Hard-to-maintain layout code

The new gap properties solve these issues by allowing spacing to be defined at the container level, making layouts cleaner and more predictable.

When to Use What?

- Use `rowGap` → when spacing vertically stacked elements
- Use `columnGap` → when spacing horizontally aligned elements
- Use `gap` → when both directions need consistent spacing (especially with flexWrap)

4.2.2. Flexbox Properties on Items (Children)

In Flexbox layout, each child inside a flex container can control how it behaves and aligns within the parent layout. These properties allow individual items to grow, shrink, and align independently from other siblings.

1. `flex`—**Shorthand Property**: The flex property is a shorthand that combines three important Flexbox properties:
   - flex: 0 → Don't grow or shrink. Use only defined width/height.
   - flex: 1 → Take up remaining space (equally with other flex items).
   - flex: 2 → Take twice as much space as flex: 1 item.

2. `alignSelf`—**Override Cross-Axis Alignment**: alignSelf allows a child to override the container's alignItems setting.

   - Works on the cross axis
   - Useful for exceptions in layout

3. `flexBasis`—**Initial Size of an Item**: `flexBasis` defines the default size of a flex item before remaining space is distributed.

   - Acts like width (row) or height (column)
   - Accepts numbers (React Native units) or percentages

4. `flexGrow`—**Expanding to Fill Available Space**: `flexGrow` specifies how much an item should grow relative to others when extra space is available.

   - Default: 0 (no growth).
   - Values are proportional.

5. `flexShrink`—**Handling Overflow**: `flexShrink` controls how items reduce size when space is insufficient.

   - Default: 1
   - Higher value = shrinks more

Property	Possible Values	Description
`flex`	Numeric value (e.g., `1`, `2`, `0.5`)	Determines how item grows/shrinks to fill space
flexBasis	`auto`, number (e.g., `100`), percentage (e.g., `'50%'`)	Defines the **initial size** of the item before remaining space is distributed.
flexGrow	Number (`0`, `1`, `2`,...)	Controls how much the item **grows** relative to others when extra space is available.
flexShrink	Number (`0`, `1`, `2`,...)	Determines how much the item **shrinks** when there is not enough space.
`alignSelf`	`'auto'`, `'flex-start'`, `'flex-end'`, `'center'`, `'stretch'`, `'baseline'`	Overrides `alignItems` for a single child

(continued)

Property	Possible Values	Description
`width`, `height`	Numeric values or percentage	Sets item size directly
`margin`, `padding`	Standard CSS shorthand	Adds spacing around the item

4.3. Summary

This chapter covered the essential skills for creating an effective user interface in React Native. You learned that styling works with a subset of CSS-like properties for colors, spacing, typography, and borders. For laying out components, Flexbox is the primary system. You now understand how to use properties like `flexDirection`, `justifyContent`, and `alignItems` to control the arrangement and alignment of components. Specifically, `justifyContent` aligns items along the main axis, while `alignItems` handles the cross axis. You also learned that the flex property on a child component dictates how it grows or shrinks to fill available space, with `flex: 1` being a common way to make a component expand to fill its parent.

To ensure your app is performant and maintainable, remember these key best practices:

- Always use `StyleSheet.create()` for readability.
- Keep your styles separate from your component's logic.
- For larger projects, a theming system is crucial for consistency.
- Avoid duplicating values; instead, use a single source of truth for colors, fonts, and spacing.

In the next chapter, we'll dive deeper into React Native's core components.

CHAPTER 5

Building Interfaces with Core Components

> *"Great design is not just what it looks like and feels like. Great design is how it works."*
>
> –Steve Jobs

Chapter 4 introduced the fundamental concepts of `StyleSheet` and `Flexbox`. Building upon that foundation, this chapter advances into the study of React Native Core Components, which form the essential building blocks of user interface design. The topics addressed in this chapter include

- Layout and container components
- List components
- Interactive components
- Animations

A comprehensive understanding of these components is crucial for developing robust mobile applications. They enable developers to structure interfaces effectively, manage user interactions with precision, and incorporate animations that enhance both usability and user experience. This progression marks a significant step toward creating applications that are not only functional but also visually engaging and responsive.

A. Nalwaya and A. Paul, *React Native for Mobile Development*, https://doi.org/10.1007/979-8-8688-2977-2_5

5.1 React Native Core Components

React Native provides a comprehensive set of built-in components that serve as the foundation for building mobile applications. These Core Components are essential building blocks that translate to native UI elements on both iOS and Android platforms, ensuring optimal performance and a native look and feel. Understanding these components is crucial for any developer working with React Native, as they form the backbone of mobile app development in this framework.

Core Components in React Native are pre-built, ready-to-use components that map directly to native views on the target platform. Unlike web development, where you work with HTML elements, React Native components bridge the gap between JavaScript and native mobile components. Each component renders as platform-specific native elements: a View becomes a `UIView` on iOS and an `android.view` on Android while maintaining the same API across platforms. These components are designed with strong isolation in mind, meaning you can drop a component anywhere in your application and trust that it will look and behave consistently as long as the props remain the same. This architectural decision ensures predictable behavior and simplifies development across different screens and contexts.

5.1.1 Core Components at a Glance

React Native exposes a set of primitive components that map to native UI views. Think of them as HTML tags for mobile UI.

Component	Purpose	Typical Use
`View`	Container/layout block	Flexbox layout, cards, rows
`Text`	Render text	Labels, paragraphs, inline links
`Image`	Render images	Avatars, banners, icons
`TextInput`	Editable text field	Forms, search bars
`ScrollView`	Scrollable container	Short lists, carousels, rich content
`FlatList`	Virtualized list	Long/large lists with recycling
`SectionList`	Grouped lists	Settings screens, categorized data

(*continued*)

Component	Purpose	Typical Use
`Pressable`	Touch interactions	Buttons, tappable rows
`Button`	Simple button	Quick CTAs without custom styling
`Switch`	On/off toggle	Settings
`ActivityIndicator`	Loading spinner	Pending network or computation
`Modal`	Overlays content	Dialogs, pickers
`SafeAreaView`	Respect notches	Layout padding for insets
`StatusBar`	Status bar control	Light/dark content, hidden

There are many more components, but most screens can be built with 10–15 primitives—master those first.

By mastering these components, you will be equipped to design and implement virtually any mobile user interface while maintaining performance, accessibility, and native behavior.

This chapter introduces the most essential React Native Core Components, organized into the following categories:

Category	Component
Layout and Container Components	`View, SafeAreaView, Modal, KeyboardAvoidingView`
Text and Input Components	`Text, TextInput`
List Components	`ScrollView, FlatList, SectionList`
Interactive Components	`Button, Pressable, Touchables`

5.2 Layout and Container Components

Every app requires a foundation on which UI elements are arranged. In React Native, this foundation is provided by layout and container components. These components help structure the screen, handle spacing, and ensure that your design adapts gracefully to different devices.

The key layout and container components we will explore are

- **View**: The most fundamental building block of UI
- **SafeAreaView**: Prevents UI from overlapping notches and system bars
- **Modal**: Renders content above everything else, like dialogs or overlays
- **KeyboardAvoidingView**: Shifts UI to prevent text inputs from being hidden by the keyboard

5.2.1 View: The Building Block

The View component is the most fundamental building block in React Native. It serves as a container that supports layout with Flexbox, styling, touch handling, and accessibility controls. Think of it as the equivalent of a <div> in HTML, but specifically designed for mobile interfaces.

View components can be nested infinitely and support various props including `style`, `onLayout`,`pointerEvents`, and accessibility properties. The component automatically handles platform-specific optimizations and can be configured for touch interactions through responder props.

Use View to create rows/columns.

Think in boxes. Each View is one box in a flexible grid.

React Native uses Flexbox, which makes it easier to create responsive layouts across devices.

```
import React from 'react';
import { View, Text, StyleSheet } from 'react-native';

export default function App() {
  return (
    <View style={styles.container}>
      <Text style={styles.text}>Hello, inside a View!</Text>
    </View>
  );
}
```

```
const styles = StyleSheet.create({
  container: {
    flex: 1,
    backgroundColor: '#f5f5f5',
    alignItems: 'center',
    justifyContent: 'center',
  },
  text: {
    fontSize: 20,
    color: '#333',
  },
});
```

In the example, the main component App returns a `View` styled with `styles.container`. The container uses `flex: 1`, which allows it to expand and fill the entire screen. With `alignItems: 'center'` and `justifyContent: 'center'`, the children inside the View (in this case, the Text) are perfectly centered both vertically and horizontally. This example demonstrates how View acts as a flexible container to manage layout and how styles are applied using the StyleSheet API.

- `flex: 1` makes the View take up the full available screen.
- `alignItems` and `justifyContent` position the children (here, `Text`).
- `backgroundColor` adds visual styling.

5.2.2 SafeAreaView: Respecting Device Boundaries

Modern devices often have notches, curved corners, and system bars. Without proper handling, your UI may overlap these areas.

- `SafeAreaView` ensures content is placed inside the safe visible area.
- The original `SafeAreaView` shipped within the core `react-native` package has been **deprecated** because it only supported iOS and had layout limitations. Today, the industry standard is to use the `react-native-safe-area-context` library.

The best use case is for wrapping the root app container. It ensures headers, footers, and navigation bars don't overlap notches. This is the code snippet.

```
import { SafeAreaView } from 'react-native-safe-area-context';
import { Text } from "react-native";
export default function App() {
  return (
    <SafeAreaView style={{ flex: 1, backgroundColor: "white" }}>
      <Text>Inside Safe Area</Text>
    </SafeAreaView>
  );
}
```

This code defines a simple React Native application that uses a `SafeAreaView` to ensure that the content is displayed within the safe boundaries of the device screen, avoiding overlaps with elements such as notches, status bars, or rounded corners. The `SafeAreaView` is styled to occupy the full available screen space (`flex: 1`) with a white background. Inside it, a Text component is rendered, which displays the message *"Inside Safe Area."* In effect, this example demonstrates how `SafeAreaView` helps maintain a clean and consistent layout across devices with different screen designs, ensuring that the text is always visible and properly positioned.

5.2.3 Modal: Overlays and Pop-ups

The Modal component is used to present content above the main interface of an application. It is particularly useful for creating dialogs, forms, menus, alerts, or confirmation prompts that require the user's immediate attention. When a modal is active, it appears over the existing content and prevents interaction with the background elements, ensuring focus remains on the displayed content. Depending on the design needs, a modal can either cover the entire screen or be made transparent, allowing the background to remain partially visible while still emphasizing the modal's content.

Here is a code snippet to understand it better:

```
import { Modal, View, Text, Button } from "react-native";
import { useRef, useState } from "react";

export default function App() {
```

```
  const [visible, setVisible] = useState(false);

  return (
    <View style={{ flex: 1, justifyContent: "center", alignItems:
    "center" }}>
      <Button title="Open Modal" onPress={() => setVisible(true)} />
      <Modal visible={visible} transparent={true} animationType="slide"
      onRequestClose={() => setVisible(false)} >
        <View style={{ flex: 1, justifyContent: "center", alignItems:
        "center", backgroundColor: "rgba(0,0,0,0.5)" }}>
          <View style={{ backgroundColor: "white", padding: 20,
          borderRadius: 10 }}>
            <Text>This is a modal!</Text>
            <Button title="Close" onPress={() => setVisible(false)} />
          </View>
        </View>
      </Modal>
    </View>
  );
}
```

This example shows a button that opens a modal when pressed. The modal appears over the app's content with a semi-transparent background, drawing the user's attention to the dialog box while preventing interaction with anything behind it.

In React Native, Android devices have a physical "Back" button. If a user presses the Android Back button while your Modal is open, the app needs to know what to do. If you don't provide the `onRequestClose` prop to the `<Modal>`, Android will throw a warning, and the back button behavior will be broken.

5.2.4 KeyboardAvoidingView: Handling Keyboard Overlap

On mobile devices, when a user focuses on an input field, the on-screen keyboard often slides up from the bottom. This can sometimes hide the input field, forcing the user to type without being able to see what they are entering, which creates a frustrating experience. The `KeyboardAvoidingView` component in React Native addresses this issue by automatically adjusting the layout when the keyboard is open, ensuring that input fields remain visible and accessible. This makes it particularly valuable in scenarios such as forms with multiple text inputs, where the user needs to move between fields, or chat applications where the message input is located at the bottom of the screen. By using KeyboardAvoidingView, developers can provide a smoother and more user-friendly experience across devices with varying screen sizes.

```
import React, { useState } from "react";
import { View, TextInput, Button, KeyboardAvoidingView, Platform } from
"react-native";

export default function App() {
  const [text, setText] = useState("");

  return (
    <KeyboardAvoidingView
      style={{ flex: 1, justifyContent: "center", alignItems: "center" }}
      behavior={Platform.OS === "ios" ? "padding" : "height"}
    >
      <View style={{ width: "80%" }}>
        <TextInput
          style={{
            borderWidth: 1,
            borderColor: "gray",
            padding: 10,
            marginBottom: 10,
            borderRadius: 5,
          }}
          placeholder="Enter text"
          value={text}
          onChangeText={setText}
        />
        <Button title="Submit" onPress={() => alert(text)} />
      </View>
    </KeyboardAvoidingView>
  );
}
```

In this example, the `KeyboardAvoidingView` ensures that the text input remains visible when the keyboard is opened, preventing it from being hidden. The behavior prop adjusts how the view shifts—using "padding" on iOS and "height" on Android for optimal results.

⚠ **Limitations of KeyboardAvoidingView**

KeyboardAvoidingView is known to be unreliable in practice. It requires different tweaking for different OS versions and frequently does not work well with complex layouts, nested ScrollViews, or nested navigators.

The community widely recommends more robust alternatives:

react-native-keyboard-aware-scroll-view: Handles most use cases reliably

react-native-keyboard-controller: A newer, more powerful option with native backing

Be aware of these limitations when using KeyboardAvoidingView in production, and consider the alternatives above if you encounter issues.

5.3 Text and Input Components

Text is one of the most fundamental elements in any application. From labels and titles to paragraphs and messages, text carries meaning and guides users. Equally important are input fields, which allow users to type, search, or interact with your app.

In React Native, text-related UI is handled by two core components:

- **Text**: For displaying content
- **TextInput**: For capturing user input

5.3.1 Text: Displaying Information

The `Text` component is used to render text in React Native. It supports styling, nesting, accessibility, and touch interactions. Text supports these key features:

- **Styling**: Apply properties like `color`, `fontSize`, `fontFamily`, and `textAlign` to make text look good.

- **Nested Text**: You can nest multiple `<Text>` components to apply different styles to different parts of the same text block.
- **Touch Events**: Supports the `onPress` event to handle user interactions.
- **Accessibility**: Supports properties like `accessibilityLabel` to make your app screen-reader friendly.

Let's understand this through an example:

```
import { Text, View } from "react-native";

export default function App() {
  return (
    <View style={{ padding: 20 }}>
      <Text style={{ fontSize: 24, fontWeight: "bold" }}>Hello, Text
      Component!</Text>
      <Text style={{ color: "gray" }}>This is a subtitle.</Text>
    </View>
  );
}
```

In this code, we use the `Text` component from React Native to display text on the screen. The app consists of a main `View` container with some padding. Inside the View, there are two `Text` components. The first Text displays the message `"Hello, Text Component!"` with a larger font size (`fontSize: 24`) and bold weight (`fontWeight: "bold"`), making it stand out as a heading. The second Text shows `"This is a subtitle."` with gray color styling (`color: "gray"`), giving it a lighter appearance. This simple example demonstrates how the Text component allows easy styling of text content in React Native apps.

We can use nesting also:

```
<View style={{ padding: 20 }}>
    <Text style={{ fontSize: 24, fontWeight: "bold" }}>Hello, Text
    Component!</Text>
    <Text style={{ color: "gray" }}>This is a <Text style={{ fontWeight:
    "bold" }}>subtitle.</Text></Text>
 </View>
```

In this code, we demonstrate nested Text components in React Native. The outer Text has a gray color style (`color: "gray"`), which applies to the entire text block by default. Inside it, there is another Text component that wraps the word "subtitle." with a bold style (`fontWeight: "bold"`). As a result, the full text displayed on the screen is "This is a subtitle." where most of the text appears in gray, but the word "`subtitle.`" appears in bold gray. This shows how nesting Text components allows us to apply different styles to parts of the same text block.

5.3.2 TextInput: Capturing User Input

The `TextInput` component in React Native is a fundamental and highly interactive component that allows users to enter and edit text directly within a mobile application. It plays a crucial role in building forms, search bars, chat interfaces, and any other feature where user input is required. The `TextInput` component is designed to offer a smooth and customizable input experience across both iOS and Android platforms. A few of the key concepts are features for `TextInput`:

- **Placeholder Text**: Displays a hint or description inside the input field when it is empty, helping users understand the expected input

- **Single-Line or Multiline Support**: Can be configured to accept single-line input (like for usernames or passwords) or multiline input for longer text entries, such as comments or messages
- **Keyboard Type Control**: Allows developers to specify the keyboard type based on the expected input (e.g., numeric keypad for phone numbers, email keyboard for email addresses, or password keyboard with masked characters)
- **Event Handlers**
    - **`onChangeText`**: Called whenever the text inside the input changes, allowing for real-time input handling (e.g., live search)
    - **`onSubmitEditing`**: Triggered when the user submits the input (like pressing "Enter"), useful for handling form submissions
    - **`onFocus`**: Fires when the input gains focus, allowing the app to perform actions like showing helper text or adjusting the view

Additionally, `TextInput` offers customization options such as styling, text alignment, auto-correction, secure text entry (for passwords), and more, making it a powerful tool for capturing user input in a variety of scenarios. It ensures a consistent user experience while giving developers flexibility to tailor its behavior to specific needs.

Let's create a basic `TextInput`:

```
import { TextInput, View } from "react-native";
import { useState } from "react";

export default function App() {
  const [value, setValue] = useState("");

  return (
    <View style={{ padding: 20 }}>
      <TextInput
        placeholder="Enter your name"
        value={value}
        onChangeText={setValue}
        style={{ borderWidth: 1, padding: 10, borderRadius: 5 }}
      />
```

```
    </View>
  );
}
```

The TextInput component allows users to type text into the app and captures their input in real time. It uses a state variable to store the text and updates it via the onChangeText handler. The placeholder guides users on what to enter, while styling adds a border, padding, and rounded corners. This makes the input easy to use and visually clear within the app's layout.

Password Input with secureTextEntry

For password fields, use the secureTextEntry prop to mask user input. This hides characters as the user types, which is essential for login and registration screens:

```
import { TextInput, View, StyleSheet } from "react-native";
import { useState } from "react";

export default function PasswordInput() {
  const [password, setPassword] = useState("");

  return (
    <View style={styles.container}>
      <TextInput
        style={styles.input}
        placeholder="Enter password"
        secureTextEntry={true}
        value={password}
        onChangeText={setPassword}
      />
    </View>
  );
}

const styles = StyleSheet.create({
  container: { padding: 20 },
  input: { borderWidth: 1, borderColor: "#ccc", padding: 10,
borderRadius: 8 },
});
```

Useful Props for Email and Form Inputs

When building forms, two props significantly improve usability:

autoCapitalize="none": Prevents the keyboard from auto-capitalizing the first letter. Essential for email and username fields.

autoCorrect={false}: Disables autocorrect, which can interfere with email addresses and technical strings.

```
<TextInput
  placeholder="Email address"
  autoCapitalize="none"
  autoCorrect={false}
  keyboardType="email-address"
/>
```

5.4 Lists in React Native: ScrollView, FlatList, and SectionList

Modern mobile applications often need to display lists of data—whether it's a search page, a chat feed, or a settings menu. In React Native, lists are a fundamental part of building efficient and responsive user interfaces. React Native provides three primary ways to render lists: `ScrollView,` `FlatList`, and `SectionList`. Each has its strengths and trade-offs, and choosing the right one depends on the complexity and size of your data.

In this chapter, we will explore these three components in detail, understand their differences, and learn when to use each.

5.4.1 ScrollView

A `ScrollView` is the simplest way to display a scrollable list of content. It renders all items at once, which makes it best suited for short lists.

- **Purpose:** Displays a scrollable container that holds multiple child components

- **Best For:** Small to medium lists where the number of items is known and not very large
- **Limitation:** Renders all children at once, which may lead to performance issues for large lists

```
import { ScrollView, Text } from "react-native";

export default function App() {
  return (
    <ScrollView>
      {Array.from({ length: 10 }, (_, i) => (
        <Text key={i}>Item {i + 1}</Text>
      ))}
    </ScrollView>
  );
}
```

This is how the output will appear when we run the code, since no styling has been applied:

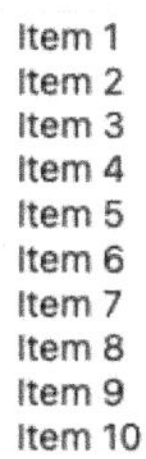

In this code, the `ScrollView` component is used to render a list of items that can be scrolled vertically. Inside it, `Array.from` generates ten elements, and each one is displayed as a `<Text>` component labeled from *Item 1* to *Item 10*. Each item is given a unique key to help React efficiently manage updates and rendering. Since `ScrollView` renders all its children at once, this approach works well for small lists but becomes inefficient with large datasets, where memory usage and performance may suffer. For handling bigger lists, a virtualized list component like `FlatList` is recommended.

Horizontal Scrolling with ScrollView

ScrollView also supports horizontal scrolling via the horizontal prop. This is extremely common in mobile apps for carousels, image galleries, and horizontal card lists:

```
import { ScrollView, View, Text, StyleSheet } from "react-native";

export default function HorizontalCarousel() {
  const items = ["Card 1", "Card 2", "Card 3", "Card 4"];

  return (
    <ScrollView horizontal={true} showsHorizontalScrollIndicator={false}>
      {items.map((item) => (
        <View key={item} style={styles.card}>
          <Text>{item}</Text>
        </View>
      ))}
    </ScrollView>
  );
}

const styles = StyleSheet.create({
  card: { width: 160, height: 100, backgroundColor: "#e0e0e0",
          marginRight: 12, borderRadius: 8, justifyContent: "center",
          alignItems: "center" },
});
```

Use showsHorizontalScrollIndicator={false} to hide the scroll bar for a cleaner look, which is standard practice in most carousel implementations.

Since `ScrollView` renders the entire list into memory and mounts all components simultaneously, it can lead to significant performance overhead and increased memory consumption when working with large datasets (hundreds or thousands of items). For scalable and optimized rendering, `FlatList` should be used instead, as it implements virtualization to render only the visible items and efficiently recycle views.

5.4.2 FlatList

`FlatList` is React Native's optimized solution for rendering large datasets efficiently. It leverages virtualization, which ensures that only the items visible on the screen (along with a small buffer) are rendered at any given time. This makes it far more memory-efficient compared to `ScrollView`, which renders all items simultaneously. It is one of the most widely used list components in React Native for handling scalable lists.

- **Purpose:** Optimized component for rendering large lists of data.
- **Best For:** Large datasets where only visible items should render.
- **Features:** It supports lazy loading, where items are rendered only as they come into view, reducing memory consumption and improving performance. You can also add item separators to visually distinguish between list entries, making the UI more structured and readable. Additionally, `FlatList` includes pull-to-refresh support, allowing users to refresh the list data with a simple swipe gesture, which enhances the overall user experience.

Let's try to run the following code:

```
import { FlatList, Text } from "react-native";

const data = Array.from({ length: 1000 }, (_, i) => `Item ${i + 1}`);

export default function App() {
  return (
    <FlatList
      data={data}
      renderItem={({ item }) => <Text>{item}</Text>}
      keyExtractor={(item) => item}
```

Note: Avoid Using Index As Key

Using the array index as a key is a well-known anti-pattern in React (and React Native). When items are reordered, filtered, or deleted, index-based keys cause React to incorrectly reuse component instances, leading to subtle UI bugs and performance issues.

Best Practices for keyExtractor:

Use a unique field from your data object (e.g., item.id, item.uuid).

If your data items are simple unique strings, the item itself can serve as the key (as shown above).

In real-world apps, always prefer a stable unique identifier such as a database ID.

```
// x Anti-pattern - avoid
keyExtractor={(item, index) => index.toString()}

// ✅ Correct - use a unique field from your data
keyExtractor={(item) => item.id.toString()}

    />
  );
}
```

This code demonstrates how to use `FlatList` in React Native to efficiently render a large dataset. Here, an array of 1,000 items is generated, each labeled as *Item 1* through *Item 1000*. Instead of rendering all items at once, `FlatList` virtualizes the list—meaning it only renders the items currently visible on the screen plus a small buffer around them, which makes it much more memory-efficient than `ScrollView`. The data prop supplies the list of items, and the `renderItem` function defines how each item should be displayed—in this case, as a simple `<Text>` element. The `keyExtractor` ensures each item has a unique key; in our example, each item is unique. Hence, we are using the item itself, which helps React optimize re-rendering. This setup allows you to scroll smoothly through thousands of items without performance issues.

5.4.3 SectionList

The `SectionList` is a variation of `FlatList` that allows grouping data into sections. This is especially useful when you want to render categorized lists, such as contacts grouped by the first letter of their name or products grouped by category.

- **Purpose:** Renders grouped lists with section headers.
- **Best For:** Data that needs categorization (e.g., contacts grouped alphabetically).
- **Features:** It allows you to group data into sections, rendering a header for each section to clearly separate different categories of items. It supports all the same props as `FlatList`, making it flexible and easy to use while providing the additional ability to organize and display data in a structured, sectioned format.

```
import { SectionList, Text } from "react-native";

const DATA = [
  { title: "A", data: ["Apple", "Avocado"] },
  { title: "B", data: ["Banana", "Blueberry"] },
];

export default function App() {
  return (
    <SectionList
      sections={DATA}
      keyExtractor={(item, index) => item + index}
      renderItem={({ item }) => <Text>{item}</Text>}
      renderSectionHeader={({ section }) => <Text>{section.title}</Text>}
    />
  );
}
```

The following is a tabular format that helps you decide when to use `ScrollView`, `FlatList`, or `SectionList` in React Native. Each of these components is designed for specific use cases. By comparing their features side by side, you can quickly determine which list component best fits your application's requirements.

Component	Use Case	Performance	Features
`ScrollView`	Small static lists	Renders everything at once → performance issues with large data	Simple scrolling
`FlatList`	Large dynamic lists	Virtualized rendering, efficient	Refresh control, separators
`SectionList`	Grouped large lists	Virtualized rendering, efficient	Section headers, sticky support

5.5 Interactive Components: Button, Pressable, and Touchables

Interactivity is at the heart of mobile applications. Whether a user is tapping a button, swiping through a list, or pressing an icon, apps need to respond instantly and naturally. React Native provides a set of interactive components to handle touch events, ranging from simple to highly customizable.

In this chapter, we'll explore

- **Button**: The simplest way to add a native-styled button
- **Pressable**: The modern, flexible API for touch interactions
- **Touchable Components**: Legacy but still useful options (`TouchableOpacity`, `TouchableHighlight`, `TouchableWithoutFeedback`)

By the end, you'll understand when to use each component, how to customize interactions, and how to build interactive UIs that feel natural on both iOS and Android.

5.5.1 Button

The Button component is the simplest way to add a clickable element in React Native. It renders a platform-specific native button—on iOS, it appears as a flat blue button, while on Android, it follows the raised Material-style design. The component is intentionally minimal and straightforward, as it accepts only a limited set of props such as `title`, `onPress`, and `color`. This makes it ideal for quick prototypes, small applications, or cases where you just need a straightforward action without additional styling overhead. However, because of its limited customization options, it is better suited for simple actions rather than complex UI designs.

Example

```
import { Button } from "react-native";

export default function App() {
  return <Button title="Click Me" onPress={() => alert("Pressed!")} />;
}
```

5.5.2 Pressable

The `Pressable` component is the modern and recommended way to handle user interactions in React Native. Unlike the basic Button component, which is limited in customization, Pressable can wrap any type of element such as `Text, Image, View`, or even icons, giving developers far greater flexibility in designing interactive UI elements. One of its most powerful features is support for multiple interaction states: it can detect when an element is being pressed (touched), hovered over (especially useful for web or desktop apps), or focused (important for accessibility and keyboard navigation). These states make it possible to create highly responsive designs that change appearance based on user interaction. Additionally, Pressable allows developers to apply custom styling depending on the current interaction state, enabling effects like changing colors, opacity, or scale when pressed, which results in a more engaging and intuitive user experience.

Expanding the Touch Target with hitSlop

Apple's Human Interface Guidelines require touch targets of at least 44×44 points, and Android's Material Design guidelines specify 48×48 dp. Small buttons or icons may not meet these requirements visually, but you can expand the tappable area without changing the visual size using the hitSlop prop:

```
<Pressable
  hitSlop={{ top: 10, bottom: 10, left: 10, right: 10 }}
  onPress={handlePress}
>
  <Text>Tap me</Text>
</Pressable>
```

This is especially useful for small icon buttons in toolbars or navigation bars where the visual element is compact but the tap area needs to meet accessibility standards.

- **Purpose:** Highly customizable component for handling touch gestures
- **Features:**
  - Style changes on press/hover/focus.
  - Can wrap any component, not just text.
- **Best For:** Custom UI buttons and interactive elements

Example

```
import { Pressable, Text } from "react-native";

export default function App() {
  return (
    <Pressable
      onPress={() => alert("Pressed!")}
      style={({ pressed }) => [
        { backgroundColor: pressed ? "lightblue" : "skyblue",
        padding: 10 },
      ]}
    >
      <Text>Custom Pressable</Text>
    </Pressable>
  );
}
```

5.5.3 Touchable Components: Legacy but Useful

Touchable components in React Native are the older but still widely used way to handle user interactions. They were introduced before Pressable and provide different styles of visual feedback when a user taps on an element. `TouchableOpacity` fades the element by reducing its opacity, making it useful for buttons and icons. `TouchableHighlight` darkens the background of the element, often paired with an underlayColor for a pressed effect. `TouchableWithoutFeedback` does not show any visual feedback but is helpful in special cases like dismissing the keyboard. These components are simple to implement and remain popular in existing codebases. However, they lack the flexibility and state-handling power of Pressable. Developers should prefer Pressable for new apps, but `Touchables` still have value for quick feedback effects. Understanding them is important for maintaining legacy projects. In summary, `Touchables` represent an important step in React Native's evolution of interactivity.

This is a summary of all components we discussed:

Component	Use Case	Pros	Cons
`Button`	Simple actions, forms	Fast, native look	Not customizable
`Pressable`	Custom buttons, cards, icons	Flexible, supports states	More setup needed
`TouchableOpacity`	Legacy, fading buttons	Visual feedback	Limited
`TouchableHighlight`	Legacy, highlight effect	Useful for special styles	Limited
`TouchableWithoutFeedback`	Dismiss keyboard, invisible touches	No visual effect	Can confuse users

5.6 Animation

Animations are more than visual effects—they guide user attention, provide feedback, and create delight. A well-placed animation can make your app feel polished and professional, while poorly designed or missing animations can make it feel clunky.

In React Native, animations are powered by core components and APIs such as

- **Animated API**: Flexible, declarative animations
- **LayoutAnimation**: Automatic animations for layout changes
- **InteractionManager**: Coordinating animations with heavy tasks

5.6.1 Animated API: The Core of Animations

The Animated API in React Native is a powerful system for creating smooth, high-performance animations in mobile apps. It provides a set of tools that let you animate values and apply them to style properties like position, opacity, scale, rotation, or even colors. Unlike simple CSS-like transitions, Animated is optimized to run animations on the native UI thread, which ensures they remain smooth even when the JavaScript thread is busy. These values are then connected to UI components via style properties. You can drive changes to these values using animation functions such as

- `Animated.timing`: For time-based animations (e.g., fade in/out)
- `Animated.spring`: For physics-based, spring-like effects
- `Animated.decay`: For gradually slowing down an animation (like inertia)

To run animations, you call `.start()` on them, and you can also sequence or parallelize multiple animations with helpers like `Animated.sequence` or `Animated.parallel`.

Let's understand this with code:

```
import { Animated, View, Button } from "react-native";
import { useRef } from "react";

export default function App() {
  const fadeAnim = useRef(new Animated.Value(0)).current;

  const fadeIn = () => {
    Animated.timing(fadeAnim, {
      toValue: 1,
      duration: 1000,
      useNativeDriver: true,
    }).start();
  };

  return (
    <View style={{ flex: 1, justifyContent: "center", alignItems:
    "center" }}>
      <Animated.View style={{ opacity: fadeAnim, width: 100, height: 100,
      backgroundColor: "skyblue" }} />
      <Button title="Fade In" onPress={fadeIn} />
    </View>
  );
}
```

This code demonstrates how to create a simple **fade-in animation** in React Native using the Animated API. It defines an animated value `fadeAnim` with an initial opacity of `0` (completely invisible) using `useRef`. The `fadeIn` function triggers an animation with `Animated.timing`, which gradually updates `fadeAnim` from `0` to `1` over one second, making the element fully visible. The `useNativeDriver: true` option ensures the animation runs smoothly on the native UI thread. Inside the `return`, an `Animated.View` is styled with the animated opacity value, along with fixed width, height, and background color, so it appears as a square box. A `Button` labeled "Fade In" is provided, and when pressed, it calls the `fadeIn` function, causing the sky-blue box to smoothly fade into view.

React Native provides special animated versions of core components:

- `Animated.View`
- `Animated.Text`
- `Animated.Image`
- `Animated.ScrollView`

Any property that can be animated (e.g., opacity, transform, position) can be attached to an `Animated.Value`.

5.6.2 Layout Animation: Automatic Layout Transitions

The LayoutAnimation API in React Native allows you to animate layout changes automatically without writing complex animation code. Normally, when you update the state of a component, React Native instantly re-renders the UI with the new layout—for example, if a View changes its size or position, the change happens abruptly. With `LayoutAnimation`, those changes can be smoothly animated, making the transition feel more natural and engaging.

The key idea is automatic layout transitions: instead of manually defining animations for width, height, or position, you simply tell React Native that the next layout update should be animated. When the state changes and causes the layout to reflow, React Native applies a predefined animation configuration (like ease-in, ease-out, linear, or spring).

For example, if you have a list of items and you remove one, normally the rest of the items would instantly “jump” up. By using `LayoutAnimation`, the remaining items smoothly slide into their new positions, creating a polished effect with almost no extra code.

Expands/collapses smoothly with **one line of animation code**.

```
import { Animated, View, Button } from "react-native";
import { useState } from "react";

export default function App() {
  const [expanded, setExpanded] = useState(false);   const animatedHeight =
  useRef(new Animated.Value(100)).current;

  const toggle = () => {
    const toValue = expanded ? 100 : 200;     Animated.
    timing(animatedHeight, {       toValue,       duration: 300,
    useNativeDriver: false,     }).start();
    setExpanded(!expanded);
  };

  return (
    <View style={{ padding: 20 }}>
      <Button title="Toggle" onPress={toggle} />
      <Animated.View style={{ height: animatedHeight, backgroundColor:
      "skyblue", marginTop: 20 }} />
    </View>
  );
}
```

`LayoutAnimation` enables smooth automatic transitions when a layout changes. The component maintains a state variable called expanded, which controls the height of a box—100 when collapsed and 200 when expanded. When the Toggle button is pressed, the toggle function is called. Inside this function, `LayoutAnimation.configureNext(LayoutAnimation.Presets.easeInEaseOut)` is used to tell React Native that the *next* layout change should be animated with an ease-in-ease-out effect. After that, the state is updated with `setExpanded(!expanded)`, which triggers a re-render and changes the height of the box. Normally, this change would happen instantly, but with `LayoutAnimation` applied, the height smoothly transitions between the two values, creating a polished animation without requiring any complex manual animation code.

5.6.3 Gesture-Driven Animations

Gesture-driven animations are animations that respond directly to user interactions, such as dragging, swiping, or pinching. Instead of playing automatically or based on a timer, these animations are controlled by gestures, making the UI feel interactive and intuitive. For example, when a user drags a card across the screen, the card's position, scale, or rotation can change dynamically in response to the gesture. The user can drag the box, and it springs back when released.

```
import { Animated, PanResponder } from "react-native";
import { useRef } from "react";

export default function App() {
  const pan = useRef(new Animated.ValueXY()).current;

  const panResponder = PanResponder.create({
    onMoveShouldSetPanResponder: () => true,
    onPanResponderMove: Animated.event(
      [null, { dx: pan.x, dy: pan.y }],
      { useNativeDriver: false }
    ),
    onPanResponderRelease: () => {
      Animated.spring(pan, { toValue: { x: 0, y: 0 }, useNativeDriver:
      false }).start();
    }
  });

  return (
    <Animated.View
      {...panResponder.panHandlers}
      style={[{ width: 100, height: 100, backgroundColor: "tomato" },
      pan.getLayout()]}
    />
  );
}
```

5.6.4 Advanced Animations: Combining and Sequencing

In React Native, you can create rich, professional animations by chaining or coordinating multiple animations. Think of it like a dance—one animation leads to another, or multiple animations move together in harmony. Using `Animated.sequence`, you can run animations one after another: for example, a component might first fade in using Animated.timing and then grow in size with Animated.spring, producing a smooth, eye-catching transition. With Animated.parallel, multiple animations occur simultaneously, such as moving and fading a component at the same time, while `Animated.stagger` introduces a slight delay between animations, creating cascading effects like a row of icons appearing one by one. By combining these techniques, you can craft polished and dynamic UI interactions that feel alive, engaging, and responsive—turning simple components into animated experiences that delight users.

You can chain animations with

- `Animated.sequence`: Run animations in order.
- `Animated.parallel`: Run animations together.
- `Animated.stagger`: Delay animations in sequence.

Let's try to understand how this works with a practical code snippet.

```
Animated.sequence([
  Animated.timing(opacity, { toValue: 1, duration: 500, useNativeDriver:
  true }),
  Animated.spring(scale, { toValue: 2, useNativeDriver: true })
]).start();
```

This code demonstrates how to create a **chained animation** using React Native's `Animated.sequence`. Here, two animations are combined to run one after the other. First, `Animated.timing` gradually changes the `opacity` value from its current state to `1` over 500 milliseconds, smoothly fading in the component. Once the opacity animation completes, `Animated.spring` animates the `scale` value to `2`, causing the component to grow in size with a spring-like, natural motion. The `useNativeDriver: true` option ensures that both animations are offloaded to the native thread for better performance. Finally, calling `.start()` triggers the entire sequence, so the fade-in happens first, immediately followed by the scaling effect, resulting in a smooth, coordinated visual transition.

5.7 ExpenseTracker App

Let us continue with the Expense Tracker application, which we started building in Chapter 3. In its initial version, the user interface was functional but lacked visual appeal and proper structure. In this chapter, we will transform the basic and unpolished interface into a well-designed, user-friendly application by applying the concepts learned in this and the previous chapter.

We will leverage `StyleSheet` for consistent styling, Flexbox for responsive layout design, and React Native Core Components such as `View`, `Text`, `TextInput`, `Button`, and `ScrollView` to build a clean and intuitive interface. This practical example will help consolidate your understanding of how to combine these fundamental building blocks to create a performant and visually attractive mobile application.

5.7.1 Theme in React Native

A well-structured theme is the foundation of scalable and maintainable UI design.

A consistent and well-designed theme plays a crucial role in delivering a polished and user-friendly application experience. In React Native, theming refers to defining a set of colors, font sizes, spacings, and other design tokens that can be reused throughout the application. This helps maintain visual consistency, improve maintainability, and simplify customization.

Why Use Theme?

- Centralized control of styles (colors, fonts, sizes, spacing)
- Easy to switch between light and dark modes or custom themes
- Ensures consistency across screens and components
- Improves scalability as the application grows

DefaultTheme is a predefined theme object provided by **React Navigation's** core library (`@react-navigation/native`). It defines a set of default colors and properties used by navigators such as stack navigators, tab navigators, and drawer navigators to style the navigation components like headers, backgrounds, and text.

By using DefaultTheme, developers get a consistent and well-designed appearance out of the box, but they can also customize or extend it to match the app's branding.

Now you can open App.js and modify this code:

```
// App.js
// Main entry point for the Expense Tracker React Native app
// Sets up bottom tab navigation and stack navigation for transactions

import React from 'react';
import { NavigationContainer, DefaultTheme } from '@react-navigation/
native'; // Provides navigation context
import { createBottomTabNavigator } from '@react-navigation/bottom-tabs';
// For bottom tab navigation
import { createNativeStackNavigator } from '@react-navigation/native-
stack'; // For stack navigation within tabs

// Import screen components (each displays its own screen name)
import HomeScreen from './screens/HomeScreen';
import AddAssetsScreen from './screens/AddAssetsScreen';
import TransactionScreen from './screens/TransactionScreen';
import StatsScreen from './screens/StatsScreen';
import TransactionDetailScreen from './screens/TransactionDetailScreen';

// Create navigators
const Tab = createBottomTabNavigator();
const Stack = createNativeStackNavigator();

const MyTheme = {
  ...DefaultTheme,
  colors: {
    ...DefaultTheme.colors,
    text: 'rgba(80, 3, 136, 1)',
    primary: '#C0C0C0',
    background: '#1ABC9C',
  },
};

// Stack navigator for the Transaction tab
// Allows navigation from the transaction list to transaction details
```

```
function TransactionStack() {
  return (
    <Stack.Navigator>
      <Stack.Screen name="Transactions" component={TransactionScreen} />
      <Stack.Screen name="TransactionDetail" component={TransactionDetail
      Screen} />
    </Stack.Navigator>
  );
}

export default function App() {
  return (
    <NavigationContainer theme={MyTheme}>
      <Tab.Navigator   screenOptions={{
    headerShown: false
  }}>
        <Tab.Screen name="Home" component={HomeScreen} />
        <Tab.Screen name="Add Assets" component={AddAssetsScreen} />
        <Tab.Screen name="Transaction" component={TransactionStack} />
        <Tab.Screen name="Stats" component={StatsScreen} />
      </Tab.Navigator>
    </NavigationContainer>
  );
}
```

In this code, we are creating a custom theme called `MyTheme` by extending the built-in `DefaultTheme` provided by `@react-navigation/native`. The `MyTheme` object starts by copying all the properties of `DefaultTheme` using the spread operator (`...DefaultTheme`), ensuring we keep the default structure and settings. Next, we customize the `colors` property by also spreading the default colors (`...DefaultTheme.colors`), so none of the existing color values are lost. Then, we override specific color values to apply our custom design. For example, the `text` color is set to a deep purple shade using the RGBA format (`rgba(80, 3, 136, 1)`), the `primary` color is set to `#COCOCO` (though note this appears invalid and should likely be corrected to a valid hex color like `#CCCCCC`), and the `background` color is set to a vibrant turquoise (`#1ABC9C`). This custom theme allows the app to have a unique look and feel while still maintaining the structure and functionality of React Navigation's default theming system.

Let's run the app in simulator:

5.8 App Layout

To build a production-grade application, it is important to create a consistent layout that is used throughout the app. A well-structured layout helps provide a seamless user experience across different devices and screen sizes.

The App Layout defines how we arrange and organize components within the main structure of a React Native application. A properly designed layout ensures that key elements such as headers, content areas, footers, and navigation bars are positioned correctly and remain responsive.

Let's go ahead and create our first app layout. For this, we will use gradient.

```
npm install expo-linear-gradient
```

Create the AppLayout.js file in the Component folder and copy this code:

```
import React from 'react';
import {  StyleSheet, StatusBar, View, Dimensions } from 'react-native';
import { LinearGradient } from 'expo-linear-gradient';
import { useTheme } from '@react-navigation/native';

const { height, width } = Dimensions.get('window');

export default function AppLayout({ children }) {
  const { colors } = useTheme();
  return (
    <View style={styles.screen}>
      <LinearGradient
        colors={[colors.backgroundColor, 'transparent']}
        style={styles.gradient}
      />
        <StatusBar barStyle="dark-content" backgroundColor={colors.
        background} />
        <View style={styles.container}>{children}</View>
    </View>
  );
}

const styles = StyleSheet.create({
  screen: {
        flex: 1,
    },

  container: {
    flex: 1,
  },
  gradient: {
    height: height / 1.2,
    width: width,
```

```
    position: 'absolute',
    top: 0,
    left: 0,
  },
});
```

This code defines a reusable AppLayout component in React Native that serves as a consistent layout wrapper for the entire application. It uses the useTheme hook from @react-navigation/native to access the current theme's colors, ensuring the layout adapts to light or dark mode automatically. The layout consists of a full-screen View container styled with flex: 1 to occupy the entire screen space. At the top layer, a LinearGradient is applied, which creates a smooth gradient background that blends the app's background color into transparency. The gradient is sized based on the device's screen dimensions (height and width) and positioned absolutely to cover the top portion of the screen. The StatusBar component is configured to use the theme's background color and set the text style to dark content for better visibility. Finally, the children prop is placed inside an inner View, allowing any content passed to AppLayout to render within this structured layout. This approach ensures consistent styling, theme support, and a visually appealing background throughout the app.

And update App.js:

```
// App.js
// Main entry point for the Expense Tracker React Native app
// Sets up bottom tab navigation and stack navigation for transactions

import React from 'react';
import { NavigationContainer, DefaultTheme } from '@react-navigation/
native'; // Provides navigation context
import { createBottomTabNavigator } from '@react-navigation/bottom-tabs';
// For bottom tab navigation
import { createNativeStackNavigator } from '@react-navigation/native-
stack'; // For stack navigation within tabs
import AppLayout from './components/AppLayout';

// Import screen components (each displays its own screen name)
import HomeScreen from './screens/HomeScreen';
import AddAssetsScreen from './screens/AddAssetsScreen';
```

```
import TransactionScreen from './screens/TransactionScreen';
import StatsScreen from './screens/StatsScreen';
import TransactionDetailScreen from './screens/TransactionDetailScreen';

// Create navigators
const Tab = createBottomTabNavigator();
const Stack = createNativeStackNavigator();

const MyTheme = {
  ...DefaultTheme,
  colors: {
    ...DefaultTheme.colors,
    text: 'rgba(80, 3, 136, 1)',
    primary: '#C0C0C0',
    backgroundColor: '#1ABC9C', // Background color set to a light shade
  },
};

// Helper HOC to wrap screens with AppLayout
function withAppLayout(Component) {
  return function Wrapper(props) {
    return (
      <AppLayout>
        <Component {...props} />
      </AppLayout>
    );
  };
}

const HomeScreenWithLayout = withAppLayout(HomeScreen);
const AddAssetsScreenWithLayout = withAppLayout(AddAssetsScreen);
const TransactionScreenWithLayout = withAppLayout(TransactionScreen);
const StatsScreenWithLayout = withAppLayout(StatsScreen);
const TransactionDetailScreenWithLayout =
withAppLayout(TransactionDetailScreen);

// Stack navigator for the Transaction tab
// Allows navigation from the transaction list to transaction details
```

```
function TransactionStack() {
  return (
    <Stack.Navigator>
      <Stack.Screen name="Transactions" component={TransactionScreenWith
      Layout} />
      <Stack.Screen name="TransactionDetail" component={TransactionDetailSc
      reenWithLayout} />
    </Stack.Navigator>
  );
}

export default function App() {
  return (
    <NavigationContainer theme={MyTheme}>
      <Tab.Navigator   screenOptions={{
    headerShown: false
  }}>
        <Tab.Screen name="Home" component={HomeScreenWithLayout} />
        <Tab.Screen name="Add Assets" component={AddAssetsScreenWith
        Layout} />
        {/* Hide the default header for the Transaction tab to avoid double
        headers */}
        <Tab.Screen name="Transaction" component={TransactionStack}
        options={{ headerShown: false }} />
        <Tab.Screen name="Stats" component={StatsScreenWithLayout} />
      </Tab.Navigator>
    </NavigationContainer>
  );
}
```

This code defines a Higher-Order Component (HOC) named `withAppLayout`, which is used to wrap any screen component with a consistent layout structure. The `withAppLayout` function takes a component (e.g., `HomeScreen`, `AddAssetsScreen`) as its argument and returns a new functional component called Wrapper. Inside the Wrapper, the original component is rendered as a child of the reusable `AppLayout` component. The props passed to the wrapped component are forwarded using {...props}, ensuring the component receives all the necessary data and functions it expects.

By using this pattern, we apply the same layout structure—such as background gradient, status bar, and consistent padding—across multiple screens without repeating layout code in every screen.

In this example, five screen components are wrapped:

- HomeScreenWithLayout
- AddAssetsScreenWithLayout
- TransactionScreenWithLayout
- StatsScreenWithLayout
- TransactionDetailScreenWithLayout

Each of these new components now automatically includes the app's common layout, improving code reusability and ensuring a consistent user experience throughout the application.

Let's put icons in the app:

```
// App.js
// Main entry point for the Expense Tracker React Native app
// Sets up bottom tab navigation and stack navigation for transactions

import React from 'react';
import { NavigationContainer, DefaultTheme } from '@react-navigation/
native'; // Provides navigation context
import { createBottomTabNavigator } from '@react-navigation/bottom-tabs';
// For bottom tab navigation
import { createNativeStackNavigator } from '@react-navigation/native-
stack'; // For stack navigation within tabs
import AppLayout from './components/AppLayout';

// Import screen components (each displays its own screen name)
import HomeScreen from './screens/HomeScreen';
import AddAssetsScreen from './screens/AddAssetsScreen';
import TransactionScreen from './screens/TransactionScreen';
import StatsScreen from './screens/StatsScreen';
import TransactionDetailScreen from './screens/TransactionDetailScreen';
import { Ionicons } from '@expo/vector-icons';

// Create navigators
const Tab = createBottomTabNavigator();
const Stack = createNativeStackNavigator();
```

```
const MyTheme = {
  ...DefaultTheme,
  colors: {
    ...DefaultTheme.colors,
    text: 'rgba(80, 3, 136, 1)',
    primary: '#C0C0C0',
    backgroundColor: '#1ABC9C', // Background color set to a light shade
  },
};

// Helper HOC to wrap screens with AppLayout
function withAppLayout(Component) {
  return function Wrapper(props) {
    return (
      <AppLayout>
        <Component {...props} />
      </AppLayout>
    );
  };
}

const HomeScreenWithLayout = withAppLayout(HomeScreen);
const AddAssetsScreenWithLayout = withAppLayout(AddAssetsScreen);
const TransactionScreenWithLayout = withAppLayout(TransactionScreen);
const StatsScreenWithLayout = withAppLayout(StatsScreen);
const TransactionDetailScreenWithLayout = withAppLayout(TransactionDeta
ilScreen);

function getTabIcon(routeName, focused) {
  if (routeName === 'Home') {
    return focused ? 'home' : 'home-outline';
  } else if (routeName === 'Stats') {
    return focused ? 'bar-chart' : 'bar-chart-outline';
  }
    else if (routeName === 'Add Assets') {
        return focused ? 'add-circle' : 'add-circle-outline';
    } else if (routeName === 'Transaction') {
```

```
        return focused ? 'wallet' : 'wallet-outline';
    }
  return 'ellipse-outline';
}
// Stack navigator for the Transaction tab
// Allows navigation from the transaction list to transaction details
function TransactionStack() {
  return (
    <Stack.Navigator>
      <Stack.Screen name="Transactions" component={TransactionScreenWith
      Layout} />
      <Stack.Screen name="TransactionDetail" component={TransactionDetailSc
      reenWithLayout} />
    </Stack.Navigator>
  );
}

export default function App() {
  return (
    <NavigationContainer theme={MyTheme}>
    <Tab.Navigator
      screenOptions={({ route }) => ({
        headerShown: false,
        tabBarShowLabel: true,
        tabBarActiveTintColor: '#5F9EA0',
        tabBarInactiveTintColor: '#5F9EA0',
        tabBarIcon: ({ focused, color, size }) => (
          <Ionicons name={getTabIcon(route.name, focused)} size={size ||
          24} color={color} />
        ),
      })}
    >
        <Tab.Screen name="Home" component={HomeScreenWithLayout} />
        <Tab.Screen name="Add Assets" component={AddAssetsScreenWith
        Layout} />
```

```
      {/* Hide the default header for the Transaction tab to avoid double
      headers */}
      <Tab.Screen name="Transaction" component={TransactionStack}
      options={{ headerShown: false }} />
      <Tab.Screen name="Stats" component={StatsScreenWithLayout} />
    </Tab.Navigator>
  </NavigationContainer>
 );
}
```

5.8.1 Create an Add and Remove Expense

Now, let's create an Add Assets screen where you can add or remove any expense. To build this, we'll use several core components we've already learned in this chapter. Along with that, we'll introduce Context to store all expenses in one place and provide helper functions like addExpense and deleteExpense to update them. By wrapping our components inside a Provider, every child component can access this shared data directly, without the need to pass props through multiple levels.

In an Expense Tracker, different screens and components often need to work with the same expense data. If we try to pass this information down manually through props at each level, the code becomes hard to manage—a problem known as prop drilling.

React solves this problem with the Context API, which lets us create a central "store" of data and functions that can be accessed by any component, no matter how deeply nested. When combined with React's state management (using hooks like useState), **Context** provides a clean, scalable way to manage data and keep applications well-organized.

Update AddAssetsScreen.js. It wraps the AddAssets component inside the ExpenseProvider, giving it access to shared expense-related state and functions.

```
import React from 'react';
import { ExpenseProvider } from '../context/ExpenseContext';
import AddAssets from '../components/AddAssets';

export default function AddAssetsScreen() {
  return (
    <ExpenseProvider>
      <AddAssets />
    </ExpenseProvider>
  );
}
```

Create a file ExpenseContext.js inside the context folder:

```
import React, { createContext, useContext, useState } from 'react';

const ExpenseContext = createContext();

export function ExpenseProvider({ children }) {
  const [expenses, setExpenses] = useState([]);
```

```
  const addExpense = (expense) => {
    setExpenses((prev) => [
      ...prev,
      { ...expense, id: Date.now().toString() },
    ]);
  };

  const deleteExpense = (id) => {
    setExpenses((prev) => prev.filter((exp) => exp.id !== id));
  };

  return (
    <ExpenseContext.Provider value={{ expenses, addExpense,
    deleteExpense }}>
      {children}
    </ExpenseContext.Provider>
  );
}

export function useExpenses() {
  return useContext(ExpenseContext);
}
```

This code creates a shared Expense Context in React so that multiple components can access and update expense data without passing props manually. The `ExpenseProvider` component uses `useState` to store a list of expenses and provides two functions: `addExpense`, which adds a new expense with a unique ID, and deleteExpense, which removes an expense by its ID. These values are passed through `ExpenseContext.Provider` so that any child component can use them. The useExpenses hook makes it easier for other components to access this context directly.

Create `AddAssets.js` inside the component folder:

```
import { StatusBar } from 'expo-status-bar';
import { StyleSheet, Text, View, TextInput, Button, FlatList,
TouchableOpacity } from 'react-native';

import React, { useState } from 'react';
import { useExpenses } from '../context/ExpenseContext';
```

```
export default function AddAssets() {

  const { expenses, addExpense, deleteExpense } = useExpenses();
  const [type, setType] = useState('Expense'); // 'Expense' or 'Income'
  const [name, setName] = useState('');
  const [amount, setAmount] = useState('');
  const [category, setCategory] = useState('');
  const [date, setDate] = useState('');

  const handleAddExpense = () => {
    if (!name || !amount || !category || !date) return;
    addExpense({ type, name, amount, category, date });
    setName('');
    setAmount('');
    setCategory('');
    setDate('');
  };
  return (
    <View style={styles.container}>
      <View style={styles.typeRow}>
        <TouchableOpacity
          style={[styles.typeBtn, type === 'Expense' && styles.
          typeBtnActive]}
          onPress={() => setType('Expense')}
        >
          <Text style={[styles.typeBtnText, type === 'Expense' && styles.
          typeBtnTextActive]}>Expense</Text>
        </TouchableOpacity>
        <TouchableOpacity
          style={[styles.typeBtn, type === 'Income' && styles.
          typeBtnActive]}
          onPress={() => setType('Income')}
        >
          <Text style={[styles.typeBtnText, type === 'Income' && styles.
          typeBtnTextActive]}>Income</Text>
        </TouchableOpacity>
```

```
</View>
<Text style={styles.title}>Add {type}</Text>
<View style={styles.box}>
<TextInput
  style={styles.input}
  placeholder="Name"
  value={name}
  onChangeText={setName}
/>
<TextInput
  style={styles.input}
  placeholder="Amount"
  keyboardType="numeric"
  value={amount}
  onChangeText={setAmount}
/>
<View style={styles.categoryRow}>
  {['Travel', 'Fuel', 'Food', 'Utility', 'Others'].map((cat) => (
    <TouchableOpacity
      key={cat}
      style={[styles.categoryBtn, category === cat && styles.
      categoryBtnActive]}
      onPress={() => setCategory(cat)}
    >
      <Text style={[styles.categoryBtnText, category === cat &&
      styles.categoryBtnTextActive]}>{cat}</Text>
    </TouchableOpacity>
  ))}
</View>

<TextInput
  style={styles.input}
  placeholder="Date (YYYY-MM-DD)"
  value={date}
  onChangeText={setDate}
/>
```

```
      <Button title="Add Expense" onPress={handleAddExpense} />
      </View>
      <Text style={styles.title}>Expenses</Text>
      <FlatList
        data={expenses}
        keyExtractor={(item) => item.id}
        renderItem={({ item }) => (
          <View style={styles.expenseItem}>
            <Text>{item.type} | {item.name} | {item.amount} | {item.
            category} </Text>
            <TouchableOpacity onPress={() => deleteExpense(item.id)}>
              <Text style={styles.deleteBtn}>Delete</Text>
            </TouchableOpacity>
          </View>
        )}
        ListEmptyComponent={<Text>No expenses yet.</Text>}
      />
      <StatusBar style="auto" />
    </View>
  );}

const styles = StyleSheet.create({
  container: {
    flex: 1,
    paddingTop: 60,
    paddingHorizontal: 20,
  },
  box: {
    backgroundColor: '#fff',
    borderRadius: 16,
    padding: 20,
    marginBottom: 32,
    shadowColor: '#000',
    shadowOpacity: 0.04,
    shadowRadius: 6,
    elevation: 1,
```

```
},
title: {
  fontSize: 22,
  fontWeight: 'bold',
  marginVertical: 16,
},
input: {
  borderWidth: 1,
  borderColor: '#ccc',
  borderRadius: 5,
  padding: 10,
  marginBottom: 10,
  width: '100%',
},
expenseItem: {
  flexDirection: 'row',
  justifyContent: 'space-between',
  alignItems: 'center',
  padding: 10,
  borderBottomWidth: 1,
  borderBottomColor: '#eee',
  width: '100%',
},
deleteBtn: {
  color: 'red',
  marginLeft: 10,
},
typeRow: {
  flexDirection: 'row',
  justifyContent: 'center',
  alignItems: 'center',
  marginBottom: 16,
  gap: 12,
},
typeBtn: {
```

```
    paddingVertical: 8,
    paddingHorizontal: 24,
    borderRadius: 20,
    borderWidth: 1,
    borderColor: '#ccc',
    backgroundColor: '#f6f6f6',
    marginHorizontal: 4,
  },
  typeBtnActive: {
    backgroundColor: '#964B00',
    borderColor: '#007AFF',
  },
  typeBtnText: {
    color: '#222',
    fontWeight: '500',
    fontSize: 16,
  },
  typeBtnTextActive: {
    color: '#fff',
  },
    categoryRow: {
    flexDirection: 'row',
    flexWrap: 'wrap',
    justifyContent: 'center',
    marginBottom: 12,
    gap: 8,
  },
  categoryBtn: {
    paddingVertical: 6,
    paddingHorizontal: 16,
    borderRadius: 16,
    borderWidth: 1,
    borderColor: '#ccc',
    backgroundColor: '#f6f6f6',
    marginHorizontal: 4,
```

```
    marginBottom: 6,
  },
  categoryBtnActive: {
    backgroundColor: '#007AFF',
    borderColor: '#007AFF',
  },
  categoryBtnText: {
    color: '#222',
    fontWeight: '500',
    fontSize: 15,
  },
  categoryBtnTextActive: {
    color: '#fff',
  },
});
```

Now run the app:

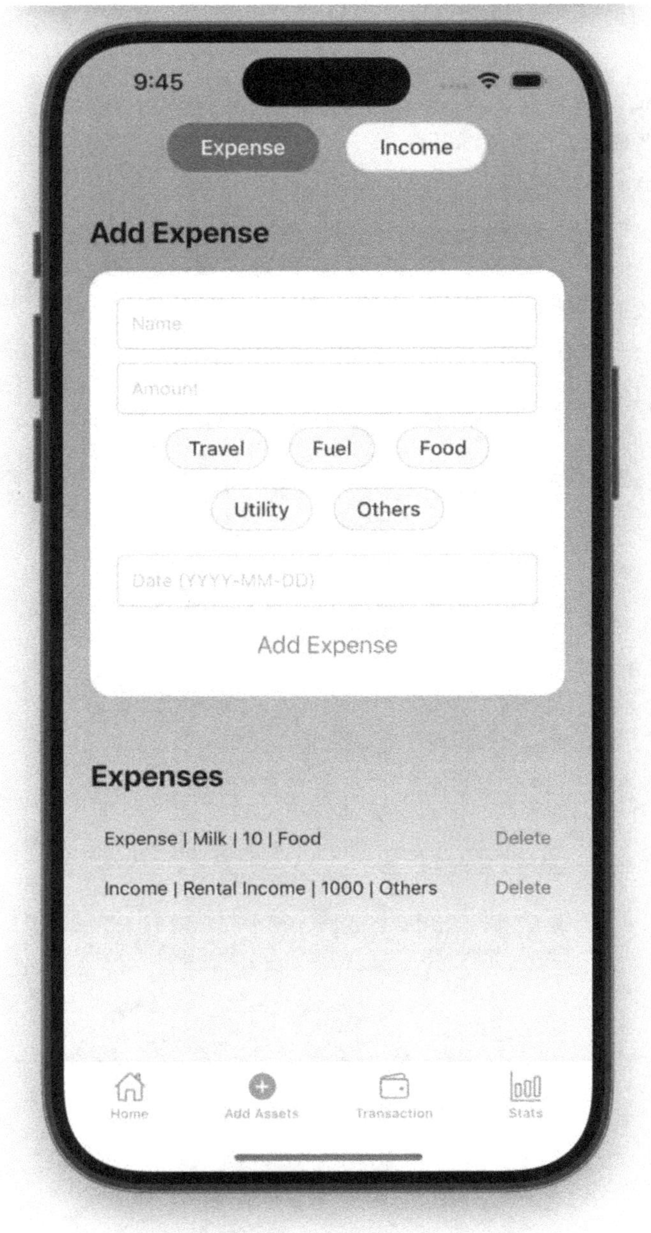
9:45
Expense
Income
Add Expense
Name
Amount
Travel
Fuel
Food
Utility
Others
Date (YYYY-MM-DD)
Add Expense
Expenses
Expense | Milk | 10 | Food
Delete
Income | Rental Income | 1000 | Others
Delete
Home
Add Assets
Transaction
Stats

Now let's understand the code:

- **React Hooks (`useState, useExpenses`)**: The component uses `useState` to manage local input states like type, name, amount, category, and date. It also uses a custom hook, `useExpenses`, which gives access to global expense data and helper functions (`addExpense, deleteExpense`) from the Context.
- **Form Inputs (`TextInput`)**: Several `TextInput` fields are used to enter details like expense name, amount, and date. Each input is connected to its state (`setName, setAmount, setDate`) to make them controlled components. For the amount field, `keyboardType="numeric"` ensures the number keypad opens.
- **Interactive Buttons (`TouchableOpacity`)**: Used for toggle buttons to switch between Expense and Income types. Also used to select categories (e.g., Travel, Fuel, Food, Utility, Others). Another `TouchableOpacity` is used inside the list for deleting an expense. This makes the UI interactive and gives visual feedback when pressed.
- **Add Expense (`Button`)**: A simple `Button` triggers the `handleAddExpense` function. This validates inputs, then adds the expense to the context and clears the fields.
- **Expense List Rendering (`FlatList`)**: Displays all the expenses dynamically from the context state. Each item shows type, name, amount, and category.
- Includes a Delete button (`TouchableOpacity`) to remove specific expenses.

Now, we have combined everything you've learned so far—core components, styling, hooks, and context—into our Expense Tracker app. This brings together the building blocks of React Native into a practical example. You've seen how inputs (`TextInput`), interactivity (`TouchableOpacity`, Button), list rendering (`FlatList`), and Context can all work together to create a complete feature. This integration not only strengthens your understanding of each concept but also shows how they fit naturally into real-world applications.

5.9 Summary

In this chapter, we explored the building blocks of React Native UI by organizing components into categories for easier understanding and usage.

- **Layout and Container Components**: We learned how View structures the UI, `SafeAreaView` ensures content fits within device boundaries, Modal displays content in overlays, and `KeyboardAvoidingView` prevents the on-screen keyboard from hiding input fields.
- **Text and Input Components**: The Text component was introduced for displaying readable content, while `TextInput` enables user entry of data and supports various customization options.
- **List Components**: We studied how `ScrollView` handles simple scrolling, while `FlatList` efficiently renders large lists, and `SectionList` organizes data into grouped sections.
- **Interactive Components**: User interaction was covered through Button, Pressable, and Touchable elements, each providing different levels of control over touch feedback and customization.
- **Animations**: Finally, we looked into creating dynamic and engaging user experiences with animations, enhancing how components transition, respond, and interact on screen.

Together, these components form the core toolkit for crafting responsive, interactive, and user-friendly mobile interfaces in React Native.

The next chapter covers different device capabilities like `MapView`, `AsyncStorage`, `NativeAlert`, `WebView`, etc.

CHAPTER 6

Working with Device Capabilities in React Native

6.1 The Role of Device Capabilities in Mobile Application Architecture

Mobile applications differ fundamentally from their web and desktop counterparts in one critical dimension: they operate atop privileged hardware subsystems, including

- Optical and depth-sensing cameras
- Secure and encrypted local storage containers
- Telephony and address book subsystems
- Calendar and event scheduling frameworks
- Orientation, proximity, motion, biometric, and geolocation sensors

Each subsystem is guarded by the operating system through strict capability-based security controls. Unlike web browsers, which provide highly abstracted and restricted access to peripherals, mobile operating systems permit high-fidelity interaction with hardware resources—but only under well-defined governance.

This governance emerges from three overlapping architectural constraints:

- **Security**: Prevent unauthorized access to private content (e.g., photos, contacts).

A. Nalwaya and A. Paul, *React Native for Mobile Development*, https://doi.org/10.1007/979-8-8688-2977-2_6

- **Performance**: Ensure hardware usage remains efficient and non-blocking.
- **User Agency**: Allow individuals to grant or revoke capability access explicitly.

Consequently, a mobile app achieves its purpose not just by rendering interfaces but by negotiating controlled access to the device's physical resources. Without this negotiation, many modern applications—such as WhatsApp, Instagram, Microsoft Outlook, and Google Pay—would be functionally non-viable.

Device capability integration is not merely an enhancement—it is the defining enabler of mobile application usefulness.

6.1.1 The Dual-World Execution Model

Every React Native application exists as a composition of two distinct computational environments:

Execution Environment	Language/Responsibilities/Performance
JavaScript Realm	JavaScript/JSX—UI definitions, business logic, event handling—managed runtime with garbage collection
Native Realm	Swift (iOS), Kotlin/Java (Android)—direct interaction with device subsystems and UI rendering—native performance, low-latency hardware access, platform-optimized UI rendering

These environments do not share memory and do not execute synchronously by default. React Native introduces a bidirectional asynchronous messaging architecture, historically called the Bridge, enabling serialized communication between realms.

6.1.2 Expo As a Managed Capability Layer

Traditional React Native development requires developers to modify Xcode .plist entitlement manifests, edit Android Manifest.xml permissions, inject Swift/Kotlin code to access native APIs, and integrate thread-safe callback interfaces manually.

Expo introduces an abstraction that pre-bundles native capability modules, controls permissions automatically through configuration metadata, supports OTA (over-the-air) updates aligned with native build compatibility, and provides a stable, unified API layer independent of OS version fragmentation.

Thus, developers operating within Expo's Managed Workflow can treat device capabilities as first-class JavaScript APIs, without direct exposure to native code semantics. This chapter leverages that transformation fully.

6.1.3 The New Architecture: JSI Replaces the Bridge

Since React Native 0.76, the New Architecture is enabled by default in all new projects. This is a significant shift that every modern React Native developer should understand.

The Legacy Bridge (pre-0.76) serialized all JS↔Native communication as JSON messages, which introduced latency and limited throughput. The New Architecture replaces this with two key technologies:

JSI (JavaScript Interface): A C++ layer that allows JavaScript to hold direct references to native objects and call native methods synchronously, without serialization. This eliminates the bridge overhead entirely.

TurboModules: Native modules built on JSI that are lazily loaded on demand, reducing app startup time. Only the modules actually used are initialized.

Fabric: The new rendering system that allows the native UI layer to synchronize directly with the JS thread, enabling concurrent rendering and improved responsiveness.

Legacy Architecture (pre-0.76)

JS Thread ➤ JSON Serialization ➤ Bridge ➤ Native Thread

New Architecture (default from 0.76+)

JS Thread ➤ JSI (Direct C++ Bindings) ➤ TurboModules/Fabric ➤ Native Thread

Throughout this chapter, when we use Expo's expo-camera, expo-contacts, and expo-calendar APIs, these are backed by TurboModules under the hood in projects running the New Architecture. The JavaScript API surface remains the same—but the execution is faster, more direct, and no longer depends on serialized message passing.

Note: If you are using Expo SDK 52+ or React Native 0.76+, the New Architecture is already active in your project. No configuration is required.

6.2 Extending the Expense Tracker with Device Capabilities

In previous chapters, we built the Expense Tracker—a fully functional app with bottom tab navigation (Home, Add Assets, Transaction, Stats), an ExpenseContext for state management, and a form-based UI for adding expenses. In this chapter, we extend this same application with four device capability modules:

Module	Capability Added to Expense Tracker
Camera	Attach receipt photos to expense entries
Contacts	Import a contact as a payee when adding an expense
Calendar	Schedule a payment reminder for an expense
AsyncStorage	Persist expenses across app restarts

This approach keeps the learning continuous: every new concept is immediately applied to code the reader already knows, making the architectural patterns easier to absorb.

6.2.1 Installing Required Packages

From the root of your ExpenseTracker project, install all capability modules at once:

```
npm install expo-camera expo-contacts expo-calendar @react-native-async-storage/async-storage
```

Expo configures native module bindings automatically in the managed workflow. No Xcode or Gradle edits are required.

6.2.2 Project Structure After This Chapter

We will add new files and modify existing ones. Here is the updated structure:

```
ExpenseTracker/
  components/
    AddAssets.js          ← modified: adds camera + contacts
```

```
context/
  ExpenseContext.js     ← modified: adds AsyncStorage persistence
screens/
  HomeScreen.js         ← modified: shows persisted balance
  AddAssetsScreen.js    ← wraps updated AddAssets
  TransactionScreen.js  ← modified: shows receipt thumbnails
  StatsScreen.js        ← (unchanged)
  TransactionDetailScreen.js ← modified: full receipt + calendar
App.js                  ← (unchanged)
```

6.2.3 Architectural Assurance

Before making any changes, verify the app still launches cleanly and all four tabs are reachable. Device capabilities will be added incrementally—one section at a time—so each feature can be tested in isolation before moving on.

Note Permission requests must always be contextual, never speculative—a principle enforced by modern OS interaction guidelines.

6.3 Permission Management in Mobile OS Ecosystems

Modern mobile operating systems enforce strict security boundaries between applications and device hardware subsystems. Because cameras, calendars, and contacts inherently involve sensitive personal data, applications cannot access them freely. Permission management is therefore a core architectural responsibility in React Native development.

Granting permission is not a mere API call—it is a legal and ethical contract between the user and the software.

6.3.1 Capability-Based Security Model

Both Android and iOS adopt a capability-based access model:

Note Applications must explicitly request capability tokens before interacting with restricted resources.

A simplified abstraction:

```
Request → User Consent → OS Grants Capability Token → Hardware
Access Enabled
```

Security Property	Description
User Consent	Human approval is mandatory for sensitive operations
Scope Restriction	App only accesses what user has approved
Revocability	User can revoke permission at any time
Least Privilege Principle	Request only what is operationally necessary

6.3.2 OS-Level Permission Governance

Even though Expo abstracts native code, underlying OS policies remain.

Android Classification

Permission Class/Examples	Approval Type
Normal—Internet, Vibration	Granted at install time
Dangerous—Camera, Contacts, Microphone, Calendar	User prompt required

iOS Permission Lifecycle

iOS treats all sensitive capabilities as requiring user consent. Once denied, iOS will not prompt again automatically—the developer must guide the user to Settings.

Note Apple's Privacy Philosophy: iOS assumes users own their data. Apps must earn trust—not assume it.

6.3.3 Architectural Placement of Permission Logic

Permission requests should always be

✔ Contextual → ask only when the user initiates the related action

✔ Incremental → one capability at a time

✔ Explainable → provide rationale before OS dialog appears

✔ Recoverable → handle denial with UI alternatives

What you must NOT do: ask for Camera, Contacts, and Calendar permissions all at once on first launch. This violates both usability and OS review guidelines.

6.3.4 Permission Handling in React Native + Expo

Expo exposes unified permission interfaces as asynchronous contracts with three outcomes:

- Granted
- Denied

Understanding canAskAgain: Two Sub-states of Denial

When a permission is denied, there are actually two distinct sub-states that require different handling:

1. **Recoverable Denial (canAskAgain: true)**: The user denied the prompt, but the OS will show the dialog again if requested. You can call requestPermission() once more, and the system prompt will re-appear.
2. **Permanent Denial (canAskAgain: false)**: The user selected "Never Ask Again" (Android) or has denied the permission twice on iOS. The OS will never show the dialog again. Calling requestPermission() has no effect. The only recovery path is to direct the user to the app's system Settings page using Linking.openSettings().

Always inspect canAskAgain from the PermissionResponse object before deciding how to handle a denial.

```
const { status, canAskAgain } = await requestPermission();
if (status !== 'granted') {
  if (canAskAgain) {
    // Show rationale and offer retry
  } else {
    // Direct user to Settings - OS will not prompt again
    Linking.openSettings();
  }
}
```

- Undetermined (no prompt shown yet)

In the latest Expo SDKs, API-specific permission hooks are preferred. We will use that modern pattern throughout this chapter.

6.3.5 Permission Request Lifecycle

The flow can be decomposed into a series of well-defined states:

- **JS Initiates Permission Request**: The app determines a privileged action is about to occur (e.g., "Attach Receipt Photo"). JavaScript calls the relevant Expo permission API. No OS dialog is shown yet.
- **OS Presents Permission Dialog**: The underlying OS takes over and surfaces the system permission modal. This dialog is non-customizable by the app.
- **User Responds—Branch A: Approve**: OS grants a capability token. Control returns to JavaScript with a 'granted' status.
- **User Responds—Branch B: Deny**: Control returns to JavaScript with a 'denied' status. App must not crash or hang.
- **Capability Granted → Execute Feature**: Camera opens, contacts load, calendar writes, or storage persists.
- **Capability Denied → User Education UI**: App presents a helpful message explaining why the permission is needed and offers a retry path.

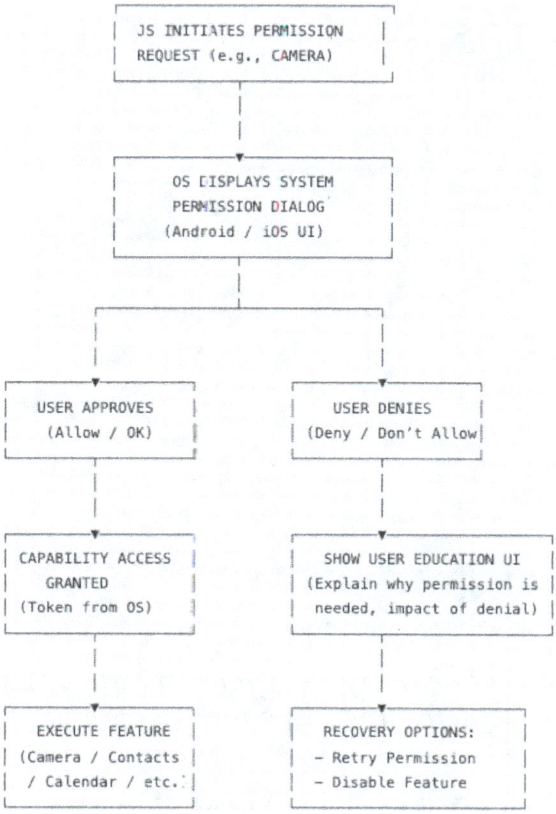

Permission Validation and Recovery Flow in React Native/Expo

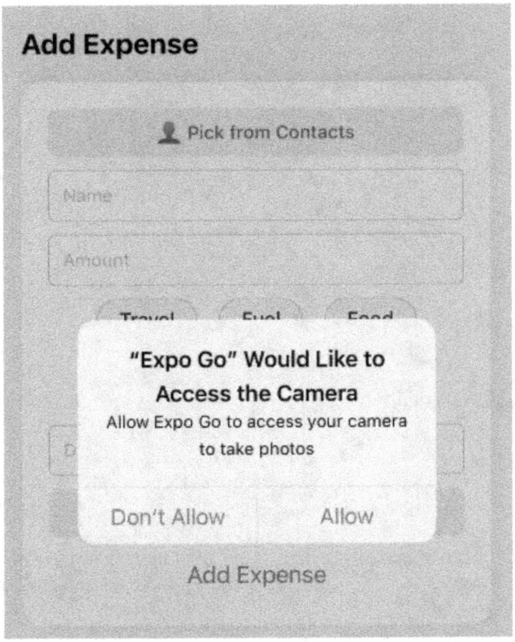

Permission Validation and Recovery Flow in React Native / Expo
OS Permission Dialog Triggered from Expense Tracker Add Assets Screen

6.3.6 Permission UX Design: Best Practice Rules

Guideline	Example in Expense Tracker
Ask permission immediately after user intent	User taps "Attach Receipt" → Request Camera Access
Provide a short rationale before OS dialog	"We need camera access to attach receipt photos to your expenses."
Handle 'denied' gracefully	Disable "Attach Receipt" button but keep full form functional
Allow retry pathway	Provide a "Retry Permission" button below the form
Do not beg	If denied twice → direct to system settings silently

Note Modern app reviews reject apps lacking clear justification messaging.

6.3.7 Permission Revalidation Must Be Continuous

Permissions must be checked every time a feature requiring them is invoked:

- App update? Permission may reset.
- Device policy change? Permission revoked.
- OS upgrade? Privacy sandbox may shift.

```
checkPermission → requestIfNotGranted → execute → re-check later
```

Permission evaluation is not a one-time setup—it is a continuous system compliance loop.

6.4 Camera: Attaching Receipt Photos to Expenses

The camera is not merely a media capture device—it is a real-time optical sensor array, managed by low-latency native frameworks: AVFoundation (iOS) and CameraX/Camera2 API (Android). Expo's expo-camera library abstracts these subsystems through a controlled JavaScript interface.

In the context of the Expense Tracker, the camera serves a practical purpose: allowing users to photograph receipts and attach them to an expense entry. This transforms the AddAssets screen from a data-entry form into a document-capture workflow.

This section will

✓ Request camera permission contextually from AddAssets

✓ Display a live camera preview when "Attach Receipt" is pressed

✓ Capture the receipt photo and attach its URI to the expense

✓ Render the attached photo thumbnail in the expense list

✓ Discuss memory and performance implications

6.4.1 Installing and Importing the Camera Module

The package was installed in the "Installing Required Packages" section. Now add the import to the AddAssets component:

```
// components/AddAssets.js – updated importss
import { StatusBar } from 'expo-status-bar';
import {
  StyleSheet, Text, View, TextInput, Button,
  FlatList, TouchableOpacity, Image
} from 'react-native';
import React, { useState, useRef } from 'react';
import { CameraView, useCameraPermissions } from 'expo-camera';
import { useExpenses } from '../context/ExpenseContext';
```

Import	Technical Importance
useCameraPermissions	Modern hook-based permission API—cleaner than the old Camera.requestCameraPermissionsAsync()
CameraView	React Native wrapper over native AVFoundation/CameraX capture pipeline
useRef	Provides stable camera instance reference across renders for issuing capture commands
Image	Renders the captured receipt thumbnail URI in the expense list

6.4.2 Adding Camera State to AddAssets

Inside the AddAssets functional component, add camera-related state alongside the existing form state:

```
export default function AddAssets() {
  const { expenses, addExpense, deleteExpense } = useExpenses();

  // Existing form state
  const [type, setType] = useState('Expense');
  const [name, setName] = useState('');
  const [amount, setAmount] = useState('');
```

```
  const [category, setCategory] = useState('');
  const [date, setDate] = useState('');

  // New: camera state
  const [permission, requestPermission] = useCameraPermissions();
  const [showCamera, setShowCamera] = useState(false);
  const [receiptUri, setReceiptUri] = useState(null);
  const cameraRef = useRef(null);
```

Code	Engineering Rationale
useCameraPermissions()	Hook returns [permission, requestPermission]—permission.status tracks OS authorization state at runtime
showCamera	Controls whether to render the CameraView overlay—keeps native sensor idle until needed
receiptUri	Stores the file URI returned by takePictureAsync—references native temp directory, not pixel data
cameraRef	Without this ref, JS cannot issue capture commands to the native camera instance

6.4.3 Conditional Camera Permission Logic

Add the receipt capture handler that checks and requests permission contextually—only when the user taps "Attach Receipt":

```
const handleAttachReceipt = async () => {
  if (!permission?.granted) {
    const { granted } = await requestPermission();
    if (!granted) {
      alert('Camera permission is required to attach receipts.');
      return;
    }
  }
  setShowCamera(true);
};
```

```
const handleCapture = async () => {
  if (cameraRef.current) {
    const photo = await cameraRef.current.takePictureAsync({
    quality: 0.5 });
    setReceiptUri(photo.uri);
    setShowCamera(false);
  }
};
```

Notice that permission is requested only when the user explicitly taps "Attach Receipt"—not on component mount. This is the contextual permission pattern required by modern OS guidelines.

Note Null/Undefined Case Matters: Before the user responds, permission?. granted is falsy. The optional chaining prevents a runtime crash during the indeterminate state.

6.4.4 Rendering the Camera View Overlay

When showCamera is true, render a full-screen camera overlay instead of the form. Update the return JSX:

```
if (showCamera) {
  return (
    <View style={styles.cameraContainer}>
      <CameraView
        style={styles.cameraView}
        ref={cameraRef}
      />
      <View style={styles.cameraControls}>
        <TouchableOpacity style={styles.captureBtn}
        onPress={handleCapture}>
          <Text style={styles.captureBtnText}>📷 Capture Receipt</Text>
```

```
        </TouchableOpacity>
        <TouchableOpacity
          style={styles.cancelBtn}
          onPress={() => setShowCamera(false)}
        >
          <Text style={styles.cancelBtnText}>Cancel</Text>
        </TouchableOpacity>
      </View>
    </View>
  );
}
```

Component	Native Implication
<CameraView />	Spins up hardware optical pipeline in a separate native thread—GPU-accelerated preview
ref={cameraRef}	Without this, JS cannot issue capture commands to the native camera instance
takePictureAsync()	Initiates sensor snapshot → encoder → temporary file; returns a URI, not pixel data
quality: 0.5	Reduces encoder workload—receipt thumbnails do not need full resolution
setShowCamera(false)	Unmounts <CameraView>—immediately releases GPU, sensor, and battery resources

6.4.5 Attaching the Receipt URI to an Expense

Update handleAddExpense to include the receiptUri in the expense object:

```
const handleAddExpense = () => {
  if (!name || !amount || !category || !date) return;
  addExpense({ type, name, amount, category, date, receiptUri });
  setName('');
  setAmount('');
  setCategory('');
```

```
  setDate('');
  setReceiptUri(null);  // reset after saving
};
```

Add an “Attach Receipt” button and receipt thumbnail preview inside the form:

```
{/* Inside the <View style={styles.box}> form section */}
<TouchableOpacity style={styles.receiptBtn} onPress={handleAttachReceipt}>
  <Text style={styles.receiptBtnText}>
    {receiptUri ? '☑ Receipt Attached' : '📷 Attach Receipt'}
  </Text>
</TouchableOpacity>

{receiptUri && (
  <Image
    source={{ uri: receiptUri }}
    style={styles.receiptThumbnail}
    resizeMode="cover"
  />
)}
```

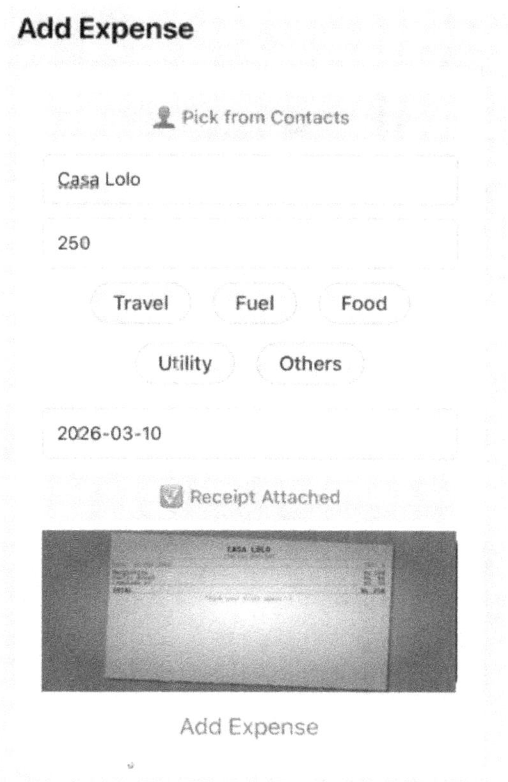

Expense Form with Attached Receipt Thumbnail in the Expense Tracker

6.4.6 Displaying Receipt Thumbnails in the Expense List

Update the FlatList renderItem in AddAssets to show receipt thumbnails alongside each expense:

```
renderItem={({ item }) => (
  <View style={styles.expenseItem}>
    <View style={styles.expenseInfo}>
      <Text>{item.type} | {item.name} | ₹{item.amount} | {item.
      category}</Text>
    </View>
    {item.receiptUri && (
      <Image
        source={{ uri: item.receiptUri }}
        style={styles.listThumbnail}
```

```
        resizeMode="cover"
      />
    )}
    <TouchableOpacity onPress={() => deleteExpense(item.id)}>
      <Text style={styles.deleteBtn}>Delete</Text>
    </TouchableOpacity>
  </View>
)}
```

Add the new styles to the existing StyleSheet:

```
cameraContainer: {
  flex: 1,
},
cameraView: {
  flex: 1,
},
cameraControls: {
  position: 'absolute',
  bottom: 40,
  left: 0,
  right: 0,
  alignItems: 'center',
  gap: 12,
},
captureBtn: {
  backgroundColor: '#007AFF',
  paddingVertical: 14,
  paddingHorizontal: 40,
  borderRadius: 30,
},
captureBtnText: {
  color: '#fff',
  fontSize: 16,
  fontWeight: '600',
},
```

```
cancelBtn: {
  backgroundColor: '#FF3B30',
  paddingVertical: 10,
  paddingHorizontal: 30,
  borderRadius: 20,
},
cancelBtnText: {
  color: '#fff',
  fontSize: 14,
},
receiptBtn: {
  backgroundColor: '#f0f0f0',
  padding: 10,
  borderRadius: 8,
  marginBottom: 10,
  alignItems: 'center',
},
receiptBtnText: {
  color: '#007AFF',
  fontWeight: '500',
},
receiptThumbnail: {
  width: '100%',
  height: 120,
  borderRadius: 8,
  marginBottom: 10,
},
expenseInfo: {
  flex: 1,
},
listThumbnail: {
  width: 48,
  height: 48,
```

```
  borderRadius: 6,
  marginLeft: 8,
},
```

6.4.7 Performance and Resource Notes

Concern	Mitigation
Camera feed consumes GPU and sensor battery	Unmount <CameraView> immediately after capture—setShowCamera(false)
takePictureAsync returns File URI, not binary	Prevents UI thread memory overload—only the path crosses the bridge
Preview decoding may spike CPU	quality: 0.5 reduces encoding work; listThumbnail is kept small
receiptUri lost on app restart	We will persist the full expense (including URI) via AsyncStorage in the "Local Storage with AsyncStorage: Persisting Expenses Across Restarts" section

Note Never block JS while the camera capture pipeline is executing. The camera is native-driven; UI remains JS-driven. They must cooperate asynchronously.

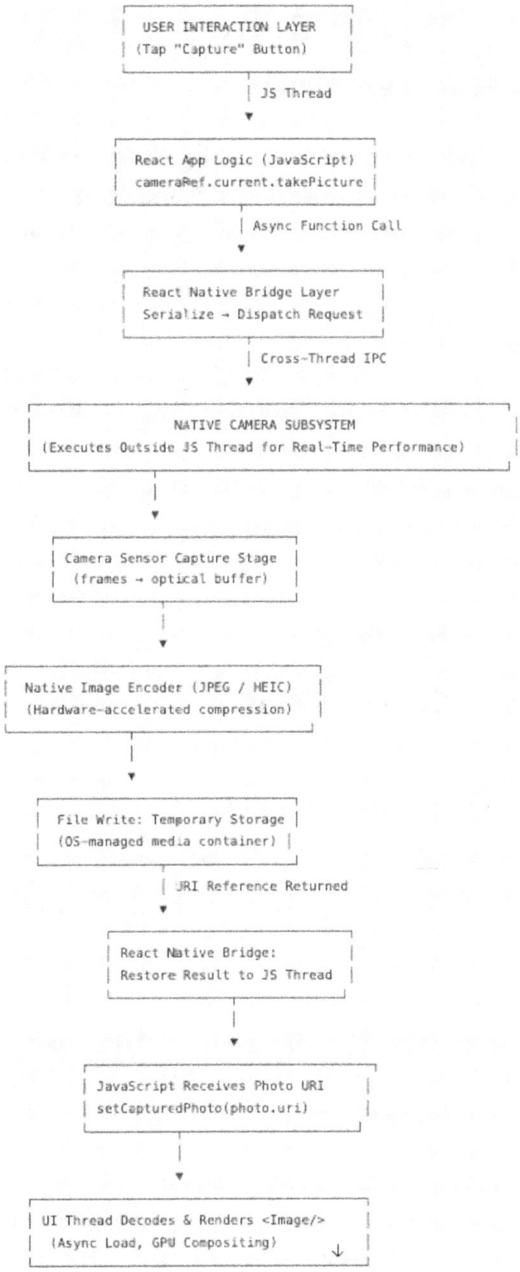

Camera Capture Lifecycle in React Native

6.5 Contacts Subsystem: Importing a Payee from the Address Book

Mobile address books contain high-risk personally identifiable information (PII): full legal names, phone numbers, email addresses, organizational roles, and residential or mailing addresses. As a result, this subsystem is guarded by the OS as a secure data domain.

In the Expense Tracker, contacts serve a concrete purpose: when adding an expense, the user may want to record who they paid. Rather than typing a payee name manually, we give them a "Pick from Contacts" option that reads the address book and populates the Name field.

This is a common pattern in finance and invoicing apps. It also demonstrates the least-privilege principle—we only request phone numbers and names, nothing else.

6.5.1 Module Installation

The package was installed in the "Installing Required Packages" section. Import it in AddAssets.js:

```
import * as Contacts from 'expo-contacts';
```

The * import is used because the Contacts API surface area is broad (query options, pagination, write ops), and this avoids constant named import changes as we expand functionality.

6.5.2 Adding Contacts State to AddAssets

Add contact picker state alongside the existing camera state:

```
// components/AddAssets.js - additional state
const [contactsPermission, setContactsPermission] = useState(null);
const [showContactPicker, setShowContactPicker] = useState(false);
const [contactList, setContactList] = useState([]);
```

Code	Architectural Purpose
contactsPermission	Tracks OS authorization state for address book access
showContactPicker	Controls a modal contact list—keeps address book data out of memory until explicitly needed
contactList	Array of native contact entries converted to JS-safe structures

6.5.3 Requesting Address Book Permission and Loading Contacts

Add the handler for the "Pick from Contacts" button—permission is requested contextually:

```
const handlePickContact = async () => {
  const { status } = await Contacts.requestPermissionsAsync();
  setContactsPermission(status);

  if (status !== 'granted') {
    alert('Contacts permission is required to pick a payee.');
    return;
  }

  const { data } = await Contacts.getContactsAsync({
    fields: [Contacts.Fields.Name, Contacts.Fields.PhoneNumbers],
    pageSize: 50,
    pageOffset: 0,
  });

  setContactList(data);
  setShowContactPicker(true);
};
```

Code	Architectural Purpose
requestPermissionsAsync()	Opens OS modal → security token grant—only called when user taps "Pick from Contacts"
fields: [Name, PhoneNumbers]	Reduces data scope → follows least-privilege principle
pageSize: 50	Protects against large address book memory spikes (enterprise users may have 2,000+ contacts)
data	Array of native contact entries—OS-sanitized snapshots, not raw database access

6.5.4 Rendering the Contact Picker

When showContactPicker is true, render an inline modal contact list. Add this inside the component return, above the camera overlay check:

```
{showContactPicker && (
  <View style={styles.contactPickerOverlay}>
    <Text style={styles.contactPickerTitle}>Pick a Payee</Text>
    <FlatList
      data={contactList}
      keyExtractor={(item) => item.id}
      renderItem={({ item }) => (
        <TouchableOpacity
          style={styles.contactRow}
          onPress={() => {
            setName(item.name);    // populate the Name field
            setShowContactPicker(false);
          }}
        >
          <Text style={styles.contactName}>{item.name}</Text>
          {item.phoneNumbers && item.phoneNumbers.length > 0 && (
            <Text style={styles.contactPhone}>
              {item.phoneNumbers[0].number}
            </Text>
```

```
          )}
        </TouchableOpacity>
      )}
      ListEmptyComponent={<Text>No contacts found.</Text>}
    />
    <TouchableOpacity
      style={styles.cancelBtn}
      onPress={() => setShowContactPicker(false)}
    >
      <Text style={styles.cancelBtnText}>Cancel</Text>
    </TouchableOpacity>
  </View>
)}
```

Element	Why it matters
FlatList	Virtualized rendering—prevents OOM issues with large contact lists
keyExtractor	Contacts have persistent IDs → no re-render chaos
setName(item.name)	Populates the existing Name TextInput in AddAssets—contacts integrate seamlessly with existing form
Conditional phone number	Fields are optional; must not assume existence
setShowContactPicker(false)	Dismisses picker—releases contact list from memory

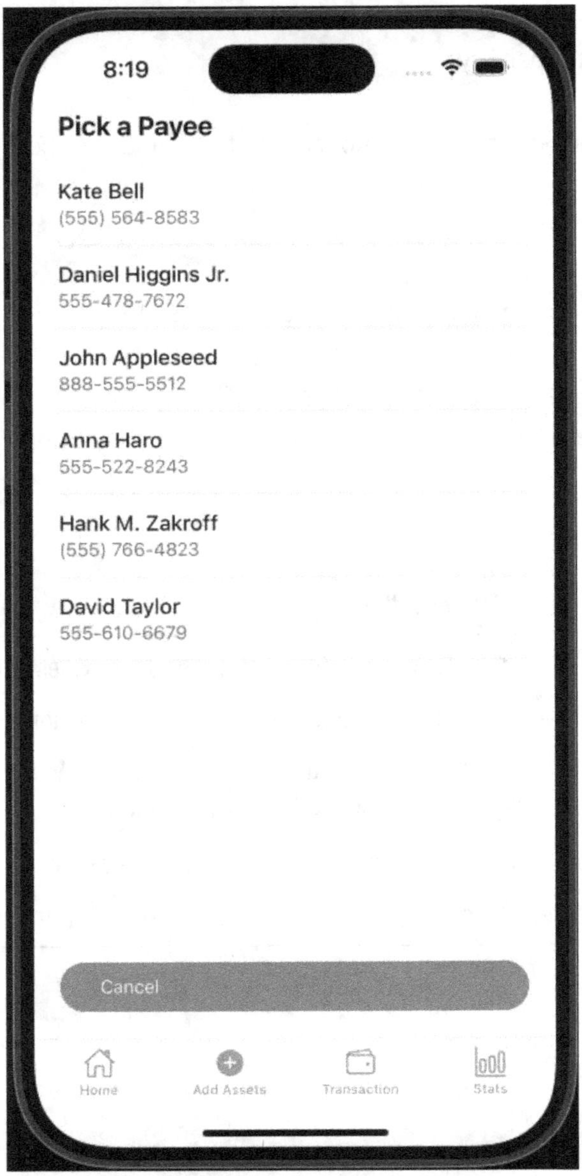

Contact Picker Overlay in the Expense Tracker Add Assets Screen

6.5.5 Adding "Pick from Contacts" Button to the Form

Add the trigger button inside the form's <View style={styles.box}> section, right above the Name TextInput:

```
<TouchableOpacity style={styles.contactPickBtn}
onPress={handlePickContact}>
  <Text style={styles.contactPickBtnText}>👤 Pick from Contacts</Text>
</TouchableOpacity>
```

And the required styles:

```
contactPickerOverlay: {
  position: 'absolute',
  top: 0, left: 0, right: 0, bottom: 0,
  backgroundColor: '#fff',
  zIndex: 10,
  padding: 20,
},
contactPickerTitle: {
  fontSize: 20,
  fontWeight: 'bold',
  marginBottom: 16,
},
contactRow: {
  paddingVertical: 12,
  borderBottomWidth: 1,
  borderColor: '#eee',
},
contactName: {
  fontSize: 16,
  fontWeight: '500',
},
contactPhone: {
  fontSize: 14,
  color: '#555',
},
contactPickBtn: {
  backgroundColor: '#f0f0f0',
  padding: 10,
```

```
  borderRadius: 8,
  marginBottom: 10,
  alignItems: 'center',
},
contactPickBtnText: {
  color: '#5856D6',
  fontWeight: '500',
},
```

📌 OS never hands raw database access to JavaScript. JS receives strictly controlled snapshotted records. React Native never owns the master contact store—it only views OS-sanitized data snapshots under temporary privilege.

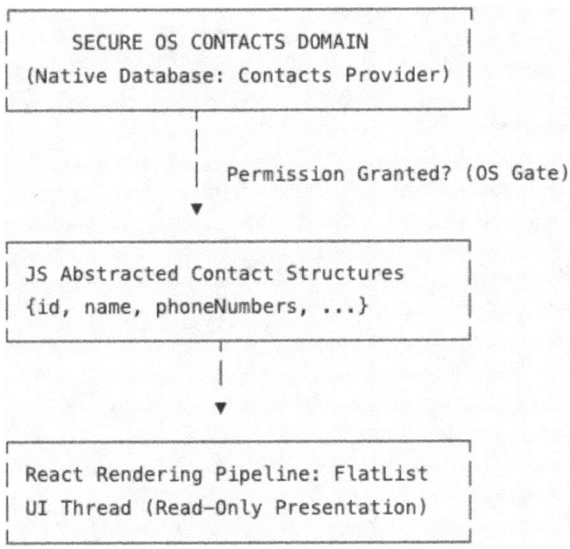

Contacts Data Security Boundary

6.5.6 Memory and Security Constraints

Risk	Mitigation
Thousands of contacts → memory load	Pagination (pageSize: 50) already applied
Slow UI while loading	Async query + FlatList virtualization
Sensitive data exposure	Only request Name and PhoneNumbers—not email, address, or full dataset
User denial → feature break	Alert message shown; Name field still editable manually

6.6 Calendar Subsystem: Scheduling Payment Reminders

The system calendar is not just a list of dates; it is a time-anchored, user-owned knowledge base managed by the operating system. Writing into the calendar means creating entries the user will see in native Calendar apps, potentially triggering system notifications and alarms, and persisting information outside your own application's storage.

In the Expense Tracker, calendar integration is placed in the TransactionDetailScreen. When a user views an expense's detail page, they can tap "Set Payment Reminder" to create a calendar event reminding them to pay by a specific date. This is a natural context for the feature—the user has already navigated to a specific transaction, indicating intent.

6.6.1 Installing the Calendar Module

The package was installed in the "Installing Required Packages" section. Open TransactionDetailScreen.js and add imports:

```
// screens/TransactionDetailScreen.js – updated imports
import React, { useState } from 'react';
import {
  View, Text, StyleSheet, Image, Button, Alert, ScrollView
```

```
} from 'react-native';
import * as Calendar from 'expo-calendar';
```

6.6.2 Updating TransactionDetailScreen to Receive Full Expense Data

In Chapter 5, TransactionDetailScreen received only an id parameter. Now it needs the full expense object to display receipt photos and schedule reminders. Update TransactionScreen.js to pass the full item:

```
// screens/TransactionScreen.js – updated navigation call
import React from 'react';
import { View, Text, StyleSheet, FlatList, TouchableOpacity, Image } from
'react-native';
import { useExpenses } from '../context/ExpenseContext';

const TransactionScreen = ({ navigation }) => {
  const { expenses } = useExpenses();

  return (
    <View style={styles.container}>
      <Text style={styles.title}>Transactions</Text>
      <FlatList
        data={expenses}
        keyExtractor={(item) => item.id}
        renderItem={({ item }) => (
          <TouchableOpacity
            style={styles.transactionItem}
            onPress={() => navigation.navigate('TransactionDetail', {
            expense: item })}
          >
            <View style={styles.transactionInfo}>
              <Text style={styles.transactionName}>{item.name}</Text>
              <Text style={styles.transactionMeta}>
                {item.category} • {item.date}
              </Text>
            </View>
```

```
            <Text style={[
              styles.transactionAmount,
              { color: item.type === 'Expense' ? '#FF3B30' : '#34C759' }
            ]}>
              {item.type === 'Expense' ? '-' : '+'}₹{item.amount}
            </Text>
            {item.receiptUri && (
              <Image
                source={{ uri: item.receiptUri }}
                style={styles.thumbnail}
                resizeMode="cover"
              />
            )}
          </TouchableOpacity>
        )}
        ListEmptyComponent={
          <Text style={styles.emptyText}>No transactions yet.</Text>
        }
      />
    </View>
  );
};

const styles = StyleSheet.create({
  container: { flex: 1, padding: 16 },
  title: { fontSize: 22, fontWeight: 'bold', marginBottom: 16 },
  transactionItem: {
    flexDirection: 'row',
    alignItems: 'center',
    paddingVertical: 12,
    borderBottomWidth: 1,
    borderColor: '#eee',
  },
  transactionInfo: { flex: 1 },
  transactionName: { fontSize: 16, fontWeight: '500' },
  transactionMeta: { fontSize: 13, color: '#888', marginTop: 2 },
```

```
  transactionAmount: { fontSize: 16, fontWeight: '600', marginRight: 8 },
  thumbnail: { width: 40, height: 40, borderRadius: 6 },
  emptyText: { textAlign: 'center', marginTop: 40, color: '#aaa' },
});

export default TransactionScreen;
```

6.6.3 Determining the Default Calendar

To create an event, we need a target calendar ID. Add this helper in TransactionDetailScreen.js:

```
async function getDefaultCalendarId() {
  const calendars = await Calendar.getCalendarsAsync(
    Calendar.EntityTypes.EVENT
  );
  if (calendars.length > 0) {
    return calendars[0].id;
  }
  throw new Error('No calendars available on this device.');
}
```

getCalendarsAsync runs in the native layer and returns metadata, not events. Selecting calendars[0] is a simplified heuristic acceptable for a demo—in production, you would filter by isPrimary or allowsModifications.

6.6.4 Implementing the Payment Reminder Feature

Now define the updated TransactionDetailScreen component:

```
export default function TransactionDetailScreen({ route }) {
  const { expense } = route.params;
  const [statusMessage, setStatusMessage] = useState('');

  const createPaymentReminder = async () => {
    try {
      // 1. Request calendar permissions
      const { status } = await Calendar.requestCalendarPermissionsAsync();
```

```
    if (status !== 'granted') {
      setStatusMessage('Calendar permission not granted.');
      return;
    }

    // 2. Resolve a default calendar ID
    const defaultCalendarId = await getDefaultCalendarId();

    // 3. Parse the expense date and set reminder for that day
    const expenseDate = new Date(expense.date);
    expenseDate.setHours(9, 0, 0, 0); // remind at 9 AM on the
    expense date
    const endDate = new Date(expenseDate.getTime() + 60 * 60 * 1000);
    // +1 hour

    // 4. Create the calendar event
    const eventId = await Calendar.createEventAsync(defaultCalendarId, {
      title: `💸 Pay: ${expense.name} – ₹${expense.amount}`,
      startDate: expenseDate,
      endDate,
      timeZone: 'Asia/Kolkata',
      notes: `Category: ${expense.category}. Created from Expense
      Tracker.`,
    });

    setStatusMessage(`Reminder set! Event ID: ${eventId}`);
    Alert.alert('Reminder Set', `Payment reminder added to your calendar
    for ${expense.date}`);

  } catch (error) {
    console.error('Error creating calendar event:', error);
    setStatusMessage('Failed to set reminder. See console for details.');
  }
};

return (
  <ScrollView style={styles.container}>
    <Text style={styles.title}>Transaction Detail</Text>
```

```
      <View style={styles.detailCard}>
        <DetailRow label="Name" value={expense.name} />
        <DetailRow label="Type" value={expense.type} />
        <DetailRow label="Amount" value={`₹${expense.amount}`} />
        <DetailRow label="Category" value={expense.category} />
        <DetailRow label="Date" value={expense.date} />
      </View>

      {expense.receiptUri && (
        <View style={styles.receiptSection}>
          <Text style={styles.sectionLabel}>Receipt</Text>
          <Image
            source={{ uri: expense.receiptUri }}
            style={styles.receiptImage}
            resizeMode="contain"
          />
        </View>
      )}
      <Button title="📅 Set Payment Reminder" onPress={createPayment
      Reminder} />
      {statusMessage ? (
        <Text style={styles.status}>{statusMessage}</Text>
      ) : null}
    </ScrollView>
  );
}

function DetailRow({ label, value }) {
  return (
    <View style={styles.detailRow}>
      <Text style={styles.detailLabel}>{label}</Text>
      <Text style={styles.detailValue}>{value}</Text>
    </View>
  );
}
```

Code Fragment	Deep Explanation
expense from route.params	Receives the full expense object passed by TransactionScreen—no need for a separate API call
expense.date parsed to calendar event	Links the reminder to the actual expense date rather than a fixed offset—contextually meaningful
timeZone: 'Asia/Kolkata'	Explicit IANA time zone avoids DST-related confusion on Indian devices—replace with user's locale in production
title includes name and amount	Calendar event is immediately informative without opening the app—user sees '💸 Pay: Lunch — ₹450' in native calendar
try/catch mandatory	All calendar interactions are IO-bound; failures may originate from permissions, device policies, or calendar store corruption

6.6.5 Styles for TransactionDetailScreen

```
const styles = StyleSheet.create({
  container: { flex: 1, padding: 16 },
  title: { fontSize: 22, fontWeight: 'bold', marginBottom: 20 },
  detailCard: {
    backgroundColor: '#fff',
    borderRadius: 12,
    padding: 16,
    marginBottom: 20,
    shadowColor: '#000',
    shadowOpacity: 0.06,
    shadowRadius: 8,
    elevation: 2,
  },
  detailRow: {
    flexDirection: 'row',
    justifyContent: 'space-between',
    paddingVertical: 10,
```

```
    borderBottomWidth: 1,
    borderColor: '#f0f0f0',
  },
  detailLabel: { fontSize: 14, color: '#888' },
  detailValue: { fontSize: 14, fontWeight: '500', color: '#222' },
  receiptSection: { marginBottom: 20 },
  sectionLabel: { fontSize: 16, fontWeight: '600', marginBottom: 10 },
  receiptImage: {
    width: '100%',
    height: 220,
    borderRadius: 10,
    backgroundColor: '#f9f9f9',
  },
  status: {
    marginTop: 12,
    fontSize: 12,
    color: '#555',
    textAlign: 'center',
  },
});
```

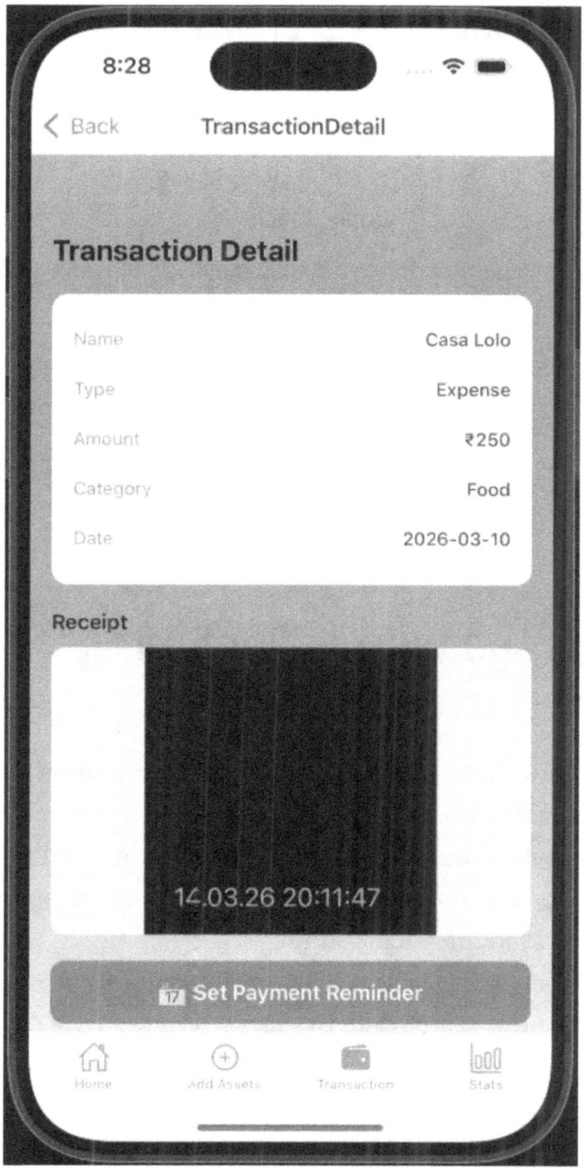

Transaction Detail Screen with Receipt Photo and Calendar Reminder Button

6.6.6 Failure Modes and Defensive Strategies

Scenario	Cause	Handling Strategy
Permission denied	User rejects OS dialog	setStatusMessage shown; Button remains—user can retry anytime
No calendars configured	Fresh emulator, restricted device	getDefaultCalendarId throws → caught in catch block; status updated
Expense date invalid	User typed non-ISO date	expenseDate will be Invalid Date—guard with isNaN(expenseDate) check in production
Calendar store locked	Rare OS-level issue	createEventAsync rejects; error captured, logged, status shown

6.7 Local Storage with AsyncStorage: Persisting Expenses Across Restarts

In every non-trivial application, you eventually face a fundamental requirement: some data must survive app restarts.

React component state alone cannot satisfy this requirement. State lives entirely in memory and is destroyed when the app process is killed, the user restarts the device, or the OS reclaims resources in the background.

For the Expense Tracker, this is a critical problem: all expenses added by the user vanish every time the app is closed. In this section, we wire AsyncStorage into ExpenseContext so that the expense list is automatically saved on every change and restored on every app launch.

AsyncStorage IS	AsyncStorage is NOT
A lightweight persistence layer for preferences, flags, and small JSON blobs	A relational database, full-text search engine, or analytics store
Appropriate for user-entered expense records	Suitable for large binary media or unbounded data growth
An async API similar to localStorage but more explicit	A synchronous blocking store

6.7.1 Installing AsyncStorage

The package was installed in the "Installing Required Packages" section. It may use different backing implementations internally (SQLite, files, or platform-specific key-value stores), but the API contract remains the same.

Note: Recommendation—expo-sqlite for Structured Data

If your data needs grow beyond AsyncStorage—complex queries, relational data, or larger datasets—use expo-sqlite (not the bare react-native-sqlite-storage package):

```
npm install expo-sqlite
```

```
import * as SQLite from 'expo-sqlite';
const db = await SQLite.openDatabaseAsync('expenses.db');
await db.execAsync(`
  CREATE TABLE IF NOT EXISTS expenses (
    id TEXT PRIMARY KEY, name TEXT,
    amount TEXT, category TEXT, date TEXT
  );`),
```

expo-sqlite works in Expo Go and managed workflow without ejecting, and supports SQLite 3.x features. Use AsyncStorage for simple key/value persistence; graduate to expo-sqlite when you need relational queries or multiple data entities.

6.7.2 Updating ExpenseContext to Use AsyncStorage

This is the most impactful change in this chapter. We modify ExpenseContext.js so that

- On mount, it loads any previously saved expenses from storage (hydration)
- Whenever expenses change, it saves the updated array to storage (persistence)

Open context/ExpenseContext.js and replace its contents:

```
// context/ExpenseContext.js
import React, { createContext, useContext, useState, useEffect } from
'react';
import AsyncStorage from '@react-native-async-storage/async-storage';
```

```
const ExpenseContext = createContext();

const STORAGE_KEY = '@expensetracker:expenses';

export function ExpenseProvider({ children }) {
  const [expenses, setExpenses] = useState([]);
  const [isLoaded, setIsLoaded] = useState(false);

  // —— Hydration: load saved expenses on first mount
————————————————————————————

  useEffect(() => {
    const loadExpenses = async () => {
      try {
        const stored = await AsyncStorage.getItem(STORAGE_KEY);
        if (stored !== null) {
          setExpenses(JSON.parse(stored));
        }
      } catch (error) {
        console.error('Failed to load expenses from storage:', error);
      } finally {
        setIsLoaded(true);
      }
    };
    loadExpenses();
  }, []);

  // —— Persistence: save expenses whenever they change
——————————————————————

  useEffect(() => {
    if (!isLoaded) return; // don't overwrite storage during initial
    hydration
    const saveExpenses = async () => {
      try {
        await AsyncStorage.setItem(STORAGE_KEY, JSON.stringify(expenses));
      } catch (error) {
        console.error('Failed to save expenses to storage:', error);
      }
```

```
    };
    saveExpenses();
  }, [expenses, isLoaded]);

  const addExpense = (expense) => {
    setExpenses((prev) => [
      ...prev,
      { ...expense, id: Date.now().toString() },
    ]);
  };

  const deleteExpense = (id) => {
    setExpenses((prev) => prev.filter((exp) => exp.id !== id));
  };

  return (
    <ExpenseContext.Provider value={{ expenses, addExpense, deleteExpense,
    isLoaded }}>
      {children}
    </ExpenseContext.Provider>
  );
}

export function useExpenses() {
  return useContext(ExpenseContext);
}
```

Code	Engineering Explanation
isLoaded flag	Prevents the persistence useEffect from running during hydration—avoids overwriting stored data with an empty array on first render
getItem(STORAGE_KEY)	Asynchronously retrieves the JSON string from native storage. Returns null if no entry exists—null is a meaningful sentinel, not an error
JSON.parse(stored)	AsyncStorage is string-only; the expense array must be deserialized explicitly. Wrap in try/catch because corrupted or partially written data may be present

(continued)

Code	Engineering Explanation
JSON.stringify(expenses)	Serializes the full array on every change. For large expense lists, consider debouncing this write in production
setIsLoaded(true) in finally	Ensures the persistence hook is unblocked even if hydration fails—app remains functional
isLoaded in context value	Consumers can show a loading indicator while initial hydration is in progress

Note This pattern—hydrate on mount, persist on change—is the recommended approach for mirroring persistent state into component state in React Native.

6.7.3 Showing a Loading State While Hydrating

Update AddAssetsScreen.js (which wraps ExpenseProvider) to show a brief loading indicator while the stored expenses are being read:

```
// screens/AddAssetsScreen.js
import React from 'react';
import { View, Text, ActivityIndicator } from 'react-native';
import { ExpenseProvider } from '../context/ExpenseContext';
import AddAssets from '../components/AddAssets';
import { useExpenses } from '../context/ExpenseContext';

function AddAssetsContent() {
  const { isLoaded } = useExpenses();
  if (!isLoaded) {
    return (
      <View style={{ flex: 1, justifyContent: 'center', alignItems:
      'center' }}>
        <ActivityIndicator size="large" color="#007AFF" />
        <Text style={{ marginTop: 12, color: '#888' }}>Loading your
        expenses...</Text>
      </View>
```

```
    );
  }
  return <AddAssets />;
}

export default function AddAssetsScreen() {
  return (
    <ExpenseProvider>
      <AddAssetsContent />
    </ExpenseProvider>
  );
}
```

6.7.4 AsyncStorage Data Flow

The following describes the complete execution path for both Save and Load operations:

Save (on expenses state change)

- User adds or deletes expense → setExpenses called → React re-renders.
- Persistence useEffect fires (isLoaded is true).
- JSON.stringify(expenses) serializes the array.
- AsyncStorage.setItem crosses JS→Native bridge.
- Native IO thread writes to device storage asynchronously.
- Promise resolves → no UI thread blocking.

Load (on app launch)

- ExpenseProvider mounts → hydration useEffect fires.
- AsyncStorage.getItem crosses JS → Native bridge.
- Native IO thread reads from device storage.
- Stored JSON string returns to JS → JSON.parse → setExpenses.
- React re-renders with restored expense list → isLoaded set to true.

Importantly: at no point does JavaScript hold references to the underlying storage engine. The storage back end may change across OS versions or devices, but the AsyncStorage API remains stable.

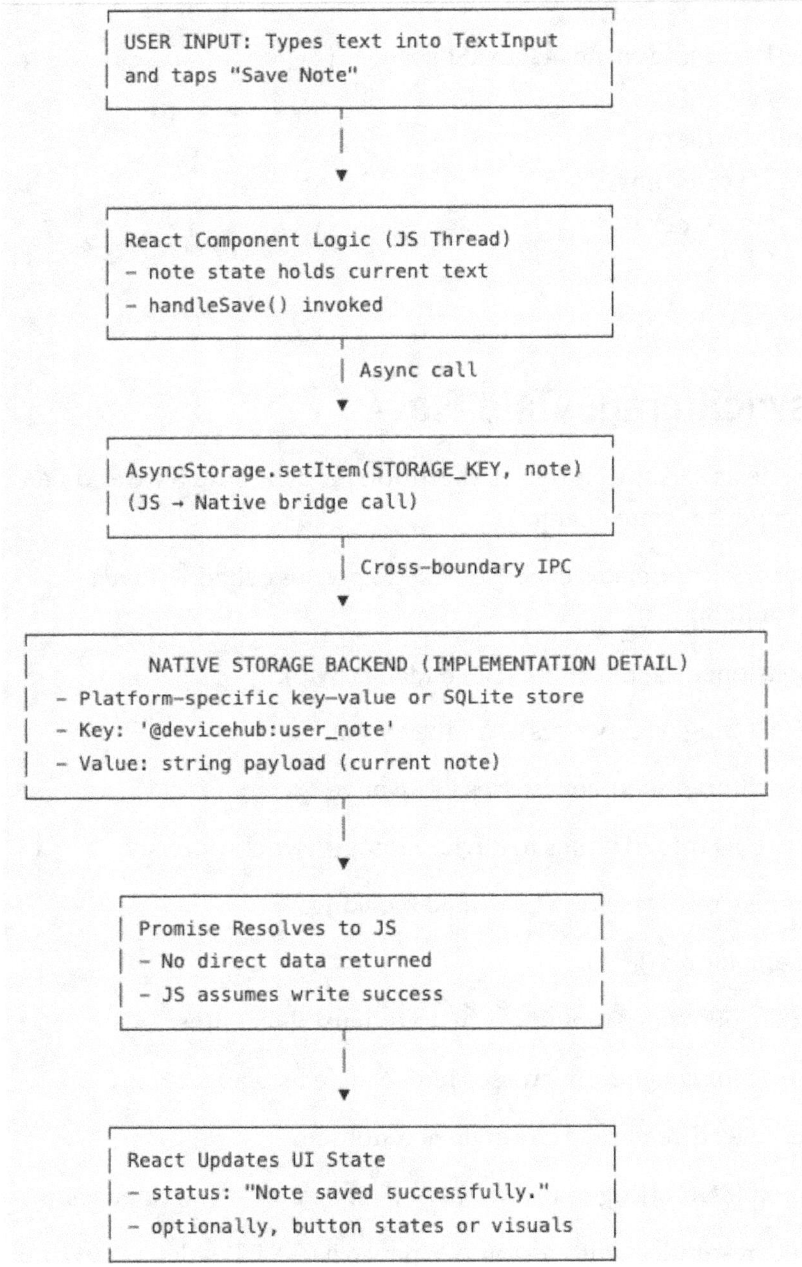

AsyncStorage Save Flow

6.7.5 Constraints, Patterns, and Best Practices

Capacity and Data Size

AsyncStorage is optimized for small to moderate volumes of data. Use it for

- User preferences and feature flags
- Small session caches and recently opened item lists
- The Expense Tracker's expense records (each entry is a small JSON object)

Do NOT use it for

- Media blobs (receipt images should stay as file URIs, not base64 strings)
- Large logs or analytics events
- High-write-frequency transactional data

Serialization Patterns

For non-primitive data (objects, arrays), use explicit JSON operations—exactly as we do in ExpenseContext:

```
await AsyncStorage.setItem(STORAGE_KEY, JSON.stringify(expenses));
const raw = await AsyncStorage.getItem(STORAGE_KEY);
const loaded = raw ? JSON.parse(raw) : [];
```

Always wrap JSON.parse in try/catch, because corrupted or partially written data may be present. Version your serialized schema if the structure is expected to evolve.

6.7.6 Verifying Persistence

To verify that AsyncStorage is working correctly:

- Add a few expenses in the Add Assets tab.
- Fully close the app (kill the process on your device or emulator).

- Relaunch the app.
- Navigate to the Transaction tab—all previously added expenses should still be listed.

This confirms that the expense data survived the app restart and was successfully restored from native storage.

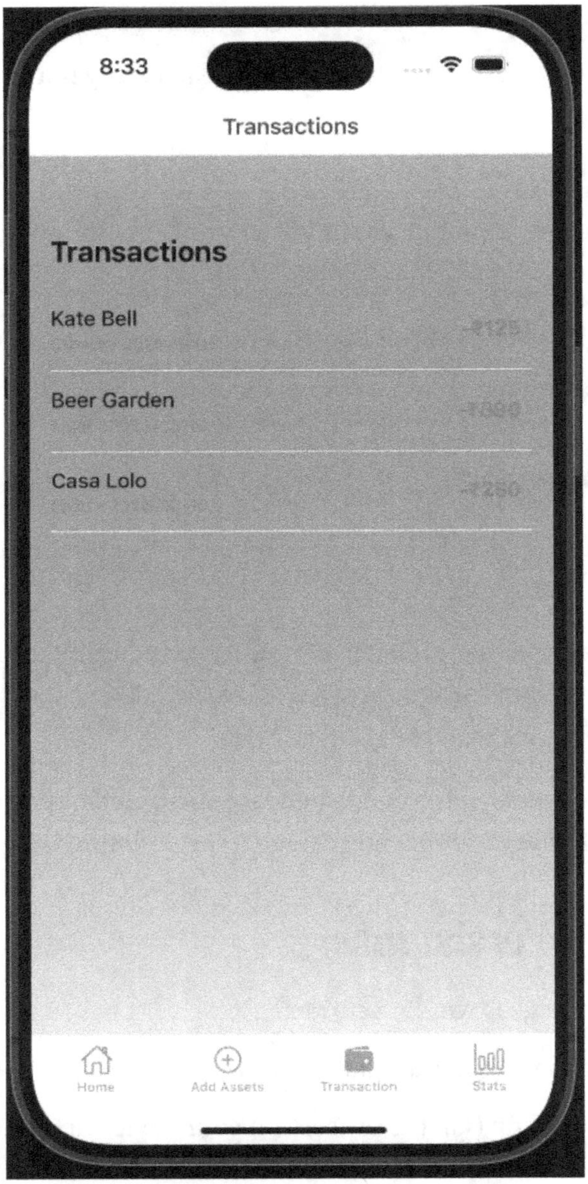

Expenses Persisted Across App Restart via AsyncStorage

6.8 How Native Modules Work in React Native

Every capability explored in this chapter—Camera, Contacts, Calendar, AsyncStorage—is fundamentally delivered by native code running outside the JavaScript sandbox. Expo provides JavaScript bindings so that hardware interactions feel like regular JS, but under the hood, the system follows strict principles.

6.8.1 The JavaScript ↔ Native Execution Boundary

Layer/Language	Purpose/Characteristics
JavaScript Realm—JS/React	UI logic, state, event handlers—single-threaded, asynchronous event loop
Native Realm—Swift (iOS), Kotlin/Java (Android)	Rendering + Hardware access—multi-threaded, real-time execution

These realms cannot directly share memory. They communicate exclusively through asynchronous message passing.

Allowed	Not Allowed
Strings	Objects with cycles
Numbers	Functions/closures
Booleans	Raw pointers/memory references
Plain arrays	Non-serializable native handles
JSON-like objects	Huge binary buffers

This is why camera APIs return URI references instead of pixel arrays. A large binary payload would require chunking, worker-based decoding, and avoiding UI thread stalls.

6.8.2 Native Module Methods: Always Asynchronous

Hardware operations are IO-bound, latency-variable, permission-dependent, and often compute-heavy. Therefore: JS must not block while waiting for native results.

This leads to a mandatory design rule:

✓ Native Methods = Promise-based or callback-based

Examples from the Expense Tracker:

```
// Camera – may take 50-300ms on sensor + encoder
const photo = await cameraRef.current.takePictureAsync();

// Contacts – may query hundreds or thousands of records
const { data } = await Contacts.getContactsAsync({ ... });

// Calendar – writes to OS-managed storage layer
const eventId = await Calendar.createEventAsync(calendarId, { ... });

// AsyncStorage – reads from native key-value store
const stored = await AsyncStorage.getItem(STORAGE_KEY);
```

Task	Thread
React rendering, user events	JavaScript thread
Camera capture	Dedicated camera thread
Storage read/write	Native IO thread
Contact query	Native data provider thread
Screen drawing	Native UI thread

6.8.3 Native-to-JS Events

Some hardware operations produce events over time, not one-time results: accelerometer updates, GPS location changes, push notifications, media playback progress. These cannot be represented as one request/one response.

Instead, native modules emit events that JavaScript subscribes to. This allows multiple events delivered per second and real-time streaming of hardware data. Camera's frame processing pipeline is a classic example—each preview frame is an emitted event.

```
Native subsystem triggers event
        |
        ▼
┌───────────────────────────┐
| Native Event Emitter      |
| - queues message          |
| - fires over bridge       |
└───────────────────────────┘
           |
           ▼
┌───────────────────────────┐
| JS Event Listener Callback |
| (runs asynchronously)      |
└───────────────────────────┘
```

Native-to-JS Event Emission Flow

6.8.4 Failure States and Isolation Guarantees

Native modules can fail due to permission revocation, hardware unavailability, OS policy changes, thermal throttling, or IO lock contention. But thanks to architectural isolation:

✓ JavaScript remains alive.

✓ UI remains actionable.

✓ Errors are surfaced as rejected promises.

Failure in Expense Tracker	JS Experience
Camera blocked/permission denied	Promise rejection → alert shown, form still accessible
Storage quota exceeded	Error thrown → expenses not saved, console log available
Contacts read denied	Data array empty → user can type name manually
Calendar event write forbidden	Rejected async call → statusMessage shown, app remains functional

Note Native code errors must be handled in JavaScript—every try/catch in this chapter exists for this reason.

6.9 Summary and Best Practices

By this point, the Expense Tracker has been transformed from a stateless form into a fully capable mobile application. We have extended every layer of the existing code base:

Module	What Changed in the Expense Tracker
Camera (expo-camera)	AddAssets now captures receipt photos and attaches them to expense entries
Contacts (expo-contacts)	AddAssets allows picking a payee from the system address book
Calendar (expo-calendar)	TransactionDetailScreen can schedule a payment reminder in the native calendar
AsyncStorage	ExpenseContext persists and restores the full expense list across app restarts

Each domain is mediated by OS-level permission governance, native execution and thread scheduling, serialized message passing via the React Native bridge, asynchronous control flow in JavaScript, and graceful handling of denial and failure states.

This separation is not an obstacle—it is what keeps apps secure, performant, and reliable on real devices.

6.9.1 Architectural Lessons to Retain

Core Principle	Why It Matters
JavaScript and Native are isolated	Prevents direct memory corruption and UI hangs
Async is mandatory	Hardware latency must never block user interactions

(*continued*)

Core Principle	Why It Matters
Permission handling is a lifecycle	Consent can change at any moment—check before every use
Data crossing the bridge must be serializable	Ensures safe marshaling and predictable behavior
Native owns hardware and system data	App receives controlled snapshots only
Check access before use—always	Prevents crashes and security violations

Do not treat the hardware as a JavaScript-owned domain. It belongs to the user and OS governance, not to your app.

6.9.2 Checklist of Best Practices

Security and Permissions

- Request permissions only in context—'Attach Receipt' triggers camera; 'Pick from Contacts' triggers contacts.
- Provide a clear explanation before OS dialogs appear.
- Never assume permissions remain granted—check on every use.
- Handle the denial path as a first-class flow—keep the rest of the app functional.
- Offer a Settings redirect when recovery requires OS action.

Execution Behavior

- Keep all hardware calls asynchronous—every camera, contacts, calendar, and storage call in this chapter is awaited.
- Avoid heavy operations on the JS thread.
- Ensure CameraView unmounts when the overlay is dismissed—setShowCamera(false) releases GPU and sensor resources.
- Perform pagination when querying large contact sets (pageSize: 50).

State and Storage Hygiene

- Treat AsyncStorage as a cache or preference store, not a database.
- Always validate serialized data on load—wrap JSON.parse in try/catch.
- Mirror persistent state into component/UI state before use—the isLoaded flag pattern.
- Do not save media blobs in AsyncStorage—store file URIs instead.

Error and Recovery

- Wrap all native calls in try/catch.
- Show helpful recovery UI on permission denial.
- Maintain app usability even when hardware is unavailable.

6.9.3 What You Can Build Now

With the foundations covered in this chapter and the Expense Tracker as your base, you are fully equipped to

- Build a receipt scanning workflow (camera + OCR for amount extraction)
- Add a payee management screen backed by the contacts subsystem
- Send due-date reminders for scheduled expenses via the calendar
- Persist user settings, budget limits, and preferences across sessions
- Extend to SQLite or a remote API when AsyncStorage capacity is outgrown

CHAPTER 7

Networking, Data Layers, and Native Module Integration

"The network is the computer."

—John Gage, former Chief Scientist, Sun Microsystems

Modern mobile applications do not operate in isolation. Unlike early desktop software, where most computation and data lived locally, today's mobile apps are primarily **clients of distributed systems**. Almost every meaningful interaction—authentication, content retrieval, payments, analytics, personalization—depends on communication with remote services over the network.

In this sense, a React Native application is not merely a UI rendered on a device. It is a **coordinator** between three distinct domains:

- The **user interface** running in the JavaScript runtime
- The **networked back-end systems** accessed over HTTP-based protocols
- The **native execution environment** that mediates performance, security, and platform access

This chapter examines how React Native applications communicate beyond their local execution context—first with **remote servers** and then with **custom native code** when JavaScript abstractions are no longer sufficient.

A. Nalwaya and A. Paul, *React Native for Mobile Development*, https://doi.org/10.1007/979-8-8688-2977-2_7

Where Chapter 6 focused on accessing *device-owned capabilities* (camera, contacts, calendar, storage), this chapter shifts focus to **system-to-system interaction** and **execution extensibility**:

- How data moves between a mobile app and remote services
- How networking behaves under mobile constraints such as latency, intermittent connectivity, and background execution
- How and why developers extend React Native using **Native Modules** to bridge gaps that JavaScript alone cannot cover

The goal is not to merely demonstrate API calls, but to build a **mental model** for networking and native integration that scales to real-world, production-grade applications.

7.1 The Role of Networking in Mobile Application Architecture

Networking is not an implementation detail in mobile applications—it is a **foundational architectural concern**.

A mobile app rarely "owns" its data. Instead, it participates in a distributed system where responsibility is divided across multiple services:

- Authentication servers
- Data APIs
- Content delivery networks
- Analytics and telemetry pipelines
- Third-party integrations

From the perspective of a React Native application, every network request represents an **interaction with an external system that it does not control**. This immediately introduces uncertainty:

- The server may be slow or unreachable.
- The response may be partial, malformed, or stale.
- Connectivity may change while a request is in flight.
- The app may be backgrounded or terminated mid-operation.

Unlike desktop or server environments, mobile networking operates under **strict constraints**:

- Limited and variable bandwidth
- Aggressive power and background execution limits
- OS-level scheduling that can pause or delay network activity
- User-driven connectivity changes (airplane mode, Wi-Fi ↔ cellular transitions)

As a result, networking must be treated as a **first-class architectural system**, not as a simple function call that returns data.

In React Native, this complexity is further amplified by the **JavaScript–Native boundary**. While network requests are initiated from JavaScript, their execution is delegated to native networking stacks controlled by the operating system. The JavaScript runtime never sends packets directly; instead, it issues **intent**, and the native layer performs the actual IO.

This separation has important consequences:

- All networking is inherently **asynchronous**.
- JavaScript must be resilient to delayed, cancelled, or failed responses.
- UI state must remain consistent even when network operations fail.

Understanding this model is essential before examining how REST and GraphQL APIs are consumed in React Native—and before deciding when native extensions are required.

In the sections that follow, we will progressively move from **conceptual foundations** to **practical implementations**, beginning with REST-based communication and the native systems that power it.

7.2 REST APIs in React Native

REST (Representational State Transfer) remains the most widely adopted architectural style for client-server communication in mobile applications. Despite the rise of GraphQL and other query-based systems, REST continues to dominate for reasons that matter deeply in mobile contexts: simplicity, cacheability, debuggability, and broad tooling support.

In React Native, REST APIs are not accessed through a browser environment, nor through Node.js networking primitives. Instead, they are executed via **native networking stacks**, with JavaScript acting as an orchestration layer.

Understanding this distinction is critical before writing even a single `fetch()` call.

7.2.1 Native Networking Stack Behind `fetch`

At first glance, networking in React Native appears deceptively familiar:

```
fetch(url)
  .then(response => response.json())
  .then(data => { /* use data */ });
```

However, unlike web applications, this code does **not** execute inside a browser, and unlike back-end JavaScript, it does **not** run on Node.js.

Instead, the execution model looks like this:

JavaScript Intent ➤ Native Networking Stack ➤ OS Network APIs ➤ Remote Server ➤ Native Response ➤ JavaScript Promise Resolution

What Actually Happens When `fetch()` Is Called

1. **JavaScript Initiates a Request**
    - The React Native JavaScript runtime constructs a request descriptor (URL, method, headers, body).
    - No network socket is opened by JavaScript itself.
2. **The Request Crosses the JS–Native Boundary**
    - The request metadata is serialized and passed to the native layer via the React Native JSI layer (JavaScript Interface), which in the New Architecture provides direct C++ bindings without JSON serialization overhead.
    - This handoff is asynchronous and non-blocking.

3. **Native Networking Stack Executes the Request**

    - On iOS, networking is handled by URLSession—the modern Swift networking API (formerly NSURLSession in Objective-C). URLSession provides full support for HTTP/2, background transfers, authentication challenges, and TLS configuration.
    - On Android, networking is handled by OkHttp—a production-grade HTTP client maintained by Square and used by Android itself. OkHttp supports HTTP/2, connection pooling, response caching, and is the recommended foundation for advanced production features such as request interceptors, certificate pinning, and custom DNS resolvers.
    - DNS resolution, TLS negotiation, and redirects are all handled natively. Note: neither URLSession nor OkHttp automatically retry failed HTTP requests by default. Retry logic is the responsibility of the application layer—the client must implement any retry strategy explicitly.

4. **Response Data Flows Back to JavaScript**

    - Once the native layer receives a response, it streams the data back to JavaScript in a controlled, serialized form.
    - JavaScript receives the result as a resolved or rejected Promise.

Important fetch() Has No Built-In Timeout Unlike many HTTP clients, fetch() in React Native has no built-in timeout mechanism. A request to a slow or unresponsive server will hang indefinitely—there is no default timeout that will cancel it automatically.

For production apps, always wrap fetch() with an explicit timeout using AbortController:

```
const fetchWithTimeout = (url, ms = 10000) => {
  const controller = new AbortController();
  const timeout = setTimeout(() => controller.abort(), ms);
  return fetch(url, { signal: controller.signal })
    .finally(() => clearTimeout(timeout));
};
```

Ten seconds is a reasonable default for most mobile API calls. Adjust based on the expected response time of your specific endpoints.

This architecture has several important implications.

Asynchronous by Design: No Exceptions

Because networking is performed outside the JavaScript runtime:

- **All network calls are asynchronous**.
- JavaScript never blocks waiting for a response.
- UI rendering and user interaction remain responsive.

Any attempt to treat networking as synchronous would freeze the application and violate OS execution rules. React Native enforces this separation strictly.

JavaScript Does Not Own the Connection

JavaScript

- Does not manage sockets
- Does not control retries at the TCP level
- Does not handle TLS directly

Instead, it **requests** that the operating system perform a network operation on its behalf.

This is why

- Network behavior can vary across devices and OS versions
- Timeouts and failures must always be handled defensively
- The same code can behave differently under poor connectivity

Why This Matters Architecturally

Treating `fetch()` as "just another function call" leads to fragile applications. A robust React Native app must assume

- Requests may complete out of order
- Responses may arrive after a screen has unmounted

- The app may be backgrounded or killed mid-request
- Network availability may change at any moment

Therefore, networking logic must always be

- **Lifecycle-aware**
- **Failure-tolerant**
- **Explicitly asynchronous**

These principles will guide the implementation choices in the following sections.

7.2.2 Performing a REST API Call

To ground the discussion of REST-based networking in something concrete, we will work with a single, persistent example throughout this chapter: a screen that displays a **feed of posts** retrieved from a remote service. Conceptually, this screen could represent articles, updates, messages, or any other server-driven content stream commonly found in mobile applications. The specific domain is intentionally unimportant; what matters is the structure and behavior of the network interaction.

For this example, we use **JSONPlaceholder**, a public, read-only REST API designed for testing and prototyping. The endpoint `/posts` returns a list of post objects, each containing a title and body. Although the data is synthetic, its shape and behavior closely resemble real-world back-end responses, making it suitable for architectural discussion without introducing setup overhead.

At a high level, the responsibility of the posts feed screen is simple: initiate a network request when the screen appears, retrieve a list of posts, and render their titles and bodies in a scrolling list. Despite this apparent simplicity, even this basic requirement already touches several aspects of mobile networking architecture.

The execution flow for the posts feed request can be visualized as follows:

```
PostsFeedScreen mounted
        |
        ▼
JavaScript initiates fetch(/posts)
        |
        ▼
Native networking stack
```

```
        |
        ▼
Remote REST API (JSONPlaceholder)
        |
        ▼
Response delivered to JavaScript
        |
        ▼
UI rendered with post data
```

The important observation here is that only the first and last steps occur in JavaScript. The actual network operation is executed entirely by the native networking layer, with JavaScript acting as an orchestrator rather than an executor.

A minimal, correct implementation of this screen begins by explicitly modeling its networking state. Even before adding error handling or cancellation logic, the screen must be able to represent three fundamental conditions: loading, success, and failure.

```
import React, { useEffect, useState } from 'react';
import { View, Text, FlatList } from 'react-native';

export default function PostsFeedScreen() {
  const [posts, setPosts] = useState([]);
  const [loading, setLoading] = useState(true);
  const [error, setError] = useState(null);

  useEffect(() => {
    async function loadPosts() {
      try {
        const response = await fetch(
          'https://jsonplaceholder.typicode.com/posts'
        );

        if (!response.ok) {
          throw new Error(`HTTP error: ${response.status}`);
        }

        const data = await response.json();
        setPosts(data);
```

```
    } catch (err) {
      setError(err.message);
    } finally {
      setLoading(false);
    }
  }

  loadPosts();
}, []);
```

This code expresses a number of architectural decisions that are worth examining carefully. The network request is initiated inside a `useEffect` hook, ensuring that it runs when the screen mounts rather than during rendering. The use of `async/await` makes the asynchronous nature of the operation explicit, reinforcing the fact that data arrival is decoupled from UI creation.

The response is validated using `response.ok` before any attempt is made to parse the body. This distinction is critical: a resolved `fetch()` Promise does not imply application-level success. Parsing and state updates are performed only after the response is known to be semantically valid.

Rendering logic then reflects the explicit networking state:

```
if (loading) {
  return <Text>Loading posts...</Text>;
}

if (error) {
  return <Text>Unable to load posts.</Text>;
}

return (
  <FlatList
    data={posts}
    keyExtractor={(item) => item.id.toString()}
    renderItem={({ item }) => (
      <View style={{ padding: 12 }}>
        <Text style={{ fontWeight: '600' }}>{item.title}</Text>
        <Text>{item.body}</Text>
      </View>
```

```
      )}
    />
  );
}
```

At this stage, the posts feed screen is functionally correct. It loads data from a remote service, renders meaningful content, and communicates failure to the user. Importantly, it does so without assuming ideal network conditions or hiding uncertainty behind implicit behavior.

However, this implementation is intentionally incomplete.

The request cannot be cancelled if the user navigates away mid-load. Errors are surfaced but not classified or recoverable. The screen assumes that its lifecycle will outlast the network request. These are not mistakes; they are deliberate omissions that allow us to examine each concern in isolation.

In the following sections, we will return to this same posts feed screen and progressively harden it. We will analyze how different classes of failures surface, how lifecycle mismatches introduce subtle bugs, and how networking state must be treated as a first-class concern in mobile applications.

For now, this example serves as a stable reference point—a simple, honest baseline against which more robust patterns can be evaluated.

7.2.3 Error Handling and Network Failures

In mobile applications, failure is not an exceptional condition that occurs at the margins of normal execution; it is the default state that engineers must assume from the outset. Unlike server-to-server communication—where networks are relatively stable, latency is predictable, and execution environments are controlled—mobile networking exists in a continuously volatile context. Signal strength fluctuates, devices move between networks, applications are backgrounded without warning, radio handoffs interrupt connections, captive portals intercept traffic, and operating systems aggressively suspend or terminate background activity in the interest of power efficiency.

Because of this volatility, error handling in React Native cannot be treated as a generic catch-all mechanism layered on top of networking code. It must begin with a precise understanding of *what kind of failure has occurred* and at which layer of the system that failure originated.

From an architectural perspective, all networking failures in a React Native application fall into three broad categories. These categories are not arbitrary; they correspond directly to distinct execution layers involved in fulfilling a network request.

A typical REST request initiated from React Native follows the execution path shown below:

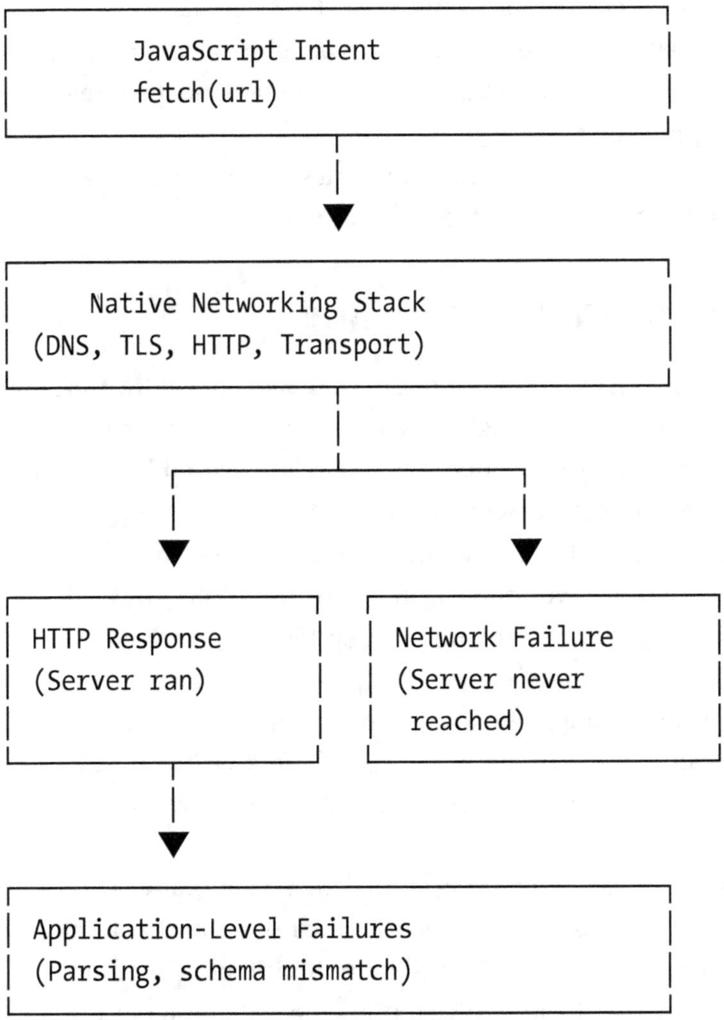

Failures can occur after the server has processed the request, before the server is ever reached, or after a successful response has been delivered but cannot be safely consumed by the application. Although these failures may look similar at the UI level, they are fundamentally different in cause, behavior, and recovery strategy.

The first category consists of **HTTP-level errors**, which occur when a request successfully reaches the server and the server returns a response indicating failure through its HTTP status code. Typical examples include authentication failures, missing resources, and server-side exceptions, commonly represented by status codes such as 400, 401, 403, or 500.

In React Native, these failures are often misunderstood by developers new to mobile networking. When the server responds with an error status, the `fetch()` Promise still resolves successfully. From the perspective of the networking stack, the request completed as intended: a response was received. The failure is semantic rather than transport-related. As a result, the application must explicitly inspect the response status to determine whether the operation was successful in application terms.

This is why checking `response.ok` is not optional but mandatory:

```
if (!response.ok) {
  throw new Error(`HTTP error: ${response.status}`);
}
```

Without this check, applications silently treat server failures as valid responses, often proceeding to parse error payloads as if they were usable data. Such bugs rarely surface during development and typically emerge only under real-world conditions.

The second category consists of **network-level failures**, where the request never reaches the server at all. These failures occur when the device is offline, DNS resolution fails, a TLS handshake cannot be completed, or a connection is interrupted mid-flight due to environmental conditions or operating system intervention. In these cases, no HTTP response exists because the server never received the request.

React Native exposes these failures by rejecting the Promise returned by `fetch()`. There is no status code to inspect and no response body to parse. These failures are environmental rather than logical, and treating them as server-side errors leads to incorrect retry strategies and misleading user feedback.

The third category consists of **application-level failures**, which occur after the network request itself has succeeded. In these cases, the network worked correctly and the server returned a response, but the data cannot be safely used. The response body may be malformed, JSON parsing may fail, required fields may be missing, or the API contract may have changed without coordination.

From the application's point of view, this category represents a failure of assumptions rather than infrastructure. The network worked. The server worked. The application's expectations did not. This is why even seemingly harmless lines of code such as the following must be treated as potential failure points:

```
const data = await response.json(); // may throw
```

Because failures can occur at all three layers, a production-safe networking implementation must handle them in a unified and explicit control flow. The following pattern captures this requirement and represents the minimum structure necessary for robust REST consumption in React Native:

```
try {
  const response = await fetch(url);

  if (!response.ok) {
    throw new Error(`HTTP error: ${response.status}`);
  }

  const data = await response.json();
  // safe to use data here

} catch (error) {
  // network failure OR parsing failure
}
```

This structure is not stylistic. It is architecturally necessary. It ensures that transport failures, protocol-level failures, and data-level failures are all intercepted at a single boundary, where the application can decide how to recover and how to communicate failure to the user.

At this point, experienced mobile engineers recognize that error handling is not merely a technical concern but a user experience concern. Raw error messages such as "Network request failed" or "Unexpected token < in JSON" may be technically accurate, but they are meaningless to users. Users do not care what failed internally; they care what action, if any, they should take next. Effective applications translate technical failures into clear, actionable UI feedback such as checking connectivity, retrying later, or understanding that content is temporarily unavailable.

Error handling in mobile applications is further complicated by differences from the web environment. In browsers, reloading often resolves transient failures, network stability is assumed, and page lifecycles are relatively simple. In mobile applications, reloading is not intuitive, apps frequently resume from partially completed states, requests can outlive the screens that initiated them, and operating systems may terminate processes silently without notice. Under these conditions, every network request must assume that the UI initiating it may disappear before the request completes.

For this reason, failure-state UI is not optional. A professional mobile application must explicitly encode network state, moving predictably through loading, success, and recoverable error states. When any of these states are missing, users lose trust, bugs become difficult to reproduce, and support costs increase dramatically.

Finally, there is one production reality that experienced engineers encounter repeatedly: the most common networking bug in real applications is not that a request failed, but that a request succeeded *after the user had already left the screen*. This leads to attempts to update unmounted components, memory leaks, and subtle UI corruption. Addressing this class of bug requires explicit coordination between request lifetime and component lifecycle, which we address directly in the next section.

Observing Failure Modes in the Posts Feed

To make these failure categories concrete, we return to the **posts feed screen** introduced in the "Performing a REST API Call" section. The implementation of this screen has not changed. What changes instead is the **environment in which it runs** and, in one case, the **endpoint it targets**. By doing so, we can observe how each class of failure surfaces in practice, even though the user-facing UI may look identical.

To observe an **HTTP-level error**, the posts feed can be pointed temporarily to an invalid endpoint, such as `/posts-invalid`. In this case, the request successfully reaches the server, and a response is returned, but the HTTP status code indicates failure. The `fetch()` Promise resolves, `response.ok` evaluates to `false`, and the error-handling path is triggered. From the user's perspective, the screen transitions from the loading state to the error state, even though network connectivity is intact.

To observe a **network-level failure**, the endpoint remains unchanged, but the device is taken offline before launching the application. In this scenario, the request never reaches the server. The Promise returned by `fetch()` rejects immediately, no HTTP status code exists, and execution jumps directly to the `catch` block. The UI again displays an error state, but the underlying cause is fundamentally different from the previous case.

Finally, an **application-level failure** can be demonstrated by forcing a parsing error after a successful response, for example, by corrupting the response before calling `response.json()`. Here, both the network and the server behave correctly, yet the application still fails because its assumptions about the data no longer hold. Once again, the UI enters the same error state, even though the failure originates entirely within the JavaScript runtime.

In all three cases, the posts feed screen presents a similar visual outcome, but the architectural cause differs. This distinction is precisely why experienced engineers reason about failures in terms of execution layers rather than UI symptoms.

7.2.4 Request Cancellation and Component Lifecycle

In React Native applications, network requests and user interfaces operate on fundamentally different timelines. Network requests are long-lived, asynchronous operations whose completion time depends on external systems and environmental conditions. User interfaces, by contrast, are ephemeral. Screens mount and unmount in response to user navigation, gesture-driven transitions, and operating system interventions. When these two timelines are not explicitly coordinated, subtle but serious bugs emerge.

A common assumption among less experienced developers is that a network request "belongs" to the screen that initiated it. In practice, this assumption is false. Once a request has been handed off from JavaScript to the native networking stack, it continues to execute independently of the component that triggered it. Navigation away from the screen, re-rendering, or even partial teardown of the JavaScript tree does not automatically cancel the underlying request.

This mismatch between request lifetime and component lifetime is one of the primary sources of instability in mobile applications.

Conceptually, the sequence often unfolds as follows:

```
Component mounted
       |
       ├── Network request initiated
       |
       ├── User navigates away
       |
Component unmounted
       |
       ├── Network response arrives
       |
Attempt to update UI state that no longer exists
```

From React's perspective, this manifests as warnings about state updates on unmounted components. From a production perspective, the consequences are more severe. Memory leaks accumulate over time, UI state becomes corrupted in ways that are difficult to reproduce, and application behavior diverges depending on network speed and user interaction patterns.

Historically, React Native developers attempted to mitigate this problem by introducing ad hoc flags—typically boolean variables that track whether a component is still mounted. While such patterns can reduce surface-level warnings, they do not address the underlying issue: the network request itself continues to consume resources and may still trigger downstream side effects.

A more principled approach is to explicitly cancel network requests when they are no longer relevant.

Modern React Native environments support request cancellation through the `AbortController` API. This mechanism allows JavaScript to signal intent to cancel an in-flight request, which is then propagated to the native networking layer. When cancellation occurs, the request is terminated at the transport level rather than merely ignored at the UI level.

A lifecycle-aware REST request using `AbortController` typically follows this structure:

```
import { useEffect } from 'react';

useEffect(() => {
  const controller = new AbortController();

  async function loadData() {
    try {
      const response = await fetch(url, {
        signal: controller.signal,
      });

      if (!response.ok) {
        throw new Error(`HTTP error: ${response.status}`);
      }

      const data = await response.json();
      // update state safely here
```

```
    } catch (error) {
      if (error.name === 'AbortError') {
        // request was cancelled intentionally
      } else {
        // handle genuine network or parsing errors
      }
    }
  }

  loadData();

  return () => {
    controller.abort();
  };
}, []);
```

In this pattern, the network request is explicitly tied to the lifecycle of the component. When the component unmounts, the cleanup function aborts the request, ensuring that no response will arrive after the UI context has been destroyed. This eliminates an entire class of bugs rather than merely masking their symptoms.

It is important to note that cancellation is not an error condition in the traditional sense. An aborted request does not represent a failure of the network or the server; it represents a change in application intent. Treating cancellation as a normal, expected outcome leads to cleaner control flow and more predictable behavior. Distinguishing aborted requests from genuine failures allows applications to avoid unnecessary error messaging and redundant retries.

From an architectural standpoint, request cancellation reinforces an important principle: **networking logic must be lifecycle-aware**. Any request that is scoped to a screen, a component, or a user interaction must be cancellable when that scope ends. Requests that outlive their relevance waste resources at best and corrupt application state at worst.

Experienced mobile engineers internalize this principle early. They assume that users will navigate rapidly, that networks will be slow, and that operating systems will interrupt execution unpredictably. Under these assumptions, cancellation is not an optimization—it is a requirement for correctness.

This discussion of lifecycle-aware networking also clarifies why mobile error handling cannot be copied directly from web applications. On the web, page reloads reset state and terminate outstanding requests. In mobile applications, state persists across navigation and backgrounding, and requests continue unless explicitly cancelled. React Native therefore demands a higher level of discipline around request management.

With lifecycle-safe REST communication in place, we can now turn our attention to a different but related question: how data itself should be shaped, cached, and requested in mobile applications. In the next section, we introduce GraphQL and examine how it addresses some of the structural limitations of REST in data-driven mobile interfaces.

7.3 GraphQL in React Native

As mobile applications grow in complexity, the limitations of traditional REST-based data fetching become increasingly visible. REST remains a powerful and widely adopted architectural style, but it encodes assumptions that do not always align with the demands of modern, data-driven mobile interfaces. Chief among these assumptions is that the server determines the shape of the data returned to clients. In practice, mobile applications increasingly require data to be shaped around screens rather than resources.

GraphQL emerged in response to this mismatch. Instead of exposing a collection of fixed endpoints, a GraphQL service exposes a strongly typed schema describing the entire data graph available to clients. The client specifies exactly which fields it needs and how those fields should be structured in the response. For mobile applications—where bandwidth, latency, and rendering efficiency are tightly constrained—this shift has significant architectural consequences.

GraphQL should not be approached as a replacement for REST, but as an alternative data access model with different trade-offs. Understanding when and why it is useful requires examining the specific problems it was designed to solve.

7.3.1 Why GraphQL Exists in Mobile Applications

In REST-based systems, endpoints are typically designed around server-side resources rather than client-side views. A single endpoint often returns far more data than a specific screen requires, while another screen may require data from multiple endpoints to assemble a complete view. These patterns give rise to two well-known problems: over-fetching and under-fetching.

Over-fetching occurs when an endpoint returns fields that the mobile application does not use. While this may appear harmless in desktop or server environments, it has real costs on mobile devices. Larger payloads increase network latency, consume additional bandwidth, and require extra parsing work on the JavaScript thread. Under ideal network conditions, these costs may go unnoticed; under constrained or unreliable connectivity, they directly impact perceived performance.

Under-fetching occurs when a single screen requires data from multiple endpoints. In such cases, the application must issue multiple requests, coordinate their completion, and handle partial failure scenarios. This increases implementation complexity and introduces additional uncertainty at runtime, particularly when requests are interdependent.

GraphQL addresses both problems by allowing the client to describe its data requirements declaratively. Instead of requesting a predefined resource representation, the client submits a query that specifies the precise shape of the data it needs. The server resolves that query against its schema and returns a response that mirrors the requested structure exactly—no more and no less.

From a mobile perspective, this yields two immediate benefits. First, payload size is reduced by eliminating unused fields. Second, multiple data requirements can often be satisfied by a single request, reducing round trips and simplifying client-side coordination. These benefits are especially pronounced on screens that aggregate data from multiple back-end domains.

However, these advantages are not free. GraphQL shifts responsibility for query construction and data shape from the server to the client, increasing coupling between UI components and back-end schemas. This trade-off must be understood clearly before adopting GraphQL in a React Native application.

7.3.2 GraphQL Client Architecture

Using GraphQL in React Native typically involves introducing a dedicated client library that manages query execution, caching, and result normalization. While specific tooling varies, the underlying architectural principles remain consistent.

At a high level, a GraphQL client sits between the UI layer and the network layer. UI components declare their data requirements in the form of queries. The client determines whether those requirements can be satisfied from its local cache, whether a network request is required, or whether a combination of cached and fresh data should be returned. This decision-making process is opaque to the component, which reacts only to loading, success, and error states.

This architecture introduces a fundamentally different data flow from REST-based fetching. Instead of treating each request as an isolated operation, the client maintains a normalized representation of the application's data graph. Screens and components become views onto this shared data model rather than owners of independent copies of remote data.

For mobile applications, this approach offers clear advantages. Cached data can be reused across screens without refetching, transitions appear faster, and parts of the application may remain functional even when the network is unavailable. At the same time, this model introduces new complexity around cache invalidation, schema evolution, and memory usage—concerns that must be evaluated carefully in resource-constrained environments.

Before examining these trade-offs further, it is useful to look at a concrete example of executing a GraphQL query from a React Native screen.

7.3.3 Executing a GraphQL Query

Installing Apollo Client

Before executing any GraphQL queries, install Apollo Client and its peer dependency:

```
npm install @apollo/client graphql
```

Then wrap your app's root component with ApolloProvider, passing a configured ApolloClient instance:

```
import { ApolloClient, InMemoryCache, ApolloProvider } from '@apollo/
client';

const client = new ApolloClient({
  uri: 'https://countries.trevorblades.com/',
  cache: new InMemoryCache(),
});

export default function App() {
  return (
    <ApolloProvider client={client}>
      <YourNavigator />
    </ApolloProvider>
  );
}
```

Every component that calls useQuery, useMutation, or useLazyQuery must be a descendant of ApolloProvider. Without this, hook calls will throw a runtime error.

To illustrate GraphQL usage in React Native without introducing unnecessary setup complexity, we use a public, read-only GraphQL endpoint. This allows us to focus on execution flow, data shaping, and runtime behavior rather than authentication, mutations, or back-end configuration.

In a GraphQL-based application, a screen does not request a resource in the traditional REST sense. Instead, it declares a query that describes exactly what data it requires. The response returned by the server mirrors this structure precisely. This symmetry between query and response is one of GraphQL's defining characteristics and a key reason for its appeal in UI-driven applications. In this section, we use the public Countries GraphQL API (`https://countries.trevorblades.com/`), which provides read-only access to structured country data without requiring authentication.

Before useQuery can be called, the query itself must be defined using the gql template literal from @apollo/client. The GET_COUNTRIES variable wraps the GraphQL query string in a parsed document that Apollo can execute:

```
import { gql } from '@apollo/client';

const GET_COUNTRIES = gql`
  query GetCountries {
    countries {
      code
      name
      capital
    }
  }
`;
```

This component must also be rendered inside the ApolloProvider set up in the app root (see installation section above). Without ApolloProvider in the tree, useQuery will throw: "No Apollo Client found".

A simple query might request a list of countries along with a limited subset of their fields:

```
query {
  countries {
```

```
    code
    name
    capital
  }
}
```

From the perspective of the React Native application, this query represents a contract between the UI and the back-end schema. The UI expresses its needs explicitly, and the server guarantees that the response will conform to the declared shape, provided the schema remains stable.

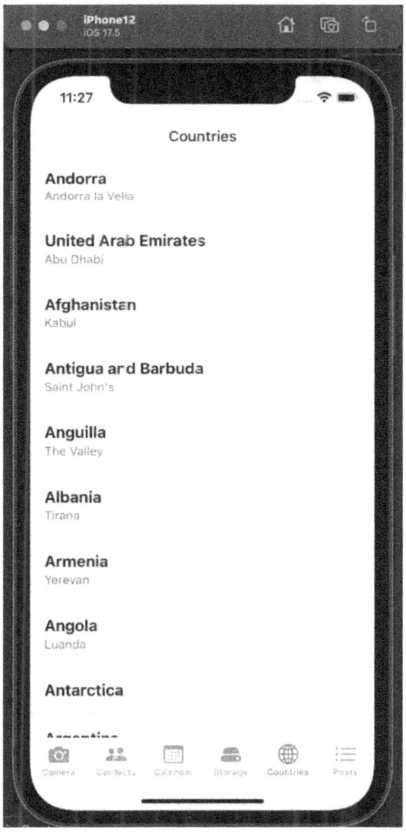

In practice, executing this query from a React Native screen involves defining the query, invoking it through a GraphQL client, and responding to the resulting loading, success, or error state. A typical client hook exposes these states directly:

```
const { loading, error, data } = useQuery(GET_COUNTRIES);
```

Although concise, this line hides substantial machinery. Under the hood, the GraphQL client determines whether the requested data already exists in its cache, whether a network request is required, and how the resulting data should be normalized and stored. From the component's point of view, however, the interaction remains declarative: the component describes *what* it needs, not *how* that data is fetched.

Experienced Perspective

A common mistake when adopting GraphQL is treating it as "REST with nicer responses." GraphQL changes where decisions are made. Data-shape decisions move from the server to the client, which gives UI components more power—and more responsibility.

As with REST, GraphQL does not eliminate uncertainty. Network failures, schema changes, and partial data availability remain realities that the UI must handle explicitly:

```
if (loading) {
  return <Text>Loading...</Text>;
}

if (error) {
  return <Text>Unable to load data.</Text>;
}
```

At first glance, this pattern resembles REST-based fetching. The critical difference lies not in UI reaction, but in data flow over time. With GraphQL, multiple screens may depend on overlapping subsets of the same underlying data. Changes in one part of the application can therefore influence what other screens observe, even without additional network requests.

Production Insight

GraphQL caching is both its greatest strength and its most common source of subtle bugs. When data appears to update "mysteriously" across screens, the cache is usually behaving correctly. Problems arise when teams do not fully understand identity, normalization, and cache keys.

Schema evolution introduces another important distinction. In REST systems, back-end changes often break clients implicitly. In GraphQL systems, schema changes are explicit and immediately visible. Removing or renaming a field breaks any query that depends on it, shifting coordination requirements between front-end and back-end teams.

Experienced Perspective

GraphQL works best when front-end and back-end teams treat the schema as a shared product rather than an implementation detail. Without this collaboration, GraphQL can amplify friction instead of reducing it.

Despite these trade-offs, GraphQL's ability to align data fetching closely with UI requirements makes it particularly attractive in mobile applications, where minimizing unnecessary data transfer and coordinating complex screens are persistent challenges.

7.3.4 REST vs. GraphQL: Choosing the Right Approach

Both REST and GraphQL are viable, production-proven approaches to data access in React Native applications. The choice between them is rarely absolute and often varies across different parts of the same application. The most common mistake is not choosing one over the other, but adopting either without understanding its architectural consequences.

REST excels when endpoints are stable, data models are coarse-grained, and caching can be delegated to standard HTTP mechanisms. GraphQL excels when screens have highly specific data needs, when multiple back-end domains must be composed into a single view, and when minimizing over-fetching is critical.

Note In mature mobile applications, REST and GraphQL often coexist. REST is frequently used for simple, transactional operations, while GraphQL is introduced selectively for complex, data-heavy screens. Treating this as a pragmatic architectural choice rather than an ideological one is a strong indicator of engineering maturity.

7.4 Networking State As a First-Class Concern

In many React Native applications, networking is implemented as a side effect of rendering: a component mounts, a request is issued, and the resulting data is rendered when it arrives. While this approach may work for simple demos, it breaks down quickly in real applications. The reason is that networking is not merely a data retrieval mechanism; it is a **stateful process** whose behavior directly affects user trust, perceived performance, and application correctness.

Every network request exists in one of several states, and these states are not transient implementation details. They are part of the user experience and must be represented explicitly in the UI. Failing to do so results in interfaces that appear frozen, inconsistent, or unreliable under anything but ideal conditions.

Conceptually, networking state in a mobile application progresses through a small but critical set of phases:

```
Request initiated
       |
       ▼
Loading (in flight)
       |
       ├── Success ────────► Data rendered
       |
       └── Failure ────────► Recoverable error state
```

Although this model is simple, many applications violate it implicitly by skipping one or more states. For example, screens that immediately attempt to render data without an explicit loading state often appear broken on slower networks. Conversely, applications that handle failure by simply logging errors leave users with no clear path forward.

In React Native, networking state must be modeled explicitly in component state or in a dedicated data layer. This typically involves tracking at least three orthogonal concerns: whether a request is in progress, whether it succeeded, and whether it failed in a recoverable manner. These concerns are not mutually exclusive over time; a screen may move between them repeatedly as users retry actions or as connectivity changes.

A minimal but honest representation of networking state often takes the following form:

```
const [loading, setLoading] = useState(true);
const [error, setError] = useState(null);
const [data, setData] = useState(null);
```

While this pattern may appear trivial, its importance cannot be overstated. It establishes a single source of truth for the UI and forces the developer to confront each possible state explicitly rather than relying on implicit assumptions.

An experienced engineer recognizes that the UI must never lie about network state. Showing stale data without indicating that a refresh is in progress, or hiding errors behind silent failures, erodes user trust over time. Users are generally tolerant of delays and transient failures when the application communicates clearly; they are far less tolerant of interfaces that behave unpredictably.

Experienced Perspective

One of the fastest ways to lose user trust is to let the UI imply certainty when none exists. If data may be outdated, say so. If a request is in progress, show it. Ambiguity is far more damaging than delay.

Mobile networking introduces additional complexity because connectivity itself is not stable. A request may fail and then succeed moments later without user intervention or succeed partially under constrained conditions. For this reason, recoverability must be designed into networking state from the beginning. Errors should be represented as states that the UI can exit, not terminal conditions that leave the application stuck.

Retry behavior illustrates this principle clearly. In mobile applications, retries should be intentional and visible, not automatic and opaque. Blindly retrying requests in the background can waste battery and bandwidth, while forcing users to restart the app to recover from transient failures creates unnecessary friction. A well-designed networking state exposes retry affordances clearly and allows users to regain control.

This emphasis on explicit state also explains why experienced teams often centralize networking concerns rather than scattering `fetch()` calls across components. Whether implemented through custom hooks, context providers, or dedicated data libraries, the goal is the same: to ensure that networking behavior is consistent, observable, and debuggable across the application.

Another subtle aspect of networking state is its relationship to time. Data freshness matters, particularly in mobile applications that are frequently backgrounded and resumed. A screen that renders cached data instantly may still need to indicate that a background refresh is occurring or that the data may be outdated. Treating "cached but stale" as a distinct state avoids confusing situations where users act on information that is no longer valid.

Note In many real applications, the most difficult bugs are not caused by missing data, but by *slightly outdated* data. Explicitly modeling freshness and refresh-in-progress states prevents entire classes of silent failure.

The central lesson is that networking state is not an implementation detail to be hidden behind abstractions. It is a first-class concern that must be reflected in both application architecture and user interface design. Once this is accepted, decisions about tooling—whether to use plain REST, GraphQL clients, or more sophisticated data layers—become easier to evaluate in terms of how well they expose and manage these states.

With this foundation in place, we can now turn our attention to a different boundary in React Native applications: the point at which JavaScript is no longer sufficient and native code must be introduced deliberately. The next section examines why native modules exist and when they become necessary.

7.5 Why Native Modules Exist

React Native is often described as a framework that allows developers to build mobile applications using JavaScript. While this description is directionally correct, it is incomplete in a way that matters architecturally. JavaScript does not control the device. It does not execute system code, manage hardware state, or interact directly with operating system services. React Native applications succeed precisely because they acknowledge this separation rather than attempting to abstract it away.

Mobile operating systems enforce a strict boundary between application logic and system-level capabilities. Access to device state—such as battery information, network conditions, power management, and background execution—is mediated through native APIs exposed by the operating system. JavaScript runs inside a managed runtime that is intentionally isolated from these APIs. This isolation is a feature, not a limitation. It protects system stability, enforces security guarantees, and ensures that applications remain responsive under load.

Native modules exist to bridge this boundary in a controlled and explicit manner.

There are entire categories of functionality that JavaScript cannot implement on its own, regardless of developer skill or library support. These include access to system services that are not exposed through the standard React Native API surface, integration with platform-specific SDKs distributed only as native libraries, and operations that depend on real-time system state managed by the operating system. Battery level and charging state are representative examples of this class of functionality. While they may appear simple conceptually, they are owned entirely by the operating system and are not available directly to JavaScript.

React Native does not attempt to eliminate native code from the application architecture. Instead, it formalizes its role. Native modules are not escape hatches or hacks; they are first-class participants in the React Native execution model. Even the most basic React Native application relies on native modules indirectly for rendering, networking, storage, and input handling. Writing a custom native module simply extends a mechanism that is already fundamental to how React Native works.

What distinguishes native modules from ordinary JavaScript utilities is the nature of the boundary they cross. JavaScript and native code do not share memory and cannot call each other synchronously. Communication occurs through asynchronous message passing. When JavaScript invokes a native module method, it sends a serialized request describing the desired operation. Native code receives that request, performs the work using platform APIs, and eventually returns a result back to JavaScript, where it is delivered through a Promise or an event callback.

This execution model imposes important constraints. All data crossing the boundary must be serializable. All native work must be asynchronous from JavaScript's point of view. Long-running or blocking operations must never execute on the JavaScript thread. These constraints are not incidental; they are what allow React Native applications to remain responsive while interacting with complex system services.

From an architectural standpoint, native modules exist to place responsibility where it belongs. JavaScript coordinates UI state, application logic, and user interaction. Native code interacts with the operating system, manages system state, and responds to platform-specific events. When these responsibilities are respected, applications remain predictable, performant, and maintainable. When they are blurred, complexity grows quickly and bugs become difficult to reason about.

Experienced React Native engineers learn to recognize when a requirement is fundamentally native. If accessing a capability requires polling, indirect inference, or brittle timing assumptions in JavaScript, it is often a signal that the responsibility belongs on the native side. Battery state is a clear example: the operating system already tracks this information accurately and efficiently, and exposing it through a native module is both simpler and more reliable than attempting to approximate it in JavaScript.

Experienced Perspective

Native modules are not about performance optimization first; they are about correctness. When a piece of information is owned by the operating system, the most reliable way to obtain it is from the operating system itself.

With this motivation in place, we can now examine how native modules are structured and how JavaScript interacts with them. In the next section, we focus on the execution model of native modules—the mechanics of the bridge—before implementing a concrete example that exposes battery level and charging state to a React Native application.

7.6 Introduction to Native Modules in React Native

To understand how native modules function in React Native, it is necessary to look beyond surface-level APIs and examine the execution boundary between JavaScript and the native platform. Unlike traditional mobile development, where application logic and system APIs live in the same language and runtime, React Native applications operate across two fundamentally different execution environments.

JavaScript runs inside a managed runtime with a single-threaded event loop. Native code runs inside the operating system's multi-threaded environment, with direct access to system APIs, hardware state, and platform services. These two environments do not share memory, do not execute on the same threads, and cannot call each other directly.

In the legacy architecture, a component called the Bridge coordinated this communication through asynchronous JSON message passing. Since React Native 0.76, the New Architecture is the default: the Bridge has been replaced by JSI (JavaScript Interface)—a C++ layer that provides direct bindings between JS and native code, eliminating serialization overhead and enabling synchronous native calls where appropriate. The principles below apply to both, but all new development targets the New Architecture.

First, native module interactions are typically asynchronous from JavaScript's perspective. Under the New Architecture (JSI/TurboModules), synchronous native calls are supported—TurboModules can expose synchronous methods that execute on the JS thread via direct C++ bindings, without going through an async queue. However, synchronous calls should only be used for fast, non-blocking operations such as reading a cached value. Long-running or blocking work must still be asynchronous to maintain UI responsiveness.

Second, data exchanged across the bridge must be serializable. Primitive values, plain objects, and arrays can cross the boundary safely. Complex objects, references, file handles, or pointers cannot. This requirement encourages native modules to expose simple, intention-revealing APIs rather than leaking platform-specific implementation details into JavaScript.

Third, native modules operate independently of JavaScript component lifecycles. Once JavaScript sends a request across the bridge, native code continues executing until it completes or is explicitly cancelled. This mirrors the behavior of network requests and reinforces the same lifecycle-aware discipline discussed earlier in this chapter. JavaScript must assume that native responses may arrive later or may no longer be relevant by the time they do.

Native modules can expose functionality to JavaScript in two primary ways. The first is through methods that return Promises, which resolve or reject when native work completes. This pattern is well suited to one-off queries, such as requesting the current battery level or determining whether the device is charging. The second is through event emitters, which allow native code to push updates to JavaScript when system state changes over time. This pattern is useful for long-lived signals, such as changes in battery status, connectivity, or orientation.

Choosing between these patterns is an architectural decision rather than a stylistic one. Promise-based methods emphasize request–response semantics and are easier to reason about in isolation. Event-based APIs emphasize ongoing state and require explicit subscription management and cleanup. In practice, many native modules expose both, depending on the nature of the underlying system capability.

Experienced Perspective

A good native module API feels unsurprising from JavaScript. If consumers have to guess whether a value is cached, pushed, or polled, the abstraction is probably doing too much.

Another important aspect of native modules is error propagation. Native failures—whether due to unavailable APIs, unexpected system state, or permission issues—must be translated into meaningful JavaScript errors rather than causing crashes or silent failures. From JavaScript's point of view, a native error should be indistinguishable from any other asynchronous failure and should integrate naturally with existing error-handling logic.

Finally, native modules should be treated as part of the application's public surface area. Their interfaces are contracts. Changes to method signatures, return shapes, or event semantics can break JavaScript code just as surely as changes to a back-end API can break a client. For this reason, experienced teams version native modules carefully, document their behavior explicitly, and resist the temptation to expose large, low-level APIs directly to JavaScript.

With this execution model in mind, we are now ready to examine a concrete example. In the next section, we will build a small native module that exposes battery level and charging state to JavaScript. The example is intentionally narrow in scope. Its purpose is not to provide a full-featured battery monitoring solution, but to make the mechanics of the JavaScript-native bridge explicit and understandable.

7.7 Building a Native Battery State Module

Having established why native modules exist and how the JavaScript-native bridge operates, we can now examine a concrete example. The goal of this example is not to build a comprehensive system utility, but to make the mechanics of a native module explicit and tangible.

Battery state is an ideal candidate for this purpose. Battery level and charging status are owned entirely by the operating system. They are not exposed directly to JavaScript, they change over time, and they are already tracked efficiently by native APIs. Exposing this information through a native module therefore illustrates both *why* native code is required and *how* JavaScript interacts with it.

In this section, we build a small native module that allows JavaScript to query two pieces of information:

- The current battery level
- Whether the device is charging

The module exposes this information as a Promise-based method, keeping the interface simple and easy to reason about.

7.7.1 JavaScript Interface: Codegen Spec

With the New Architecture, the JavaScript interface is defined as a typed Codegen spec. Codegen reads this file at build time to generate type-safe native stubs on both iOS and Android automatically—no more runtime reflection via NativeModules.

specs/NativeBatteryStateModule.ts

```
import type { TurboModule } from 'react-native';
import { TurboModuleRegistry } from 'react-native';

export interface BatteryState {
```

```
  level: number;
  isCharging: boolean;
}

export interface Spec extends TurboModule {
  getBatteryState(): Promise<BatteryState>;
}

export default TurboModuleRegistry.strictGet<Spec>('BatteryStateModule');
```

This file does three things: it defines the BatteryState shape that will cross the JS–Native boundary; it declares the Spec interface extending TurboModule, which tells Codegen exactly which methods to generate stubs for; and it exports the module via TurboModuleRegistry.strictGet, which throws at runtime if the native module is not registered—failing loudly rather than silently.

The call site in BatteryStateScreen.js imports directly from the spec instead of going through NativeModules:

```
import NativeBatteryStateModule from '../specs/NativeBatteryStateModule';

// Call site is identical to before:
const state = await NativeBatteryStateModule.getBatteryState();
// state.level      -> number (0.0 - 1.0)
// state.isCharging -> boolean
```

The JS-facing API—getBatteryState() returning Promise resolving to { level: number, isCharging: boolean }—is unchanged. The difference is entirely under the hood: the call now travels via JSI direct C++ bindings rather than through the legacy async JSON bridge.

7.7.2 iOS Implementation

The iOS TurboModule implementation requires two files: a Swift file for the logic and a .mm (Objective-C++) bridge file. The .mm file is mandatory—the Codegen-generated header includes C++ types so it must be compiled as Objective-C++.

modules/ios/BatteryStateModule.swift

```
import Foundation
import UIKit
```

```
// Conforms to the ObjC protocol generated by Codegen.
// No @objc on the method -- Codegen enforces the signature.
@objc(BatteryStateModule)
class BatteryStateModule: NSObject, NativeBatteryStateModuleSpec {
  func getBatteryState(
    _ resolve: @escaping RCTPromiseResolveBlock,
    reject: @escaping RCTPromiseRejectBlock
  ) {
    let device = UIDevice.current
    device.isBatteryMonitoringEnabled = true
    let level = device.batteryLevel
    let isCharging = device.batteryState == .charging
                 || device.batteryState == .full
    resolve(["level": level, "isCharging": isCharging])
  }
}
```

modules/ios/BatteryStateModule.mm

```
// Must be .mm -- Codegen header uses C++ types.
#import <React/RCTBridgeModule.h>
#import "RCTNativeBatteryStateModuleSpec.h" // generated by Codegen

@implementation BatteryStateModule
RCT_EXPORT_MODULE()

// Returns the JSI C++ dispatcher -- makes this a TurboModule.
// Without this, calls fail silently in RN 0.76+ bridgeless mode.
- (std::shared_ptr<facebook::react::TurboModule>)getTurboModule:
    (const facebook::react::ObjCTurboModule::InitParams &)params {
  return std::make_shared<
    facebook::react::NativeBatteryStateModuleSpecJSI>(params);
}
@end
```

Codegen generates RCTNativeBatteryStateModuleSpec.h during pod install. The .mm file imports it and wires up the JSI dispatcher via getTurboModule:. This is the critical difference from the legacy approach—instead of JSON serialization through a bridge queue, calls now go through direct C++ function pointers.

The config plug-in (withBatteryStateModule.js) copies both files into the ios/ app directory during expo prebuild and registers them in the Xcode build phase automatically.

7.7.3 Android Implementation

On Android, the module extends the Codegen-generated abstract class, and the package uses TurboReactPackage for lazy loading instead of eager initialization.

android/.../BatteryStateModule.kt

```
// Extends Codegen-generated spec -- no @ReactMethod annotation needed.
class BatteryStateModule(reactContext: ReactApplicationContext)
  : NativeBatteryStateModuleSpec(reactContext) {

  override fun getName(): String = NAME

  override fun getBatteryState(promise: Promise) {
    val intent = reactContext.registerReceiver(
      null, IntentFilter(Intent.ACTION_BATTERY_CHANGED)
    )
    val level  = intent?.getIntExtra(BatteryManager.EXTRA_LEVEL, -1) ?: -1
    val scale  = intent?.getIntExtra(BatteryManager.EXTRA_SCALE, -1) ?: -1
    val pct    = level.toFloat() / scale.toFloat()
    val status = intent?.getIntExtra(BatteryManager.EXTRA_STATUS, -1)
    val isCharging = status == BatteryManager.BATTERY_STATUS_CHARGING
                  || status == BatteryManager.BATTERY_STATUS_FULL
    promise.resolve(mapOf("level" to pct, "isCharging" to isCharging))
  }
  companion object { const val NAME = "BatteryStateModule" }
}
```

android/.../BatteryStatePackage.kt

```
// TurboReactPackage replaces ReactPackage.
// getModule() is lazy -- only called when JS first requests the module.
class BatteryStatePackage : TurboReactPackage() {
  override fun getModule(name: String, ctx: ReactApplicationContext) =
    if (name == BatteryStateModule.NAME) BatteryStateModule(ctx) else null

  override fun getReactModuleInfoProvider() = ReactModuleInfoProvider {
    mapOf(BatteryStateModule.NAME to ReactModuleInfo(
      BatteryStateModule.NAME, BatteryStateModule.NAME,
      canOverrideExistingModule = false,
      needsEagerInit = false,
      isTurboModule = true   // routes calls via JSI
    ))
  }
}
```

The key difference from the legacy ReactPackage is that createNativeModules()—which eagerly instantiated all modules at startup—is replaced by getModule() (lazy, on-demand) and getReactModuleInfoProvider() (returns metadata without allocating any module). The isTurboModule = true flag routes all calls through JSI at runtime.

Codegen generates NativeBatteryStateModuleSpec.kt in the build/ directory during ./gradlew build. BatteryStateModule.kt extends it, completing the type-safe contract from JavaScript spec through to native implementation on both platforms.

7.7.4 Observations from the Demo

Although the example is intentionally small, it illustrates several important architectural principles.

First, JavaScript never accesses system state directly. All privileged work occurs in native code, using APIs designed and maintained by the operating system. JavaScript receives only the data it needs, in a form it can safely consume.

Second, the asynchronous contract is preserved even when native work is fast. From JavaScript's point of view, native modules behave like network requests: they may resolve later, they may fail, and they must be handled defensively.

Third, the boundary between JavaScript and native code is explicit. Data is serialized, transferred, and deserialized. This forces native modules to expose clean, intention-revealing interfaces rather than leaking platform details across the bridge.

Experienced Perspective

A good native module does not try to be clever. It exposes exactly what JavaScript needs, no more and no less, and lets the platform do the work it already does well.

At this point, the reader has seen a complete round trip: JavaScript invoking native code, native code interacting with the operating system, and results flowing back across the bridge into the UI. This is the core pattern behind every native module in a React Native application, regardless of complexity.

7.8 JS–Native Integration

With a concrete native module example in place, it becomes possible to step back and identify a small set of architectural rules that govern effective JavaScript–native integration in React Native. These rules are not theoretical ideals; they emerge directly from the constraints of the execution model and from the kinds of bugs that appear repeatedly in real applications.

The first rule is that **native modules must expose intention, not implementation**. JavaScript should never need to know *how* a value is obtained, only *what* value is being requested. In the battery state example, JavaScript does not care whether the underlying platform uses device APIs, system broadcasts, or hardware signals. It asks for battery state and receives a simple, serializable result. When native modules leak platform details into JavaScript, they harden assumptions that make refactoring and platform parity increasingly difficult over time.

The second rule is that **every native boundary is asynchronous, even when it feels synchronous**. Native code may execute quickly, but JavaScript must always treat native calls as asynchronous operations that may resolve later or fail entirely. Designing native modules that appear synchronous encourages incorrect usage patterns and makes it easier to block rendering or introduce subtle timing bugs. Promise-based APIs force consumers to respect uncertainty and align naturally with React's rendering model.

A third rule follows directly from lifecycle behavior: **native work must never assume the continued existence of the UI that initiated it**. Once a request crosses the bridge, it is no longer owned by a component. Navigation, backgrounding, or unmounting can occur at any time. Native modules should therefore be written to tolerate cancellation, irrelevance, or delayed consumption of results. JavaScript, in turn, must be disciplined about when and how native responses are applied to UI state.

Closely related is the rule that **native modules should be narrow in scope**. A native module that attempts to expose a large surface area quickly becomes a second platform API, with all the maintenance and coordination costs that implies. Smaller modules with clearly defined responsibilities are easier to reason about, easier to test, and easier to evolve. The battery state module does one thing well and nothing more, which is precisely why it works as an example.

Another important rule concerns **data shape and serialization**. Everything that crosses the JavaScript–native boundary must be representable as plain data. This constraint is not merely technical; it is architectural. It forces native modules to define stable, language-agnostic contracts and prevents accidental coupling through shared references or implicit state. When native modules return large or deeply nested objects, they impose parsing and memory costs that are easy to underestimate on mobile devices.

Error handling deserves explicit attention. Native failures should be translated into meaningful JavaScript errors rather than crashing the application or silently failing. From JavaScript's perspective, a native error should behave like any other asynchronous failure and integrate cleanly with existing error-handling logic. This consistency allows UI components to remain agnostic about where a failure originated, focusing instead on how to recover or inform the user.

Finally, native modules should be treated as **long-lived contracts**, not internal implementation details. Changes to native module interfaces can break JavaScript code just as surely as changes to a back-end API can break a client. Experienced teams version native modules deliberately, document their behavior clearly, and resist frequent, ad hoc changes once modules are in use. This discipline becomes increasingly important as applications grow and multiple teams depend on the same native abstractions.

Taken together, these rules point to a simple conclusion: native modules are most effective when they are rare, intentional, and boring. They exist to expose capabilities that JavaScript cannot access reliably or correctly on its own. When used sparingly and designed carefully, they strengthen application architecture. When overused or poorly scoped, they introduce complexity that is difficult to unwind.

CHAPTER 8

Testing and Debugging

A common saying in software engineering is that *code is a liability*. Every line of code written is a potential location for a bug, a performance bottleneck, or a logic error. In the fast-paced world of mobile development, where users expect fluid animations and instantaneous responses, the stakes are even higher. A single crash on launch or a broken checkout button doesn't just result in a bug report—it results in a deleted app and a lost user.

Testing and debugging are not merely "final steps" in the development cycle; they are the fundamental practices that transform a fragile prototype into a professional-grade application.

Many developers view testing as a chore that slows down feature delivery. However, the opposite is true. High-quality testing suites provide developer velocity. They act as a safety net, allowing you to refactor complex code, upgrade libraries, and add new features with the confidence that you haven't inadvertently broken existing functionality.

In this chapter, we will shift our mindset from writing code that works to writing code that is proven to work.

By the end of this chapter, you will be able to

- Write unit tests using Jest to validate complex data transformations
- Simulate user behavior using the React Native Testing Library to ensure your interface responds correctly to touches and inputs
- Learn to diagnose errors quickly using industry-standard debugging tools
- Profile application performance

By the end of this chapter, you will be equipped with practical skills to maintain high-quality, reliable mobile applications.

A. Nalwaya and A. Paul, *React Native for Mobile Development*, https://doi.org/10.1007/979-8-8688-2977-2_8

8.1 Introduction to Unit Testing

A "unit" is the smallest testable part of your application. This is typically a small unit like a function, component, hook, class, etc. To test a function that takes an input, returns an output, and has no side effects (like changing a global variable or fetching data from the internet).

By testing units in isolation, we ensure that the "brain" of our app works correctly before we ever worry about how it looks on a screen.

8.1.1 The Anatomy of a Unit Test: The AAA Pattern

Professional developers follow a three-step mental framework called AAA to write clear, reliable tests. Let's look at how this applies to our Expense Tracker.

Phase	Purpose	Example in our App
Arrange	Set up the initial conditions and data.	Create an empty list and a new expense object.
Act	Execute the function you want to test.	Call the addExpense() function.
Assert	Verify that the outcome matches your expectation.	Check if the list now contains exactly one item.

Rather than testing the entire application at once, unit testing focuses on validating specific pieces of logic independently. For example, in a mobile application, unit tests may verify

- A function that calculates total expenses
- A method that validates user input
- A utility that formats dates or currency
- A service that processes API responses

Each unit test is designed to check one behavior under controlled conditions, ensuring predictable and accurate results.

Unit tests are usually automated and executed frequently during development, allowing developers to catch issues early before they affect other parts of the system.

These are the benefits of unit tests:

1. **Early Detection of Defects**: Unit tests validate individual functions and modules immediately after implementation, enabling rapid identification of logic errors and edge cases. This prevents defect propagation into higher-level components and integration layers.

2. **Improved Code Design**: Test-driven and testable code promotes loose coupling, high cohesion, and clear separation of concerns. This results in a modular architecture that is easier to refactor, extend, and scale.

3. **Faster Debugging**: Failures in unit tests precisely isolate the faulty code path, reducing the scope of investigation. Developers can quickly trace errors to specific methods or conditions without analyzing the entire system.

4. **Reliable Release:** Automated unit test suites continuously verify core business logic across code changes, ensuring functional consistency. This significantly reduces regression risks during frequent deployments.

5. **Reduced Maintenance Cost**: By minimizing post-release defects and simplifying refactoring, unit testing lowers long-term technical debt. Maintenance efforts shift from reactive bug fixing to proactive code improvement.

8.2 Setting Up Unit Testing in React Native

React Native projects include Jest by default, making it straightforward to start writing unit tests. Jest provides a fast and reliable test runner, assertion library, mocking capabilities, and code coverage reporting.

For testing React Native components from a user's perspective, install React Native Testing Library:

```
npm install --save-dev @testing-library/react-native
```

This library encourages testing application behavior rather than implementation details, helping create more maintainable and resilient tests.

8.2.1 Unit Testing in Practice: Expense Tracking Application

To understand unit testing in a real-world scenario, let us implement and test core functionalities of a simple Expense Tracking Application. This application allows users to add expenses, remove expenses, calculate total spending, and filter expenses by category. We will take a step-by-step approach, gradually building our test suite while learning the fundamental principles and best practices of unit testing in React Native.

By writing unit tests for these features, we ensure that the business logic works correctly under different conditions.

Step 1: Defining the Logic (the "Brain")

Before writing tests, we need something worth testing. A good unit test targets a piece of logic that is independent of the user interface. Think of this logic as the "brain" of the application—it takes input, processes it, and returns a predictable output.

We will create a function that is responsible for a single task: adding a new expense to an existing collection. Given the same inputs, it always produces the same output and has no dependency on React Native, APIs, or external services.

This makes it an excellent example of a unit that can be tested in isolation.

```
// expenseLogic.js

/** * Adds a new expense to the existing list.
 * We use the spread operator [...] to ensure the original list is not
modified.
 */
export const addExpense = (expenses, newExpense) => {
  return [...expenses, newExpense];
};
```

Step 2: Writing the Unit Test

Now that we have defined the business logic, we can verify that it behaves as expected.

A good unit test follows the Arrange, Act, and Assert pattern:

```
import { addExpense } from './expenseLogic';

describe('Expense Logic: addExpense', () => {

  test('should add a new expense to the list', () => {
    // 1. ARRANGE
    const initialExpenses = [];
    const newEntry = {
      id: 1,
      title: 'Groceries',
      amount: 50
    };

    // 2. ACT
    const result = addExpense(initialExpenses, newEntry);

    // 3. ASSERT
    expect(result).toHaveLength(1);              // Did the size increase?
    expect(result[0].title).toBe('Groceries'); // Is it the right data?
    expect(initialExpenses).toHaveLength(0);    // Is the original
                                                 list still empty?
                                                 (Immutability check)

  });

});
```

Before writing our first test, you may notice that functions such as `describe`, `it` (or `test`), and `expect` are used without being imported.

```
describe('addExpense', () => {
  it('adds a new expense to the list', () => {
    expect(result).toHaveLength(1);
  });
});
```

This works because Jest automatically provides these functions as globals in the test environment. When a test file is executed, Jest makes them available without requiring explicit imports.

Each function serves a specific purpose:

- `describe()` groups related test cases together.
- `it()` or `test()` defines an individual test case.
- `expect()` creates an assertion that verifies the actual result matches the expected outcome.

This code snippet demonstrates a fundamental unit test for the addExpense function, organized using the AAA (Arrange-Act-Assert) pattern to ensure logical clarity. It begins by importing the function from the `expenseLogic` module and wrapping the test in a describe block, which serves as a container for related tests. Inside the test block, the Arrange phase initializes an empty array and a mock expense object to simulate a real-world entry. The Act phase then executes the `addExpense` function with these inputs, storing the returned value in a `result` constant. Finally, the Assert phase uses Jest's expect library to verify three critical outcomes: that the new list contains exactly one item, that the item matches the provided data, and—most importantly—that the original initialExpenses array remains empty. This final check confirms immutability, proving that the function creates a new array rather than modifying the existing one, which is a vital practice for predictable state management in React Native development.

Phase	Action in Code	Purpose
Arrange	Creating initialExpenses and newEntry.	Setting the stage for the test.
Act	Running addExpense(initialExpenses, newEntry).	Executing the specific logic being tested.
Assert	Running expect() checks.	Validating that the code behaved as expected.

> ***The "Red-Green-Refactor" Pro-Tip:*** *Try changing the `addExpense` function to return an empty array and run the test. It will fail (**Red**). Then, fix the code to make it pass (**Green**). Finally, clean up the code while the test stays green (**Refactor**). This cycle is the heart of Test-Driven Development (TDD).*

Step 3: Handling Complex Logic (Filtering)

Once we are comfortable testing simple functions, we can move on to more realistic business rules. In our Expense Tracking Application, users may want to view expenses belonging to a specific category, such as Food, Travel, or Entertainment.

To support this feature, we can create a utility function that filters expenses by category.

```
// Logic
export const filterByCategory = (expenses, category) => {
  return expenses.filter(item => item.category === category);
};

// Test
test('should return only expenses matching the "Food" category', () => {
  const data = [
    { title: 'Pizza', category: 'Food' },
    { title: 'Uber', category: 'Travel' }
  ];

  const filtered = filterByCategory(data, 'Food');

  expect(filtered).toHaveLength(1);
  expect(filtered[0].title).toBe('Pizza');
});
```

Unit tests excel when logic gets complicated. For instance, filtering expenses by category requires precise logic. If we accidentally use !== instead of ===, a unit test will catch it in milliseconds.

Step 4: Building the Interface (the "Body")

So far, we have focused on testing the application's "brain"—the business logic that manages expenses and applies filtering rules. While this logic is important, users never interact with these functions directly. Instead, they interact with the user interface.

In React Native, components form the "body" of the application. They present information to the user, capture user input, and invoke business logic when actions occur. We will build an `ExpenseList` component that consumes the logic functions we previously tested.

To make this component testable, we use a custom attribute called `testID`. This acts as a stable "handle" for our tests, allowing us to find specific elements even if we change their styling or text later.

```
import React, { useState } from 'react';
import { View, Text, Button, FlatList } from 'react-native';
import { addExpense, calculateTotal } from './expenseLogic';

const ExpenseList = ({ initialExpenses = [] }) => {
  const [expenses, setExpenses] = useState(initialExpenses);

  const handlePress = () => {
    const newEntry = { id: Date.now(), title: 'Coffee', amount: 100 };
    setExpenses(addExpense(expenses, newEntry));
  };

  return (
    <View>
      {/* testID allows the test to find this specific Text node */}
      <Text testID="total-amount">
        Total: ₹{calculateTotal(expenses)}
      </Text>

      <FlatList
        data={expenses}
        keyExtractor={(item) => item.id.toString()}
        renderItem={({ item }) => <Text>{item.title}</Text>}
      />

      <Button title="Add Item" onPress={handlePress} />
    </View>
  );
};
```

While Jest runs our tests, we need a specific tool to "render" our components in a test environment. The *React Native Testing Library (RNTL)* is the industry standard. It encourages testing from the user's perspective rather than testing the internal state of the component.

The Core Tools

- `render`: Creates a virtual version of your component
- `fireEvent`: Simulates user actions like pressing a button or typing text
- `getByText / getByTestId`: Queries used to find elements on the screen

Let's test the interaction: when a user presses the "**Add Item**" button, does the list update, and does the total change?

```
import { render, fireEvent } from '@testing-library/react-native';
import ExpenseList from './ExpenseList';

describe('ExpenseList Component', () => {

  test('should update the list and total when the button is
  pressed', () => {
    // 1. ARRANGE: Render the component with an empty list
    const { getByText, getByTestId } = render(<ExpenseList
    initialExpenses={[]} />);

    // 2. ACT: Find the button and press it
    const addButton = getByText('Add Item');
    fireEvent.press(addButton);

    // 3. ASSERT: Check if the new item appears
    expect(getByText('Coffee')).toBeTruthy();

    // 4. ASSERT: Check if the total updated correctly
    const totalLabel = getByTestId('total-amount');
    expect(totalLabel.props.children).toContain('100');
  });

});
```

In this example, we use `toBeTruthy()` to verify that the element exists. However, in real-world tests, matchers such as `toBeOnTheScreen()` or `toBeVisible()` are often preferred because they more explicitly verify that the element is rendered and available to the user.

This test verifies the Integration between your UI and your Logic. It proves that

- The Button's `onPress` is correctly linked to `handlePress`.
- The `addExpense` logic function (which we unit tested earlier) is correctly updating the component's state.
- The UI is re-rendering to show the new data.

8.2.2 Unit Testing vs. UI Testing: A Quick Comparison

To help you decide which test to write and when, refer to this table:

Feature	Unit Testing (Logic)	UI Testing (Component)
Speed	Extremely Fast (ms)	Fast, but heavier than unit tests
Focus	Math, Data, Logic	User Flow, Rendering, Clicks
Environment	Pure JavaScript/Node	Virtual Mobile Environment
Best For	"Does $2 + 2 = 4$?"	"Does the total update when clicked?"

Step 5: Mocking Dependencies

In the previous examples, we tested functions and components that were completely under our control. However, real-world applications often depend on external services such as APIs, databases, analytics tools, or native modules.

When writing unit tests, we want to isolate the code being tested and avoid relying on external systems. This is where mocking becomes useful.

A mock replaces a real dependency with a controlled implementation that returns predictable results. Consider a function that retrieves expenses from an API:

```
export const fetchExpenses = async () => {
  const response = await api.get('/expenses');
  return response.data;
};
```

Instead of making an actual network request during a test, we can mock the API module.

```
import { fetchExpenses } from './expenseService';
import api from './api';

jest.mock('./api');


describe('fetchExpenses', () => {
  it('returns expenses from the API', async () => {
    api.get.mockResolvedValue({
      data: [
        { id: 1, title: 'Lunch', amount: 15 },
      ],
    });

    const result = await fetchExpenses();


    expect(result).toHaveLength(1);
    expect(result[0].title).toBe('Lunch');
  });
});
```

Mocking helps us

- Test code in isolation
- Avoid slow or unreliable network calls
- Create predictable test scenarios
- Verify how our code interacts with external dependencies

By replacing real dependencies with mocks, unit tests remain fast, reliable, and focused on the behavior we want to validate.

Mocking should be used whenever the code under test depends on something external that is outside the scope of the unit being tested. The goal is to isolate the unit and verify only its behavior.

Dependency	Why Mock It?
API calls	Avoid real network requests and make tests deterministic.
AsyncStorage	Prevent reading or writing actual device storage.
React Navigation	Focus on component behavior without setting up navigation containers.
Native modules	Many native features are unavailable in the test environment.
Analytics and logging services	Avoid sending real events during tests.
Date and time functions	Create predictable test results.

If the dependency belongs to another system (API, storage, navigation, analytics, native module), consider mocking it. If it contains the business logic you want to validate, test the real implementation.

Mock dependencies, not the unit under test.

Why Unit Testing Is Your "Secret Weapon"

- **Instant Feedback**: You don't need to wait for the Metro Bundler to load or a simulator to boot up. Jest tests run in your terminal in seconds.
- **Documentation**: A unit test tells other developers exactly what a function is supposed to do better than a comment ever could.
- **Refactor with Confidence**: Want to optimize your `addExpense` function later? If your unit tests pass, you know you haven't broken the app's core functionality.

8.3 Master the Hunt: React Native Debugging Techniques

In the previous sections, we learned how to prevent bugs through rigorous testing. But let's be realistic: bugs are inevitable. Whether it's a layout that looks perfect on iOS but breaks on Android, or a state update that feels sluggish, you need a systematic way to find the "why" behind the "what."

Debugging in React Native is unique because you are troubleshooting a multi-layered architecture:

- **The JavaScript Thread**: Where your logic and React components live
- **The Bridge/JSI**: Where data travels between JS and Native
- **The Native Thread**: Where the actual UI rendering (Java/Kotlin or Objective-C/Swift) happens

8.3.1 1. The Developer Menu: Your Control Center

The first step in any debugging session is accessing the In-App Developer Menu.

- **iOS Simulator**: Press `Cmd + D`.
- **Android Emulator**: Press `Cmd + M` (or `Ctrl + M` on Windows).
- **Physical Device**: Give the phone a literal shake.

From here, you can enable Fast Refresh, which allows you to see code changes instantly, or toggle the Element Inspector, which works like the "Inspect Element" tool in a web browser.

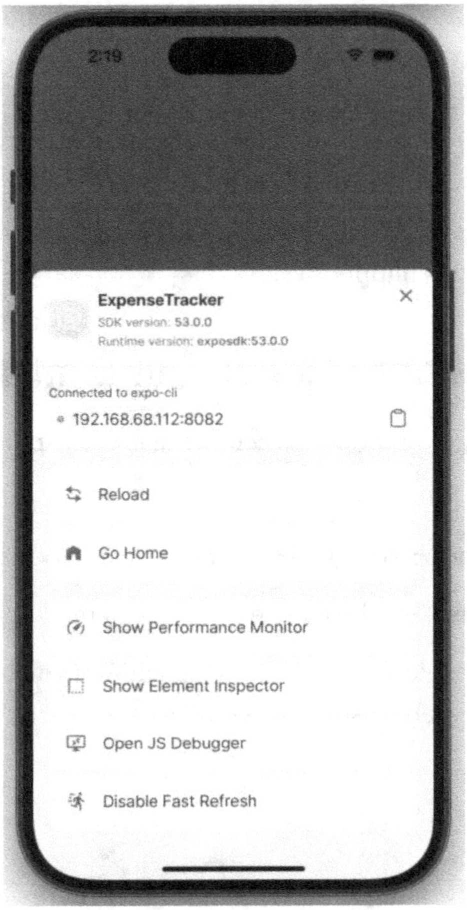

You can inspect props, state, and hooks for any component, track how and when components re-render, and quickly identify issues such as incorrect state updates or unnecessary renders. This is especially useful when bugs are caused by complex component hierarchies or shared state rather than simple logic errors.

The tool also helps answer common questions like "Which component is causing this re-render?" or "Why is this value changing?"—without modifying your code. By observing changes in real time, you can debug issues faster and with greater confidence.

To open this, go to the console form `CMD + D` in IOS or `CMD+M` in Android and click `Open JS Debugger`.

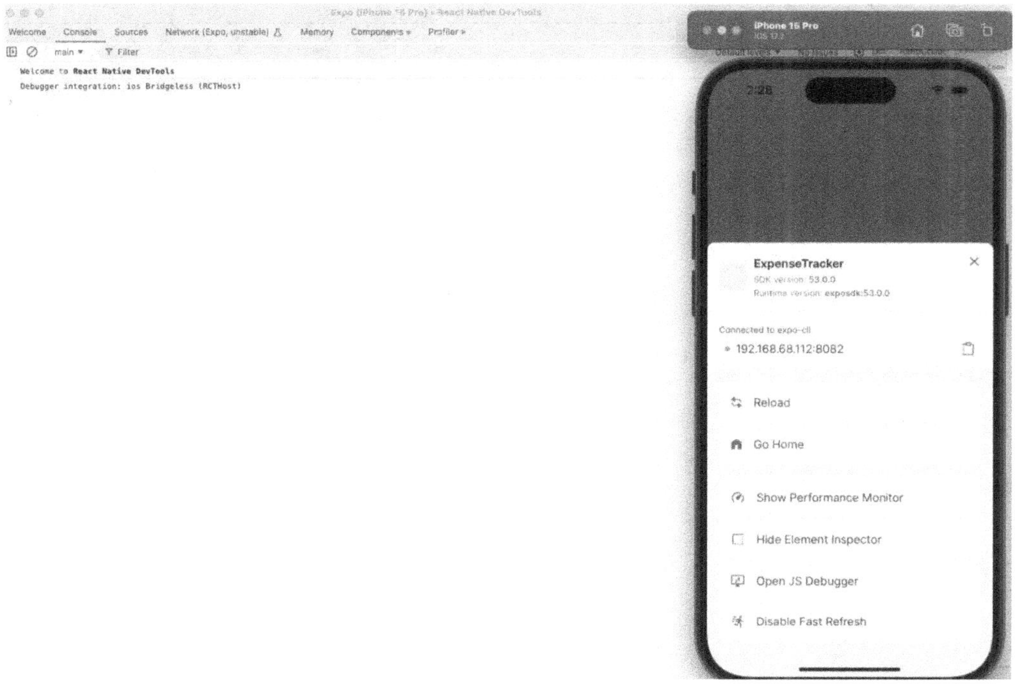

Now run the following command in the console:

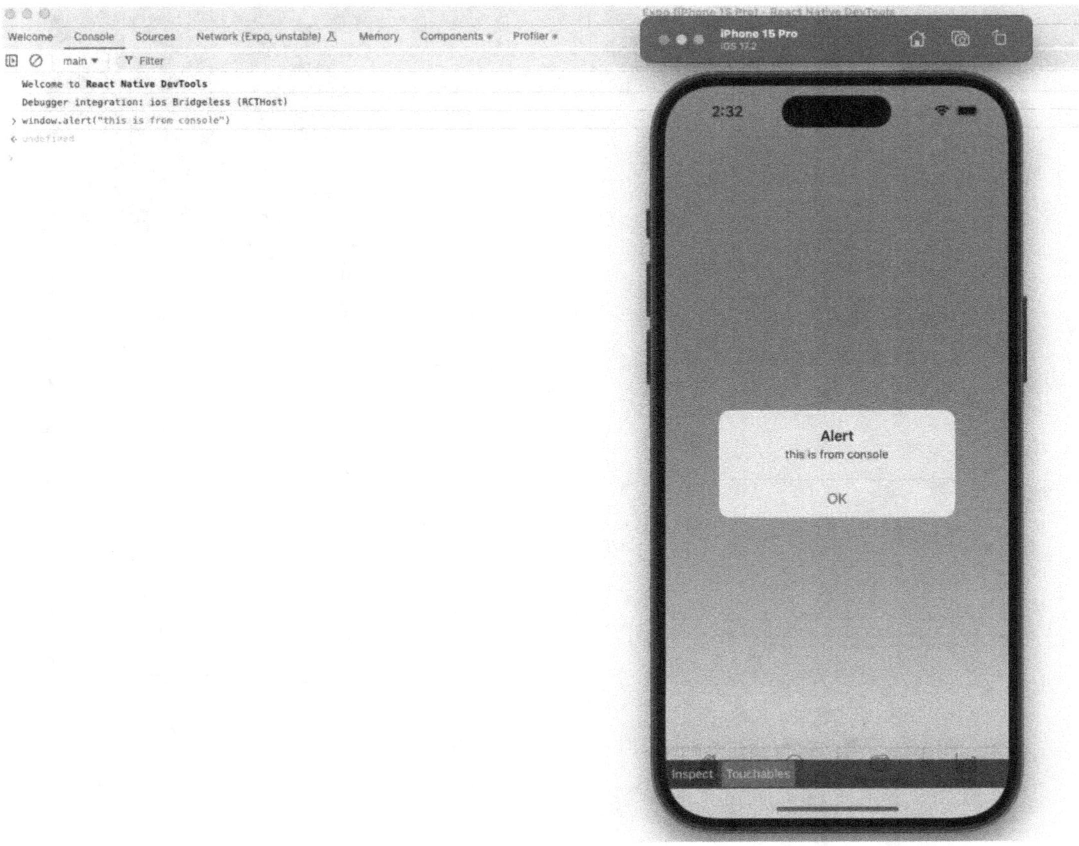

You can see from the debugger that you can interact with the app
Few More Examples: Finding a State Bug
Imagine your *ExpenseList* isn't updating when you add an item.

- Open React DevTools.
- Select the *ExpenseList* component.
- Look at the Hooks section in the right sidebar.
- Check the *useState* value. If the state updated but the UI didn't, you likely mutated the array instead of returning a new one (a classic immutability bug).

8.3.2 2. Console Logging: The Simplest Form of Debugging

`console.log()` is often the first and most approachable debugging tool developers use, and for good reason. It allows you to quickly inspect values, execution flow, and runtime behavior without setting up advanced tools or breakpoints. When something doesn't work as expected, a well-placed log can immediately answer questions like "Did this code run?", "What value do I actually have?", or "How often is this rendering?".

In React Native, `console.log()` is especially useful for tracing props, state updates, API responses, and conditional logic during development. It provides instant feedback, making it ideal for fast experimentation, early-stage development, and debugging simple issues.

However, while `console.log()` is powerful in its simplicity, it should be used intentionally and temporarily. Overusing logs can clutter the console, slow down debugging, and even impact performance if left in production builds. As applications grow in complexity, `console.log()` works best when combined with structured tools like debuggers and performance monitors.

8.3.3 3. Inspecting Network Requests

Most modern mobile applications communicate with back-end services to retrieve and update data. When developing React Native applications, it is essential to verify that network requests are being sent correctly and that the application is receiving the expected responses.

React Native DevTools provides built-in network inspection capabilities that allow developers to monitor HTTP traffic directly from the debugging environment.

To inspect network requests:

1. Open the Developer Menu.
2. Select Open DevTools.
3. Navigate to the Network tab.
4. Perform actions in your application that trigger API calls.

The Network panel displays

- Request URLs
- HTTP methods (GET, POST, PUT, DELETE)
- Request headers
- Response payloads
- Response status codes
- Request timing information

This makes it easy to verify that API requests are being sent correctly and that the application is receiving the expected responses.

8.3.4 4. Breakpoint Debugging

While console.log is a staple of every developer's diet, it has a significant limitation: it only tells you what already happened. To truly understand a complex bug, you need to see what is currently happening. Breakpoint Debugging allows you to pause the execution of your application at a specific line of code, effectively "freezing time" so you can inspect the entire state of the app at that exact microsecond.

A breakpoint is an intentional stopping point in your code. When the JavaScript engine reaches a line with a breakpoint, it pauses execution. At this point, the app hasn't crashed; it is simply suspended. This gives you the power to

- **Inspect Variables**: See the value of every local and global variable in scope.
- **Check the Call Stack**: See the "trail of breadcrumbs"—which functions were called to get you to this specific line.
- **Evaluate Expressions**: Run new code in the console using the current live state of the app.

To use breakpoints in React Native, you typically use React Native DevTools or the VS Code Debugger.

- Open React Native DevTools.
- Navigate to Sources, go to the Sources tab, and find your *.js* or *.tsx* file.

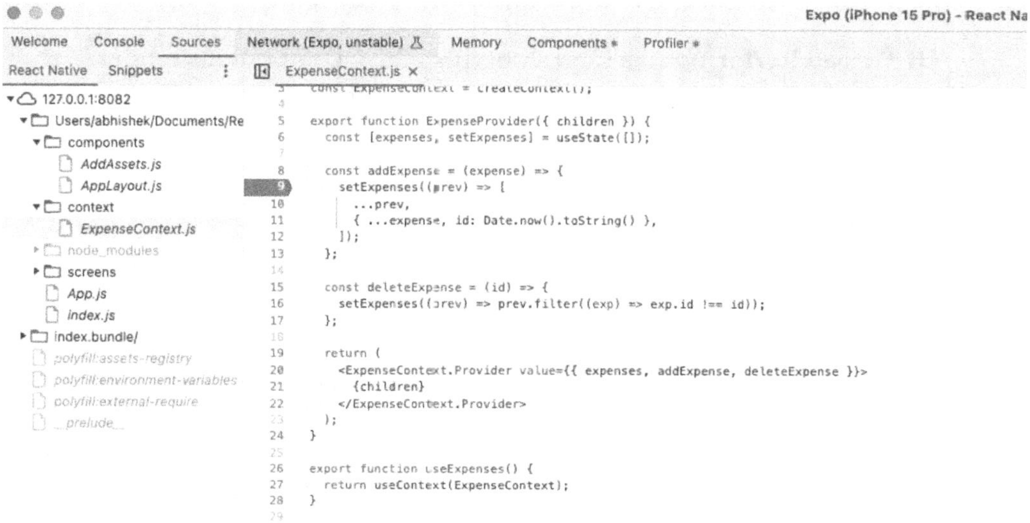

8.4 Performance Debugging: The "Why Is It Slow?" Hunt

Performance is not just about making your app run faster—it's about creating a smooth, responsive experience that users love. In React Native, performance debugging requires understanding both JavaScript execution and native rendering, making it uniquely challenging compared to traditional web or native development.

This chapter will equip you with the tools, techniques, and mental models needed to identify, diagnose, and fix performance issues in your React Native applications. You'll learn how to use profiling tools, interpret performance data, and apply targeted optimizations that make a real difference.

8.4.1 The Key Performance Areas

- **JavaScript Thread Performance**: How efficiently your business logic, state management, and component rendering execute
- **UI Thread Performance**: How smoothly native components render and animate at 60 FPS (or 120 FPS on modern devices)

8.4.2 Using the Perf Monitor

Open the Dev Menu and select "Show Perf Monitor." You will see two frame rates:

- **UI (Native)**: Usually stays at 60 fps.
- **JS**: If this drops below 60 fps during an animation or a list scroll, your JavaScript thread is overworked.

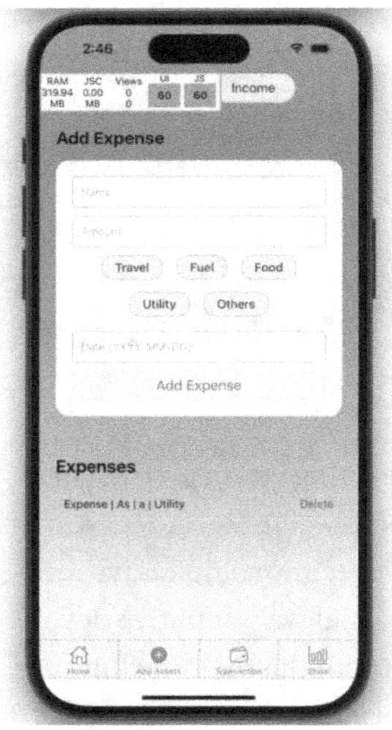

FPS (Frames Per Second) measures how many frames are rendered every second. Modern mobile devices typically refresh their displays at 60Hz or higher, meaning the application should ideally render 60 frames per second to achieve smooth animations and interactions.

When the frame rate drops significantly, users may experience

- Stuttering animations
- Delayed touch responses
- Choppy scrolling
- Screen freezes or visual lag

For production applications, developers should strive to maintain frame rates as close to 60 FPS as possible during normal interactions.

8.5 Common Performance Issues and Solutions

There are several reasons why performance issues occur, and we'll cover a few important ones to help you understand and address them.

8.5.1 Issue 1: Excessive Re-renders

The most common performance issue in React Native is components re-rendering unnecessarily. This happens when parent components pass new object or function references as props on every render.

Problem Example

```
const ParentComponent = () => {
  const [count, setCount] = useState(0);

  // Bad: Creates new function on every render
  const handlePress = () => {
    console.log('Pressed');
  };

  return <ExpensiveChild onPress={handlePress} />;
};
```

Solution: Use useCallback and React.memo

When investigating performance issues, unnecessary component re-renders are often a common cause of low JS FPS. React provides optimization techniques such as `React.memo` and `useCallback` to reduce this overhead. React.memo prevents a component from re-rendering when its props have not changed, making it particularly useful for list items and complex UI components. Similarly, `useCallback` memoizes function references, preventing new callback functions from being created on every render. When used together, these techniques can significantly reduce rendering work, improve responsiveness, and help maintain smooth performance, especially in screens that display large amounts of data or update frequently.

```
const ParentComponent = () => {
  const [count, setCount] = useState(0);

  // Good: Memoized function
  const handlePress = useCallback(() => {
    console.log('Pressed');
  }, []);

  return <ExpensiveChildMemo onPress={handlePress} />;
};

// Memoized child component
const ExpensiveChildMemo = React.memo(ExpensiveChild);
```

In this example, `ParentComponent` maintains a state variable called count. Every time the state changes, React re-renders the parent component. Without optimization, a new instance of the `handlePress` function would be created during each render, causing child components that receive it as a prop to re-render as well. To avoid this, `useCallback` memoizes the `handlePress` function and returns the same function reference across renders as long as its dependencies remain unchanged.

The `ExpensiveChild` component represents a component that performs expensive rendering operations, such as displaying a large amount of data, rendering complex UI elements, or executing computationally intensive logic. By wrapping it with `React.memo`, we create `ExpensiveChildMemo`, which only re-renders when its props change. Since handlePress is memoized using useCallback, the `onPress` prop remains stable across parent re-renders, allowing `React.memo` to skip unnecessary renders of `ExpensiveChild`.

This combination reduces rendering work on the JavaScript thread and helps maintain smooth application performance.

8.5.2 Issue 2: Heavy List Rendering

Rendering long lists with `ScrollView` loads all items at once, causing memory bloat and slow initial rendering. `FlatList` and `SectionList` implement windowing to only render visible items.

Problem Example

```
// Bad: Renders all 10,000 items immediately
<ScrollView>
  {data.map(item => <ItemCard key={item.id} {...item} />)}
</ScrollView>
```

Solution: Use FlatList with Optimization Props

When rendering large datasets, `FlatList` performance becomes critical because rendering too many items at once can overwhelm the JavaScript thread and cause dropped frames, resulting in poor JS FPS and choppy scrolling. The optimization properties shown here help React Native render list items in smaller batches, limit the number of off-screen components kept in memory, and reduce unnecessary layout calculations. In particular, `removeClippedSubviews` frees resources by removing items that are outside the visible area, while `getItemLayout` allows React Native to efficiently calculate item positions when item heights are fixed. Together, these optimizations help maintain smooth scrolling and responsive user interactions, even when displaying hundreds or thousands of list items.

```
<FlatList
  data={data}
  renderItem={renderItem}
  keyExtractor={item => item.id}
  // Optimization props
  maxToRenderPerBatch={10}
  updateCellsBatchingPeriod={50}
  initialNumToRender={10}
```

```
  windowSize={5}
  removeClippedSubviews={true}
  getItemLayout={getItemLayout} // If fixed height
/>
```

8.5.3 Issue 3: Unoptimized Images

Images are often one of the largest contributors to application size, memory consumption, and rendering overhead. Using high-resolution images without optimization can negatively impact startup time, increase network usage, and cause frame drops during scrolling or screen transitions. These issues become particularly noticeable on lower-end devices and in image-heavy screens such as product catalogs, social feeds, or gallery views.

A common mistake is loading images that are significantly larger than their displayed dimensions. For example, displaying a 4000×3000 pixel image in a 200×150 pixel container forces the device to download, decode, and process far more data than necessary.

```
<Image
      source={{ uri: imageUrl }}
      style={{ width: 200, height: 150 }}
 />
```

Solution: Implement Expo Image

To improve performance:

- Use appropriately sized images for the target device and screen.
- Compress images before distributing them.
- Prefer modern image formats such as WebP when supported.
- Avoid loading large images that are not immediately visible.
- Use image caching to reduce repeated network requests.
- Display placeholders while images are loading.

For applications that rely heavily on remote images, the `expo-image` component provides efficient image loading, caching, and decoding capabilities.

```
import { Image } from 'expo-image';

<Image
  source={{ uri: imageUrl }}
  style={styles.image}
  contentFit="cover"
/>
```

Optimizing images reduces memory usage, decreases network overhead, improves scrolling performance, and helps maintain a stable frame rate, resulting in a smoother and more responsive user experience.

8.6 Summary

In this chapter, you learned that building high-quality React Native applications requires more than simply writing code that works—it requires validating, debugging, and optimizing that code throughout its lifecycle. We explored how unit testing helps verify business logic and component behavior with confidence, reducing the risk of regressions as applications evolve. We then examined modern debugging techniques using React Native DevTools, enabling you to diagnose issues related to application state, UI rendering, network requests, and runtime behavior. Finally, we focused on performance optimization, learning how to identify bottlenecks such as unnecessary re-renders, heavy list rendering, and unoptimized assets while using tools and metrics to make data-driven improvements. Together, testing, debugging, and performance optimization form a continuous quality cycle that helps developers build reliable, maintainable, and responsive applications ready for production environments.

This is an overview of debugging and performance tools:

Tool	Best Used For...
Console Log	Immediate syntax or runtime errors.
Element Inspector	Fixing"Why is this button off-center?"
React DevTools	Investigating props, state, and re-renders.
Network Debugging	API and back-end communication issues.
Perf Monitor	Identifying drops in frame rate (FPS).
Breakpoints	Stepping through complex logic line-by-line.

CHAPTER 9

Getting Ready for the App Store and Play Store

Once the development of a React Native application is completed and the product reaches a stable state, the next essential phase is preparing it for public release. During development, applications are typically run using debug builds, which prioritize flexibility, real-time testing, and developer tools over performance and security. While these builds are ideal for rapid iteration, they are not suitable for distribution to end users. Production-ready builds, in contrast, are carefully optimized versions of the application that undergo code minification, resource optimization, and secure signing to ensure efficiency, stability, and compliance with platform requirements.

Mobile applications created with React Native are primarily distributed through the official marketplaces maintained by Apple and Google, each of which enforces specific technical standards and submission formats. Android applications are typically packaged as Android App Bundles, while iOS applications must be archived and validated using Xcode before submission. This chapter presents a comprehensive guide to generating production-ready builds for both Android and iOS platforms, detailing the necessary configurations, optimization steps, and signing processes required to ensure a smooth and successful release.

A. Nalwaya and A. Paul, *React Native for Mobile Development*, https://doi.org/10.1007/979-8-8688-2977-2_9

9.1 Creating Android Production Builds in React Native

Android production builds represent the finalized version of the application that will be distributed to users through the Play Store. Unlike development builds, production builds are optimized for performance, reduced in size, digitally signed for security, and packaged in a format approved for public release. In modern Android distribution, the mandatory format is the Android App Bundle (AAB), which enables efficient delivery of application resources based on individual device configurations.

The process of creating an Android production build in React Native involves several key steps, including version configuration, cryptographic signing, optimization through code shrinking, and final bundle generation. Each of these steps is essential to ensure compliance with platform standards and to deliver a stable, high-performance application.

9.1.1 Step 1: Configure App Versioning

Application versioning plays a critical role in managing releases, updates, and user adoption across mobile platforms. In Android, versioning is not only used to display the application's version to users but also serves as a technical mechanism for the operating system and the Play Store to determine update eligibility. Every production build must include properly configured version values to ensure seamless upgrades and compliance with store requirements.

Android uses two distinct version parameters: versionCode and versionName. The versionCode is an internal integer value that uniquely identifies each release of the application. It is never visible to users but is used by the system to determine whether a newly uploaded build is more recent than the currently published version. The versionName, on the other hand, is a user-facing string displayed within the Play Store and device settings, typically following a semantic versioning pattern such as *1.0.0* or *2.1.3*. While the versionName may change in any format preferred by the development team, the versionCode must always increase with every release.

Android uses two version values:

- `versionCode`: An integer that must increase with every release
- `versionName`: A user-visible version like 1.0.0

In a React Native Android project, versioning is configured within the Gradle build file located at `android/app/build.gradle`. Within the `defaultConfig` block, developers specify both the `versionCode` and `versionName` values. A typical configuration is shown below:

Example

```
defaultConfig {
    applicationId "com.companyname.myapp"
    minSdkVersion 21
    targetSdkVersion 34
    versionCode 3
    versionName "1.2.0"
}
```

Each time a new build is prepared for store submission, the `versionCode` must be incremented by at least one. Failure to increase this value will result in rejection during upload, as the Play Store requires each build to represent a newer release than the previous one. The `versionName` may be updated according to the release strategy adopted by the development team, such as `major`, `minor`, or `patch` updates.

9.1.2 Step 2: Create a Signing Keystore

Before an Android application can be distributed publicly, it must be digitally signed using a cryptographic key stored within a keystore file. This signing process establishes the identity of the application's developer and ensures the integrity of the application package. Every update published to the Play Store must be signed with the same keystore used for the original release. This requirement prevents unauthorized modifications and guarantees that users receive updates from a trusted source.

A keystore is a secure container that holds one or more private keys and their associated certificates. In Android development, the keystore typically contains a single key pair specifically created for signing production builds. The private key within the keystore must remain confidential, as it serves as the unique identifier for the application. If the keystore is lost or compromised, the developer may permanently lose the ability to update the application on the Play Store.

To generate a keystore, developers use the Java Development Kit (JDK) utility known as `keytool`, which is included by default with most Java installations. The keystore is created through a command-line operation that defines the encryption algorithm, key size, validity period, and alias name.

A standard command for generating a keystore appears as follows:

```
keytool -genkeypair -v -keystore my-release-key.keystore \
-keyalg RSA -keysize 2048 -validity 10000 -alias my-key-alias
```

During execution, the tool prompts the developer to enter several pieces of information, including

- Keystore password
- Key password
- Developer name and organization details

The resulting file, typically named something like release-key.keystore, is saved in the specified directory. This file should be stored in a secure location and excluded from public version control repositories to prevent unauthorized access.

The validity parameter defines how long the certificate remains active, often set to a large value such as 10,000 days to avoid expiration during the application's lifecycle. Although certificates can be renewed, maintaining a long validity period simplifies long-term maintenance.

Once the keystore is generated, it becomes a permanent part of the application's release infrastructure. Best practices include

- Creating secure backups in multiple safe locations
- Storing credentials in encrypted password managers
- Restricting access to authorized team members only

In professional environments, keystore files are often managed through secure vault systems or continuous integration pipelines to ensure controlled access.

It is important to note that the keystore used for production builds should never be replaced or regenerated for the same application. Android strictly enforces signing consistency, and uploading a build signed with a different key will result in rejection. Therefore, the initial keystore creation represents a critical one-time operation in the application's lifecycle.

9.1.3 Step 3: Configure Signing in Gradle

After generating a signing keystore, the next step is to integrate it into the Android build system so that all production builds are digitally signed automatically. Android uses Gradle as its primary build automation tool, and signing configurations are defined within the project's Gradle files. This configuration ensures that every release build is securely authenticated before being packaged for distribution.

In a React Native project, the signing setup is typically added to the file located at `android/app/build.gradle`. Within this file, developers define a signing configuration block that references the keystore file, its associated passwords, and the key alias. This configuration is then linked to the release build type, allowing Gradle to apply the signing process whenever a production build is generated.

A standard signing configuration is illustrated below:

```
signingConfigs {
    release {
        storeFile file("release-key.keystore")
        storePassword "yourStorePassword"
        keyAlias "release-key"
        keyPassword "yourKeyPassword"
    }
}
```

Each parameter in this configuration serves a specific purpose. The `storeFile` property points to the keystore file created earlier. The `storePassword` protects access to the keystore itself, while the keyAlias identifies the specific key within the keystore used for signing. The `keyPassword` secures the private key associated with the alias.

Once the signing configuration is defined, it must be associated with the release build type. This is done within the `buildTypes` section of the same Gradle file:

```
buildTypes {
    release {
        signingConfig signingConfigs.release
        minifyEnabled true
        shrinkResources true
    }
}
```

This ensures that Gradle applies the digital signature automatically whenever a production build is generated.

For improved security, it is a serious security issue to hard-code sensitive credentials directly in the Gradle file. Instead, passwords should be stored in an external properties file and loaded dynamically during the build process. This approach protects confidential information and supports safer collaboration within development teams.

9.1.4 Step 4: Enable Code Shrinking and Optimization

To deliver efficient and high-performing applications, Android production builds should enable optimization features that reduce application size and enhance runtime performance. These processes remove unused code and resources while applying obfuscation to protect the application's internal structure. In React Native projects, these tasks are handled automatically by Android's built-in R8 tool during release builds.

Code shrinking analyzes the application and its dependencies to identify components that are not required at runtime and removes them from the final bundle. Resource shrinking further reduces size by eliminating unused images and assets. Together, these optimizations result in smaller download sizes, faster installations, and improved performance on user devices.

Optimization is enabled within the Gradle release configuration:

```
buildTypes {
    release {
        minifyEnabled true
        shrinkResources true
    }
}
```

While these features provide significant benefits, developers should test the optimized build thoroughly to ensure no required components are removed. If necessary, specific rules can be added to preserve essential code.

9.1.5 Step 5: Generate Android App Bundle

Once application versioning, signing configuration, and optimization settings have been properly established, the final step in the Android build process is generating the Android App Bundle (AAB). The AAB format is the recommended and required distribution format for publishing applications on the Play Store, as it allows the platform to deliver optimized application packages tailored to each user's device configuration.

In a React Native project, the Android App Bundle is created using the Gradle build system. Developers should navigate to the Android directory within the project and execute the release build command:

```
cd android
./gradlew bundleRelease
```

During this process, Gradle compiles the application source code, applies code shrinking and resource optimization, signs the build using the configured keystore, and packages the final output in the AAB format.

Upon successful completion, the generated bundle is located in the following directory:

```
android/app/build/outputs/bundle/release/app-release.aab
```

This file represents the finalized Android production build and is the artifact uploaded to the Play Store for review and distribution.

After generating the bundle, it is recommended to perform basic validation by installing a test build on physical devices or using available testing tools. This step ensures that the application behaves correctly under release conditions and that no issues were introduced during optimization or signing.

In summary, generating the Android App Bundle marks the completion of the Android production build process in React Native. The AAB file serves as the official release package, optimized for performance and prepared for submission to the Play Store.

With the Android production build successfully generated in the form of an optimized and signed Android App Bundle, the application is now technically ready for distribution on the Android platform. This process demonstrates the importance of proper versioning, secure signing, build optimization, and thorough verification in ensuring a high-quality release.

While React Native enables a shared code base across platforms, the build and distribution workflow for iOS differs significantly from Android. Apple's ecosystem relies on a certificate-based signing system, strict provisioning profiles, and application archiving through Xcode. These platform-specific requirements introduce a distinct set of steps that developers must carefully follow to produce a valid iOS production build.

9.1.6 Step 6: Upload the Android Production Build to the Play Store

After generating the Android App Bundle (AAB) and verifying the release build, the next step is to upload the application to the Play Store for review and distribution. This process is managed through the Google Play Console, the official platform maintained by Google for publishing Android applications.

Before uploading any build, developers must create an application record within the Play Console by providing basic information such as the app name, default language, and category. This initial setup establishes the app's presence in the Play Store ecosystem and prepares the platform to receive production builds.

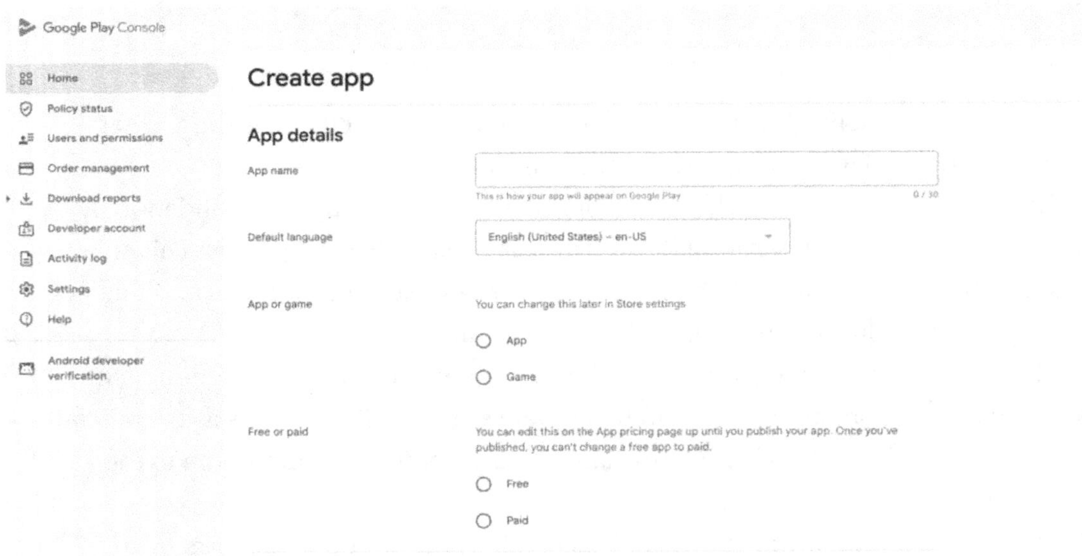

Once the application record is created, developers navigate to the **Release** section and select an appropriate release track, such as internal testing, closed testing, or production. For first-time releases, the production track is commonly used after initial testing is completed.

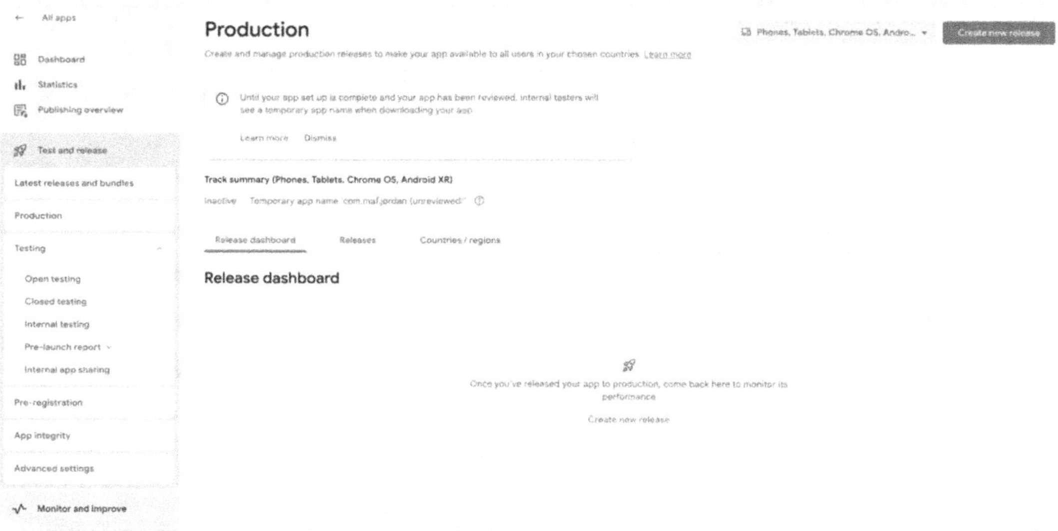

The Android App Bundle file generated during the build process is then uploaded to the selected release track.

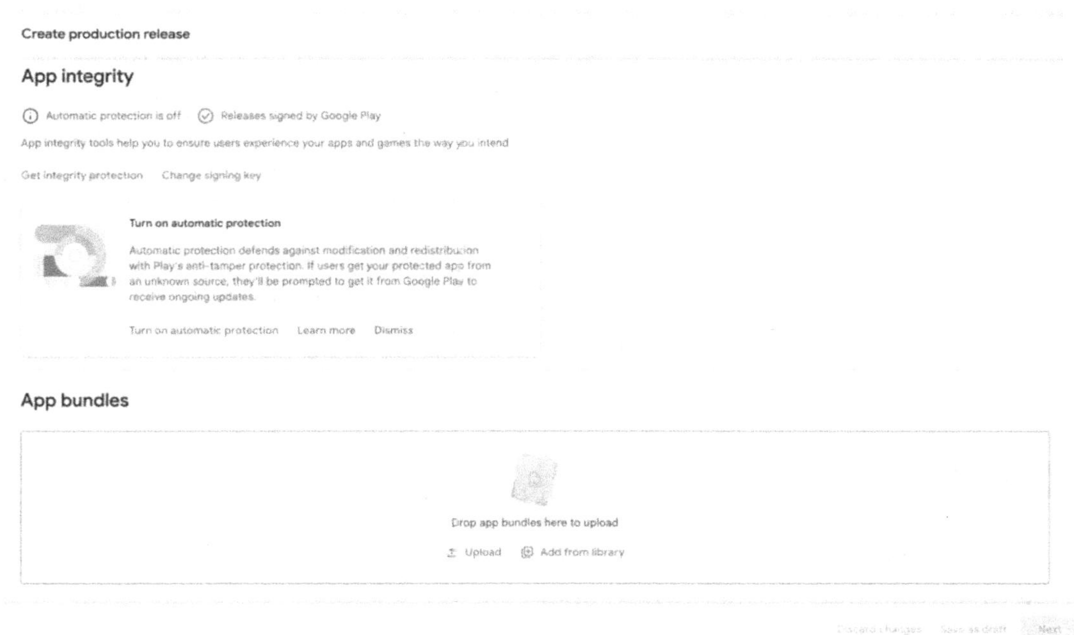

After upload, the Play Console performs automated checks to validate the bundle, ensuring correct signing, versioning, and technical compliance.

Following the successful upload, developers must complete required information including

- Store listing details such as app description and screenshots
- Content rating questionnaire
- Data safety and privacy declarations

Once all mandatory sections are completed, the release can be reviewed and submitted for approval.

Google typically processes submissions quickly, with many apps approved within hours to a few days, depending on review requirements and policy checks.

9.2 Creating iOS Production Build in React Native

Producing an iOS production build in React Native involves a structured process that integrates Apple's signing ecosystem, project configuration in Xcode, and application archiving. Unlike Android, where the build system is primarily managed through Gradle, iOS relies on certificates, provisioning profiles, and a tightly controlled distribution workflow. These mechanisms ensure application security, authenticity, and compliance with platform standards.

Applications developed for iOS are distributed through the ecosystem maintained by Apple, which enforces strict guidelines for build signing and validation. As a result, developers must carefully configure project identifiers, manage credentials, and generate properly archived builds before submission.

9.2.1 Step 1: Configuring the Bundle Identifier

The bundle identifier uniquely identifies an application within the iOS ecosystem. It follows a reverse domain naming convention, such as

```
com.companyname.applicationname
```

In a React Native project, the bundle identifier is configured within the iOS project settings in Xcode. This value must exactly match the identifier registered in the Apple Developer portal and App Store Connect.

Consistency in the bundle identifier is critical, as mismatches will prevent the application from being signed or uploaded successfully.

9.2.2 Step 2: Setting Up Certificates and Signing

Before an iOS application can be distributed publicly, it must be digitally signed using certificates issued through the developer program maintained by Apple. This signing process verifies the identity of the developer and ensures that the application has not been modified since it was built. Apple's certificate-based security model plays a critical role in protecting users and maintaining the integrity of the App Store ecosystem.

iOS signing relies on three primary components: **certificates**, **provisioning profiles**, and the **bundle identifier**.

Component	Purpose	Key Function	Where It Is Configured	Why It Is Important
Certificate	Identifies the developer	Proves the developer's digital identity	Apple Developer account and Xcode	Ensures the app is built by a trusted source
Provisioning Profile	Links app, certificate, and devices	Authorizes where and how the app can run	Apple Developer portal and Xcode	Controls app installation and distribution
Bundle Identifier	Uniquely identifies the app	Connects the app to its signing assets	Xcode project settings	Distinguishes the app within Apple's ecosystem

In React Native projects, signing configuration is managed within Xcode. Developers can choose between automatic signing and manual signing. Automatic signing is recommended for most projects, as Xcode handles certificate creation, renewal, and provisioning profile management internally. To enable this option, developers simply select their development team within the project's Signing and Capabilities settings. Xcode then generates and applies the required credentials automatically.

Manual signing, typically used in enterprise environments or complex release pipelines, requires developers to create and manage certificates and provisioning profiles through Apple's developer portal. Once created, these assets are downloaded and installed in Xcode, where they are explicitly selected for the project. While manual signing offers greater control, it also increases configuration complexity and the risk of errors.

9.2.3 Step 3: Setting Version and Build Number

iOS uses two separate values to track application releases: the Version number and the Build number. While these values serve different purposes, both must be configured correctly for every production build.

In Xcode project settings:

- **Version**: User visible (e.g., 1.0.0)
- **Build**: Increment for each upload

Apple requires the build number to increase every time.

In a React Native iOS project, both values are configured within Xcode under the project's General settings. The Version field corresponds to `CFBundleShortVersionString`, while the Build field corresponds to `CFBundleVersion` in the application's configuration file. Developers can update these values directly through Xcode's interface or within the project's property list files if manual configuration is preferred.

9.2.4 Step 4: Switching to Release Configuration and Archiving the iOS Application

Before generating a production-ready iOS build, it is essential to ensure that the project is configured to use the Release build configuration rather than the default Debug mode. The Release configuration enables compiler optimizations, removes debugging utilities, and produces a performance-optimized binary suitable for public distribution. This step is critical, as builds created in Debug mode are not intended for submission and may include development tools that violate App Store requirements.

In Xcode, the active build configuration is controlled through the project's scheme settings. Developers should verify that the scheme is set to use the Release configuration for the archive action. This ensures that when the application is compiled for distribution, it reflects the same optimized behavior expected by end users. Using the Release configuration also applies code optimizations and reduces the overall application size, contributing to improved runtime performance.

Once the Release configuration is confirmed, the next step is to create an archive of the application. Archiving compiles the project into a structured package that includes the app binary, resources, and signing information. This archive serves as the official production build that can be validated and uploaded for store submission.

To create an archive, developers select a physical device or the generic iOS device target in Xcode and then choose the Archive option from the Product menu. Xcode performs a full compilation process using the Release configuration and, upon completion, automatically opens the Organizer window displaying the newly created archive.

The archive represents the finalized version of the application prepared for distribution. From this point, developers can perform validation checks to identify potential issues related to signing, configuration, or compatibility. After successful validation, the archived build can be uploaded directly to App Store Connect for review.

In summary, switching to the Release configuration ensures that the application is optimized and free from development artifacts, while archiving transforms the project into a distributable production build. Together, these steps form the core of the iOS build preparation process and are essential for successful submission to the ecosystem maintained by Apple.

9.2.5 Step 5: Uploading to App Store Connect

Before uploading any production build, developers must first register the application in App Store Connect. This is done by logging in to the platform, navigating to the My Apps section, and selecting the Add App option. During this setup process, developers are required to enter essential information such as the application name, primary language, and the corresponding bundle identifier, followed by selecting iOS as the target platform. This step establishes the application record and links the project to Apple's distribution system.

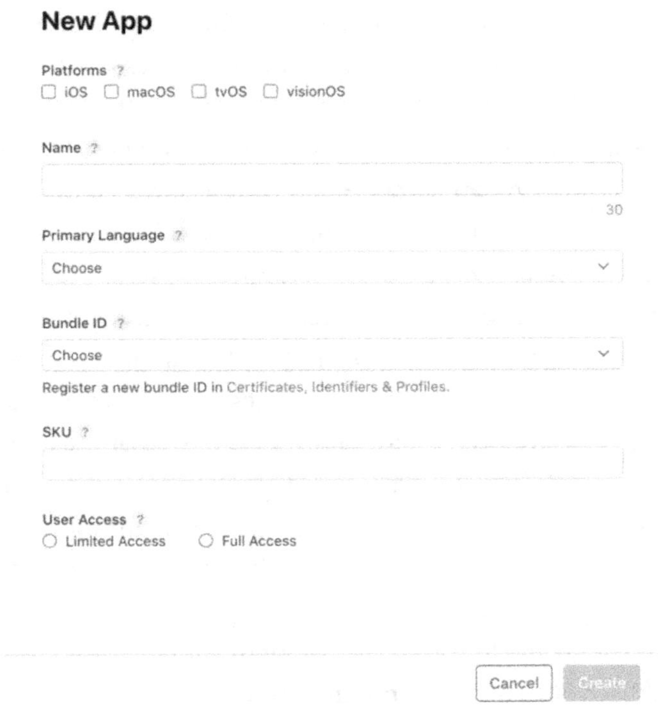

Now the production build must be uploaded to App Store Connect, the platform managed by Apple for app distribution and review. Uploading the build makes it available for assignment to an app version and submission for approval.

The upload is performed directly from Xcode through the Organizer window. Developers select the archived build, choose the distribution option for App Store deployment, and proceed with the upload. During this process, Xcode verifies signing credentials and technical requirements before securely transferring the build to Apple's servers.

Once the upload is complete and processing finishes, the build appears in App Store Connect under the application's build list. It can then be attached to a version, metadata can be finalized, and the app can be submitted for review.

9.3 Comparison of Android vs. iOS Store Submission Workflows

After generating production builds, developers must follow platform-specific workflows to publish their applications. Although both Android and iOS aim to ensure quality and security, their submission processes differ in tooling, review style, and release control mechanisms.

Android applications are submitted through the ecosystem managed by Google, while iOS applications are reviewed and distributed through the platform maintained by Apple.

Aspect	Android (React Native)	iOS (React Native)
Platform Ecosystem	Managed by Google	Managed by Apple
Primary Build Tool	Gradle	Xcode
Production Build Format	Android App Bundle (AAB)	Xcode Archive (.xcarchive)
App Identifier	Application ID (e.g., com.company.app)	Bundle identifier (e.g., com.company.app)
Versioning System	versionCode (internal), versionName (user-facing)	Build number (internal), version (user-facing)
Signing Method	Keystore file with private key	Certificates and provisioning profiles
Signing Configuration Location	android/app/build.gradle	Xcode project settings
Optimization Tools	R8/ProGuard for shrinking and obfuscation	Xcode compiler optimizations
Build Command	./gradlew bundleRelease	Product → Archive in Xcode
Validation Step	Manual testing of AAB	Built-in Xcode validation
Upload Method	Play Console upload	Direct upload via Xcode
Common Issues	Keystore mismatch, version conflicts	Certificate expiration, profile mismatch
Automation Support	Gradle + CI pipelines	Xcode + CI pipelines

9.3.1 Key Differences in Practice

- Android offers greater flexibility with testing tracks and phased rollouts, allowing gradual exposure of new versions.
- iOS emphasizes strict manual review, ensuring higher consistency with platform guidelines.
- Android submissions are largely console-driven, while iOS submissions are tightly integrated with Xcode.

9.4 Summary

This chapter explained how to prepare and release a React Native application for distribution on the mobile platforms operated by Apple and Google. It covered the creation of production-ready builds for both Android and iOS, including versioning, signing, optimization, and build generation.

The chapter also detailed the store submission workflows, highlighting how to upload builds, complete required compliance information, and submit applications for review. A comparison between Android and iOS processes helped clarify platform-specific differences in release management.

By following these practices, developers can confidently move from development to successful public release. A few of the key pointers that will help you are as follows:

- Android releases use the Android App Bundle with Gradle-based signing and optimization.
- iOS releases require certificate-based signing and archiving through Xcode.
- Version and build number management is essential for smooth updates.
- Store submission involves completing metadata and compliance forms.
- Understanding both Android and iOS workflows reduces release delays and errors.
- Production builds differ from debug builds and must be optimized and securely signed.

CHAPTER 10

Introduction: The React Native Ecosystem

React Native does not exist in isolation. While the framework provides the core abstractions for rendering native interfaces using JavaScript and React, real-world applications depend on a much larger environment of libraries, tools, and services that extend its capabilities.

In practice, a production React Native application is shaped as much by its ecosystem choices as by its internal code. Navigation frameworks determine user flow, animation libraries influence perceived performance, back-end services affect reliability and scalability, and distribution tools control how software reaches users. These concerns live outside the core framework, yet they define the quality and longevity of the final product.

As React Native has matured, this surrounding ecosystem has expanded rapidly. Thousands of third-party packages are available through npm, and a growing number of platform services offer analytics, crash reporting, feature management, and over-the-air updates tailored specifically for mobile applications. At the same time, platform evolution and architectural changes have made some tools obsolete while elevating others to critical infrastructure.

This chapter focuses on developing *ecosystem literacy*—the ability to understand, evaluate, and extend the tools that surround React Native. Rather than cataloging specific libraries, it emphasizes principles that help you make sound decisions in a fast-changing environment. You will learn how to reason about third-party dependencies, how modern services integrate into React Native workflows, and when it makes sense to extract and publish your own packages.

The goal is not to master every tool, but to understand the forces that shape the ecosystem so that your applications remain maintainable, adaptable, and professional over time.

A. Nalwaya and A. Paul, *React Native for Mobile Development*, https://doi.org/10.1007/979-8-8688-2977-2_10

10.1 Why the Ecosystem Matters More Than the Framework

When developers first encounter React Native, it is commonly presented as a framework for sharing code between iOS and Android. While accurate, this framing understates how React Native functions in real-world systems. In practice, React Native behaves less like a self-contained framework and more like a *platform* whose effectiveness depends heavily on the ecosystem that surrounds it.

Modern React Native applications rarely rely on the core APIs alone. Navigation systems, animation engines, gesture handlers, networking layers, crash reporters, analytics pipelines, feature-flag systems, and distribution tooling are almost always sourced from outside the framework. These elements are not peripheral; they are essential to delivering applications that are reliable, observable, and maintainable in production.

As a result, the architectural center of gravity in a React Native application often shifts away from the framework itself and toward the ecosystem choices made around it.

10.1.1 React Native As the Center of a Larger System

To understand why ecosystem decisions matter, it helps to visualize React Native not as the full stack, but as one layer within a broader system.

10.1.2 Conceptual Structure: The React Native Ecosystem

```
+-----------------------------------------------------+
|                External Platform Services           |
|  Analytics | Crash Reporting | Feature Flags | OTA  |
|  Auth      | Push            | Monitoring    | CI/CD |
+--------------------▲--------------------------------+
                     |
+--------------------|--------------------------------+
|          Community & Vendor Libraries               |
|  Navigation | Animations | State | Networking        |
|  Device APIs | UI Systems | Tooling                  |
```

```
+--------------------▲----------------------------+
                     |
+---------------------|---------------------------+
|             Expo (Optional Abstraction Layer)    |
|   Managed APIs | Build Tools | OTA | Dev Experience  |
+--------------------▲----------------------------+
                     |
+---------------------|---------------------------+
|            React Native Core Runtime             |
|   JS Engine | Fabric Renderer | TurboModules     |
|   JSI | Scheduling | Layout Engine            |
+--------------------▲----------------------------+
                     |
+---------------------|---------------------------+
|           Mobile Platforms (iOS / Android)       |
|   OS APIs | Hardware | System UI | Security Model |
+-------------------------------------------------+
```

This diagram makes a critical point explicit:**most production-critical behavior in a React Native app lives outside the framework itself.**

The React Native core coordinates rendering and execution, but nearly everything that determines stability, performance, observability, and release velocity is delegated upward to libraries and services.

10.1.3 A Flow-Oriented View of Responsibility

Another way to reason about the ecosystem is to view it as a flow of responsibility rather than a stack of layers:

```
User Experience
      ↑
Application Code
      ↑
Third-Party Libraries (navigation, animation, state)
      ↑
```

```
React Native Runtime
      ↑
Native Platform APIs (iOS / Android)
      ↑
Operating System & Hardware
```

Separately, but continuously interacting with this flow:

Monitoring · Analytics · Feature Flags · OTA · Distribution

These external services do not sit *inside* the application, yet they influence behavior at runtime, during rollout, and after release. This is why ecosystem decisions tend to surface later, often under production pressure.

10.1.4 The Hidden Cost of Ecosystem Decisions

Framework APIs are governed by a relatively small and stable core team. Ecosystem components, by contrast, evolve independently. Each library or service has its own

- Maintenance incentives
- Release cadence
- Compatibility guarantees
- Longevity horizon

This creates a form of hidden coupling. Over time, application architecture becomes constrained not by React Native itself, but by third-party abstractions that may lag behind platform changes or architectural shifts.

These costs are rarely visible when a dependency is first added. They tend to surface during

- Major framework upgrades
- Operating system changes
- Security or privacy reviews
- Long-term maintenance cycles

For this reason, ecosystem choices must be treated as **architectural decisions**, not convenience shortcuts.

10.1.5 Ecosystem Literacy As a Professional Skill

In professional environments, success is measured not only by how quickly features can be built, but by how reliably systems can evolve. Ecosystem literacy—the ability to evaluate, integrate, and replace third-party tools—is therefore a core engineering skill.

Ecosystem-literate teams

- Distinguish between delegation and dependency
- Contain third-party code behind clear boundaries
- Anticipate change rather than assuming permanence
- Optimize for long-term adaptability, not short-term velocity

This mindset reframes the question from *"Which library should we use?"* to

> *"What responsibility are we outsourcing, and what risks does that introduce?"*

10.1.6 Note: Treat Dependencies As Architecture

Every dependency you add becomes part of your system's architecture.

If removing a library later would require redesigning screens, rewriting state flows, or blocking framework upgrades, that dependency is no longer an implementation detail—it is a structural choice. Professional React Native teams make ecosystem decisions with the same care they apply to state management or navigation design.

10.2 Understanding the Shape of the React Native Ecosystem

The React Native ecosystem is often described using vague terms such as *large, diverse,* or *fast-moving*. While these descriptions are accurate, they do little to help developers make sound architectural decisions. Scale alone is not the challenge. The real challenge lies in understanding how different parts of the ecosystem relate to one another and what responsibilities they assume within a production application.

Without a structural model, ecosystem decisions are typically driven by surface-level signals: popularity, blog posts, conference talks, or short-term convenience. This approach may work for prototypes, but it breaks down quickly as applications grow and teams are forced to maintain software over multiple years.

To reason effectively about the React Native ecosystem, we must first understand its *shape*.

10.2.1 From a Flat List to a Structured System

At first glance, the ecosystem appears as a flat collection of libraries and services, all accessible through npm or external dashboards. In practice, however, these tools occupy very different positions relative to the React Native runtime and the underlying mobile platforms.

Some tools *define how your application is structured*. Others merely assist with implementation details. Some execute inside the app process, while others influence behavior after the app has already shipped. Treating these components as equivalent obscures important differences in risk and responsibility.

A more useful mental model divides the ecosystem into three broad zones:

1. **Core runtime components**
2. **Adjacent libraries and tooling**
3. **External services**

Each zone evolves differently, fails differently, and demands a different level of caution.

10.2.2 Core Runtime Components: The Stable Center

At the center of the ecosystem sits the React Native runtime itself. This includes the JavaScript execution environment, the rendering system, the native interoperability layer, and the scheduling mechanisms that coordinate work across threads.

This layer defines what React Native *is*. It evolves deliberately and conservatively, because changes here affect every application built on top of it. Backward compatibility, platform correctness, and long-term stability are primary concerns.

From an application developer's perspective, this layer is largely non-negotiable. You do not replace it; you adapt to it. Most ecosystem decisions therefore involve tools that sit *around* this core rather than inside it.

10.2.3 Adjacent Libraries: Extending the Runtime from Within

Surrounding the core runtime is a dense layer of adjacent libraries. These are the packages developers interact with most frequently: navigation systems, animation frameworks, state management solutions, networking abstractions, and device-level APIs.

What unites these libraries is that they execute *inside* the application process and integrate directly with React Native's APIs. Once adopted, they become part of the application's internal architecture.

This proximity comes with consequences. Adjacent libraries shape how screens are composed, how state flows through the app, and how users interact with the interface. Replacing them later is often expensive, not because the code is difficult to rewrite, but because the abstractions they introduce permeate the entire system.

This is why adjacent libraries represent the highest concentration of long-term architectural risk in the ecosystem.

10.2.4 External Services: Influencing Behavior from the Outside

Beyond the application boundary lies a different class of ecosystem components: external services. These include analytics platforms, crash reporting systems, performance monitors, feature-flag providers, over-the-air update mechanisms, and distribution pipelines.

Unlike libraries, these services do not live entirely inside the application bundle. They operate partially or entirely outside the app process and often influence behavior at runtime, during rollout, or after release.

This external position grants them significant power. Feature flags can change user experience without a new app version. OTA updates can alter code paths post-deployment. Monitoring systems shape how teams understand failures and performance regressions.

At the same time, this power introduces new forms of risk: vendor lock-in, policy changes, pricing shifts, and compliance requirements. External services must therefore be evaluated not only as technical tools, but as long-term operational commitments.

10.2.5 A Layered View of Responsibility

When viewed together, the ecosystem forms a layered system of responsibility rather than a collection of interchangeable tools:

- The **core runtime** defines execution and rendering.
- **Adjacent libraries** extend capabilities from within the app.
- **External services** influence behavior from outside the app.
- The **mobile platforms** ultimately govern hardware access, security, and policy.

Each layer moves at a different pace. Problems arise when developers assume uniform stability across layers or when volatile components are treated as foundational infrastructure.

Professional teams acknowledge these differences explicitly. They design boundaries around volatile dependencies, plan for replacement rather than permanence, and treat ecosystem evolution as an ongoing constraint rather than a one-time decision.

10.2.6 Note: Structure First, Tools Second

Before evaluating *which* library or service to use, determine *where* it sits in the ecosystem. Tools that shape application structure demand long-term commitment. Tools that operate externally demand operational discipline. Classification is the first step toward sustainable ecosystem decisions.

10.3 Categories of Third-Party Libraries in React Native

The size of the React Native ecosystem can make third-party libraries appear interchangeable. Many packages offer overlapping functionality, similar APIs, or comparable popularity metrics. However, treating libraries as generic utilities obscures the most important distinction: *the kind of architectural responsibility a library assumes once it is adopted.*

This section organizes third-party libraries not by popularity or recommendation, but by the role they play within an application. Each category carries a different level of coupling, risk, and long-term consequence. Understanding these differences allows teams to evaluate dependencies proportionally rather than uniformly.

10.3.1 Libraries That Define Application Structure

Some libraries sit so close to the root of an application that they effectively define its structure. Navigation systems are the clearest example. They determine how screens are composed, how users move through the application, and how state is scoped across routes.

Once a navigation system is in place, it influences nearly every screen and feature. Components are organized around it, deep linking logic is built into it, and testing strategies adapt to its behavior. Replacing it later is possible, but rarely trivial.

Because of this, structural libraries must be evaluated as architectural frameworks rather than conveniences. Their APIs, mental models, and long-term stability matter more than short-term ergonomics.

10.3.2 Libraries That Shape Data Flow and State

State management libraries occupy a slightly different position. They do not usually dictate screen layout, but they define how data moves through the application and how components coordinate with one another.

Over time, state abstractions become deeply embedded in component logic, side-effect handling, and debugging workflows. Even libraries that begin as thin wrappers can evolve into central organizing principles for an application.

The key risk in this category is not complexity, but permanence. Once a data flow pattern is adopted broadly, reversing it requires widespread refactoring. Teams should therefore evaluate state libraries based on clarity, longevity, and alignment with their preferred mental models rather than novelty.

10.3.3 Libraries at the JavaScript–Native Boundary

Animation, gesture, and performance-sensitive libraries occupy a particularly delicate position in the ecosystem. These tools bridge declarative JavaScript APIs with imperative native execution. They often rely on internal runtime details, specialized threads, or tight coordination with the rendering system.

Because of this proximity to the runtime, such libraries are more sensitive to architectural shifts within React Native itself. Changes to rendering, scheduling, or threading models can have disproportionate impact here.

These libraries reward careful adoption. When chosen well, they enable fluid, responsive interfaces. When chosen poorly or adopted casually, they can become sources of instability or upgrade friction.

10.3.4 Libraries That Abstract Device Capabilities

Another major category includes libraries that expose device features such as storage, sensors, media capture, and system services. At the API level, these libraries often appear simple and ergonomic. Internally, however, they manage permissions, platform divergence, and lifecycle complexity.

The architectural risk here lies less in application structure and more in platform evolution. Operating system policies change, permission models evolve, and hardware behavior differs across devices. Libraries in this category must be evaluated for platform parity, maintenance activity, and responsiveness to OS-level changes.

10.3.5 Libraries That Address Networking and Reliability

Networking, caching, and synchronization libraries operate across the entire application surface. While they may not define UI structure directly, they influence reliability, error handling, and performance in nearly every feature.

Poor choices in this category tend to surface under load, poor connectivity, or partial failure scenarios—precisely when applications are most vulnerable. As such, these libraries should be evaluated not just for API design, but for failure behavior and long-term support.

10.3.6 Libraries for Developer Experience and Tooling

Finally, there is a broad class of libraries focused on developer experience: debugging tools, logging systems, performance inspectors, and build-time validators. These tools rarely affect user-facing behavior directly, but they shape how teams build, diagnose, and maintain applications.

Architecturally, these libraries tend to be low-risk, but they can still influence workflows significantly. Teams should be mindful of how deeply such tools are embedded into development processes, especially when they affect onboarding or CI pipelines.

10.3.7 Comparing Categories by Architectural Impact

When viewed together, the categories form a spectrum rather than discrete boxes:

```
Lower Impact
↑
Developer Tooling
Networking & Reliability
Device Abstractions
Runtime-Sensitive Libraries
State Management
Structural Libraries
↓
Higher Impact
```

This spectrum reinforces a central idea: **not all dependencies deserve the same level of scrutiny**.

10.3.8 Note: Evaluate Proportionally

The deeper a library's influence on application structure and runtime behavior, the higher the standard it must meet. Lightweight utilities can be experimental. Structural dependencies should be conservative. Align evaluation effort with architectural impact, not with perceived popularity.

10.4 Evaluating Library Quality and Long-Term Risk

Once third-party libraries are classified by the role they play in an application, the next challenge is evaluation. This is where many teams struggle. Popularity metrics, conference talks, and social media recommendations provide signals, but they are often weak predictors of long-term suitability.

Evaluating a React Native library is not about determining whether it works today. It is about estimating whether it will continue to work *as the platform, the framework, and the application itself evolve.*

This section presents a set of evaluation lenses that help surface long-term risk early, when it is still inexpensive to change course.

10.4.1 Popularity Is a Signal, Not a Guarantee

Metrics such as download counts, GitHub stars, or social visibility are often the first indicators developers consider. While these signals can suggest adoption momentum, they are poor proxies for sustainability.

Highly popular libraries can still be risky if

- They are maintained by a small number of contributors
- They lag behind architectural changes in React Native
- Their APIs encourage tight coupling to internal details

Conversely, smaller libraries with focused scope and disciplined maintenance may prove far more durable over time.

Popularity should therefore be treated as an *entry point* for evaluation, not a conclusion.

10.4.2 Maintenance Health and Ownership

One of the strongest predictors of long-term viability is how a library is maintained.

Healthy libraries tend to exhibit consistent, observable behavior over time:

- Issues are acknowledged, even if not resolved immediately.
- Releases occur at a predictable cadence.
- Breaking changes are documented and justified.
- Compatibility updates track React Native releases reasonably closely.

Equally important is *ownership clarity*. Libraries maintained by identifiable teams or organizations often provide stronger continuity than those dependent on a single individual's availability. This does not imply that community-maintained projects are inferior, but it does mean their risk profile is different.

A professional evaluation acknowledges this difference explicitly.

10.4.3 Architectural Alignment with React Native

Libraries do not exist in a vacuum. They either align with React Native's architectural direction or work against it.

Well-aligned libraries

- Respect asynchronous execution models
- Avoid blocking the JavaScript thread
- Adapt as rendering and native interop mechanisms evolve
- Minimize reliance on private or unstable APIs

Misaligned libraries may work initially, but they accumulate technical debt as the framework evolves. Over time, this misalignment manifests as upgrade friction, performance regressions, or outright incompatibility.

Evaluating alignment requires more than reading documentation; it requires understanding how the library interacts with the runtime.

10.4.4 API Surface Area and Coupling

Another critical factor is how deeply a library embeds itself into application code. Libraries with broad, invasive APIs tend to increase coupling. Their abstractions spread across components, state logic, and business rules, making later replacement costly.

By contrast, libraries with narrow, well-defined responsibilities are easier to isolate and replace.

When evaluating a library, it is useful to ask:

- How many files will import this dependency?
- Will core application concepts depend on its abstractions?
- Can it be wrapped or confined behind an internal interface?

These questions help reveal whether a dependency is likely to become architectural infrastructure or remain an implementation detail.

10.4.5 Type Safety, Documentation, and Developer Ergonomics

While long-term risk is often architectural, day-to-day usability still matters. Poor documentation, unclear error behavior, or inconsistent typing can slow teams down and introduce subtle bugs.

Libraries that invest in

- Clear documentation
- Predictable error handling
- Strong type definitions

tend to scale better across teams and over time. These qualities are not cosmetic; they reduce cognitive load and make future maintenance more predictable.

10.4.6 Upgrade and Exit Strategy

Perhaps the most overlooked aspect of evaluation is planning for change. No dependency should be assumed permanent.

A responsible evaluation includes an implicit exit strategy:

- How difficult would it be to replace this library?
- Are alternatives conceptually similar or radically different?
- Does the library lock data or logic into proprietary formats?

Libraries that allow gradual migration, parallel adoption, or partial replacement are significantly less risky than those that require wholesale rewrites.

10.4.7 Note: Evaluate Libraries Under Future Pressure

Do not evaluate a library based on how it feels to adopt today.Evaluate it based on how it will behave during your *next major upgrade, next platform change*, or *next team expansion*. Libraries that age well are rarely the most exciting ones.

10.5 The Role of Expo in the Modern Ecosystem

Few topics in the React Native ecosystem generate as much polarized opinion as Expo. It is alternately described as a productivity multiplier, a beginner crutch, a strategic dependency, or an unnecessary abstraction. These labels, while emotionally charged, are not particularly useful for architectural reasoning.

To understand Expo's real role, it must be evaluated not as a competing framework, but as an **ecosystem layer** that sits alongside React Native and reshapes how developers interact with native capabilities, tooling, and distribution workflows.

10.5.1 Expo As an Ecosystem Multiplier

At its core, Expo does not replace React Native. It builds *on top of it*. The React Native runtime, rendering model, and component system remain unchanged. What Expo provides is a curated, integrated layer of tooling and APIs that reduce the friction of working with native functionality.

Expo's value lies in *coordination*:

- Pre-integrated native modules
- Unified configuration mechanisms

- Managed build and deployment workflows
- Consistent developer experience across platforms

By bundling these concerns together, Expo lowers the activation energy required to build and ship applications, particularly for teams without deep native expertise.

10.5.2 Managed vs. Bare: A Spectrum, Not a Fork

Expo is often described as offering two distinct workflows: *Managed* and *Bare*. While this distinction is real, it is more accurate to think of it as a spectrum rather than a hard boundary.

- In the **Managed workflow**, developers interact almost exclusively with JavaScript APIs and configuration files. Native code exists, but it is largely hidden and controlled by Expo.
- In the **Bare workflow**, developers retain full access to native code while still benefiting from Expo's tooling, libraries, and services.

The critical point is that adopting Expo does not permanently lock an application into a single mode of operation. Teams can move along this spectrum as requirements evolve.

This flexibility makes Expo less of a commitment than it is often perceived to be—provided teams understand the boundaries they are accepting at each stage.

10.5.3 What Expo Abstracts—And What It Does Not

Expo abstracts integration complexity, not platform reality.

On one side of that boundary, Expo handles the things that are genuinely repetitive and mechanical: wiring up device capabilities, managing permission flows, configuring builds, and smoothing over cross-platform inconsistencies. These are real costs that Expo eliminates.

On the other side, nothing changes. Platform-specific behavior, OS-level permission policies, performance constraints, and native lifecycle rules all remain exactly as the operating system defines them. Expo has no authority over these—and does not claim to.

This distinction matters in practice. Expo reduces the surface area developers must actively manage, but it does not change the underlying rules of mobile platforms. Teams that adopt Expo expecting it to remove the need for native understanding tend to encounter that reality later, usually at the worst possible moment—during a production issue or a platform rejection.

The right mental model is not "Expo instead of native" but "Expo on top of native."

10.5.4 Expo's Architectural Trade-Offs

Like any abstraction layer, Expo introduces trade-offs.

On the benefit side:

- Faster onboarding
- Reduced native boilerplate
- Consistent APIs across platforms
- Streamlined build and update workflows

On the cost side:

- Dependence on Expo's release cadence
- Limited control over certain native behaviors in Managed mode
- Need to align with Expo-supported APIs and versions

These trade-offs are neither inherently good nor bad. Their suitability depends on the application's requirements, team composition, and tolerance for abstraction.

10.5.5 Expo in Long-Lived Code Bases

In long-lived projects, Expo's role often evolves. Teams may begin in the Managed workflow to maximize speed, then gradually adopt Bare patterns as custom native requirements emerge. Others may remain fully managed for the lifetime of the application if their needs align with Expo's supported capabilities.

What matters is not whether Expo is used, but *how consciously it is adopted.*

Expo works best when treated as

- An accelerator, not a shortcut
- An abstraction, not a substitute for understanding
- A layer that can be exited deliberately if necessary

10.5.6 Note: Choose Expo for Leverage, Not Avoidance

Expo is most effective when it amplifies a team's capabilities, not when it is used to avoid understanding the platform.

If your application's requirements align with Expo's abstractions, it can dramatically reduce complexity.

If they do not, forcing alignment will create friction elsewhere.

The right question is not *"Should we use Expo?"* but *"Which responsibilities are we delegating, and why?"*

10.6 Back-End and Platform Services Around React Native Apps

As React Native applications mature, an increasing share of their behavior is shaped not by code that ships with the app, but by services that operate alongside it. These back-end and platform services provide visibility, control, and adaptability in production environments where redeploying the app for every change is impractical.

This layer of the ecosystem is often underestimated because it is not always visible during development. Yet in production systems, services for analytics, monitoring, configuration, and messaging frequently have more influence on user experience and operational success than any single library.

10.6.1 Services As Architectural Extensions

Back-end and platform services differ fundamentally from in-app libraries. They do not simply extend functionality; they *extend responsibility*.

Once integrated, these services participate in

- Runtime decision-making
- Release and rollout strategies
- Failure detection and diagnosis
- Product experimentation and iteration

From an architectural standpoint, they become part of the system even though they do not reside within the application code base.

This distinction matters because services

- Can change behavior without a new app release
- Introduce operational dependencies and policies
- Evolve independently of application versions

In effect, they act as *external control planes* for mobile applications.

10.6.2 Common Service Categories in React Native Applications

Although vendors differ, most services fall into a small number of functional categories.

Analytics and telemetry services collect usage data, user behavior metrics, and funnel information. Their value lies not in raw event counts, but in enabling teams to understand how features perform in real-world conditions.

Crash reporting and error monitoring services surface failures that cannot be reproduced easily during development. In mobile environments, where devices, OS versions, and network conditions vary widely, this visibility is essential.

Remote configuration and feature flag services allow teams to modify application behavior dynamically. They are often used to control feature rollout, enable experimentation, or mitigate issues without forcing users to update the app.

Push notification and messaging services bridge the gap between the application and the user outside active sessions. They influence engagement, retention, and time-sensitive communication.

Platforms such as **Firebase** bundle several of these capabilities together, while other providers focus on narrower problem domains. From an architectural perspective, the distinction is less important than the responsibilities being delegated.

10.6.3 Operational and Organizational Implications

Unlike libraries, services introduce concerns that extend beyond engineering. They often involve

- Vendor contracts and pricing models
- Data governance and privacy considerations
- Compliance with regional regulations
- Cross-team ownership between engineering, product, and operations

These factors influence architectural decisions as much as technical fit. A service that is easy to integrate but difficult to govern may introduce long-term risk disproportionate to its short-term benefits.

Professional teams account for these implications early, particularly in regulated or large-scale environments.

10.6.4 Latency, Reliability, and Failure Modes

Another key difference between services and libraries lies in failure behavior. Service outages, degraded performance, or misconfigurations can affect application behavior in ways that local code cannot.

For example:

- A misconfigured feature flag can disable critical functionality.
- An unavailable analytics endpoint can impact startup performance.
- A remote configuration change can alter logic paths unexpectedly.

Because these failures occur outside the app's control, defensive design is essential. Services should be integrated in ways that fail gracefully, preserve core functionality, and avoid blocking critical user flows.

10.6.5 Treating Services As First-Class Architecture

As applications scale, services should be treated with the same rigor as internal components. This includes

- Clear ownership and accountability
- Documented integration boundaries
- Explicit assumptions about availability and consistency
- Periodic reassessment of necessity and cost

When services are added incrementally without a unifying strategy, applications tend to accumulate invisible complexity that surfaces only under pressure.

10.6.6 Note: Design for Service Failure

External services should enhance your application, not hold it hostage. Assume that every service will eventually be unavailable, misconfigured, or deprecated. Integrate them defensively, and ensure that core user experiences remain intact when they fail.

10.7 Feature Flags, Experimentation, and Over-the-Air Updates

Modern mobile applications are no longer static artifacts released at fixed intervals. Increasingly, their behavior is shaped dynamically through configuration, experimentation, and controlled rollout mechanisms. Feature flags, experimentation frameworks, and over-the-air (OTA) updates sit at the center of this shift.

These tools provide significant leverage, but they also blur the boundary between development, release, and runtime execution. As a result, they must be treated as architectural infrastructure rather than tactical conveniences.

10.7.1 Feature Flags As Runtime Control

Feature flags allow teams to enable or disable functionality without releasing a new version of the application. At a basic level, this capability is used to roll out features gradually or to disable problematic behavior quickly. At scale, however, feature flags become a *control system* for application behavior.

Well-designed flag systems

- Decouple deployment from release
- Enable safer experimentation
- Reduce the blast radius of failures

Poorly designed systems, by contrast, accumulate hidden complexity. Flags multiply, interactions become opaque, and logic paths diverge in ways that are difficult to reason about or test.

Over time, unmanaged feature flags can turn application code into a maze of conditional behavior that is difficult to maintain.

10.7.2 Experimentation and Behavioral Change

Experimentation frameworks extend feature flags by enabling controlled comparison between variants. Rather than simply turning features on or off, these systems allow teams to observe how different behaviors affect user outcomes.

From an architectural standpoint, experimentation introduces additional requirements:

- Deterministic assignment of users to variants
- Stable behavior across sessions
- Clear separation between experimental and baseline logic

Without discipline, experimentation code can leak into core logic and persist long after experiments have concluded. Professional teams plan for experimentation *removal* as deliberately as they plan for experimentation *execution*.

10.7.3 Over-the-Air Updates: Power and Responsibility

OTA updates enable teams to modify application code or configuration after distribution, without requiring users to install a new version from an app store. This capability can be invaluable for bug fixes, minor adjustments, or emergency mitigations.

However, OTA updates also raise important architectural and policy considerations:

- Platform owners impose rules on what can be changed remotely.
- Users may experience behavior changes without explicit updates.
- Debugging becomes more complex when runtime code diverges from store builds.

OTA mechanisms should therefore be constrained carefully. They are best suited for incremental, reversible changes rather than structural modifications.

10.7.4 A Controlled Flow of Change

When used responsibly, feature flags, experimentation, and OTA updates form a controlled flow of change:

Build ➤ Deploy ➤ Configure ➤ Observe ➤ Adjust

Each stage introduces a feedback loop. Problems arise when changes bypass observation or when configuration becomes a substitute for proper releases.

The goal is not to eliminate release cycles, but to make them safer and more predictable.

10.7.5 Guardrails and Governance

Because these mechanisms affect runtime behavior directly, they require governance beyond code review. Effective teams establish

- Naming and lifecycle conventions for flags
- Clear ownership of configuration changes
- Auditable change histories
- Automated cleanup of expired experiments

Without such guardrails, the flexibility these tools provide can quickly turn into operational risk.

10.7.6 Note: Configuration Is Code, Even When It Isn't

Treat feature flags, experiments, and OTA updates with the same rigor as application code.

If a configuration change can break user experience, it deserves review, ownership, and rollback plans.

Flexibility without discipline is not agility—it is instability.

10.8 Distribution Pipelines for React Native Apps

Regardless of how sophisticated an application's architecture may be, it ultimately derives value only when it reaches users. Distribution is therefore not a logistical afterthought, but a core part of the React Native ecosystem that directly influences development velocity, quality assurance, and operational risk.

In mobile development, distribution constraints are imposed by platform owners. These constraints shape how quickly changes can be delivered, how issues can be mitigated, and how experimentation can be conducted. Understanding distribution pipelines is essential for making informed ecosystem and architectural decisions.

10.8.1 Distribution As a Continuation of Architecture

From an architectural perspective, distribution determines *when* and *how* changes become visible to users. It defines the boundary between development-time behavior and production reality.

Key aspects of this boundary include

- Review and approval processes
- Release timing and sequencing
- Rollback and recovery mechanisms
- User segmentation and staged rollouts

Because React Native applications share distribution channels with fully native apps, they inherit the same constraints and expectations. Cross-platform code does not imply cross-platform distribution freedom.

10.8.2 Internal Testing and Pre-release Validation

Before reaching end users, applications typically pass through one or more internal testing stages. These stages are critical for validating behavior across devices, OS versions, and network conditions.

On iOS, tools such as **TestFlight** provide a structured mechanism for internal and external beta testing. Android offers comparable tracks through its own distribution infrastructure. While the tools differ, the underlying goal is the same: detect issues in environments that more closely resemble real usage.

These pipelines influence how teams structure releases. Features may be gated, experiments limited, or monitoring intensified during pre-release phases to reduce uncertainty.

10.8.3 Staged Rollouts and Risk Management

Modern distribution pipelines support staged rollouts, where new versions are released gradually to subsets of users. This approach reduces risk by limiting exposure while real-world data is collected.

From an ecosystem perspective, staged rollouts interact closely with

- Crash reporting systems
- Analytics and telemetry
- Feature flags and configuration services

Together, these components form a feedback loop that allows teams to observe, pause, or reverse releases based on evidence rather than speculation.

10.8.4 Distribution Constraints and OTA Boundaries

While over-the-air updates and remote configuration provide flexibility, they do not eliminate the need for disciplined distribution practices. Platform policies restrict what kinds of changes can be made without a store release, particularly when behavior affects user trust, security, or monetization.

As a result, distribution pipelines remain the authoritative path for

- Structural changes
- New capabilities
- Policy-sensitive updates

Architecturally, this reinforces the importance of designing systems where critical changes flow through predictable, auditable channels.

10.8.5 Distribution As a Cross-Functional Concern

Unlike many libraries, distribution tooling affects multiple roles:

- Engineers manage builds and releases.
- Product teams plan rollout strategies.
- QA validates behavior across environments.
- Operations monitor post-release health.

This cross-functional nature makes distribution decisions especially consequential. Tooling that works well for one group but poorly for others introduces friction that slows the entire organization.

10.8.6 Note: Optimize for Repeatability, Not Speed

A fast release process that cannot be repeated reliably is a liability. Design distribution pipelines that are predictable, observable, and reversible—even if they are slightly slower. In mobile ecosystems, confidence scales better than velocity.

10.9 When and Why to Create Your Own npm Package

At some point in a mature React Native code base, teams encounter functionality that no longer feels like application logic. It may be reused across multiple projects, isolated behind a stable interface, or closely tied to a specific technical concern. This moment often raises a natural question: *Should this be extracted into a package?*

Creating an npm package is not merely a mechanical exercise. It is an architectural decision that changes how code is owned, versioned, and maintained. This section focuses on the *decision to extract,* not the mechanics of publishing.

10.9.1 Recognizing the Signals for Extraction

Not all reusable code should become a package. Premature extraction often introduces unnecessary complexity. That said, certain signals strongly suggest that extraction is appropriate.

One such signal is **cross-project reuse**. If the same functionality is being copied or reimplemented across multiple applications, a shared package can reduce duplication and improve consistency.

Another signal is **conceptual stability**. Code that has reached a relatively stable shape—with clear inputs, outputs, and responsibilities—is more suitable for packaging than code that is still evolving rapidly.

A third signal is **boundary clarity**. Functionality that can be cleanly isolated behind a narrow API is far easier to extract and maintain than code that depends heavily on internal application state.

10.9.2 Internal Packages vs. Public Packages

Extraction does not imply publication.

Many teams benefit from creating *internal packages* that are shared within an organization but never exposed publicly. These packages allow for reuse and standardization without the obligations of public support or backward compatibility guarantees.

Public packages, by contrast, introduce additional responsibilities:

- Maintaining compatibility across environments
- Communicating breaking changes clearly
- Responding to issues from unknown consumers
- Supporting use cases beyond the original application

Choosing between internal and public distribution is a strategic decision, not a technical one.

10.9.3 Designing for Unknown Consumers

Publishing a package changes the audience. Application code is written for a known team, with shared context and implicit assumptions. Package APIs must be designed for strangers.

This shift has architectural implications:

- APIs must be explicit and defensive.
- Error cases must be handled predictably.

- Assumptions must be documented or eliminated.
- Breaking changes must be rare and deliberate.

Well-designed packages tend to do *less* than application code, not more. Their power lies in restraint and clarity.

10.9.4 The Maintenance Commitment

Every published package creates an ongoing maintenance obligation. Issues will be reported. Compatibility questions will arise. Platform changes will require updates.

This maintenance burden does not scale linearly with code size; small packages can generate disproportionate support overhead if they sit on critical paths or abstract volatile behavior.

Responsible teams account for this cost upfront. Publishing a package without a plan for maintenance is effectively transferring risk to future maintainers—often without their consent.

10.9.5 When Not to Create a Package

Equally important is knowing when *not* to extract.

Extraction is usually a mistake when

- The code is tightly coupled to a specific application
- The abstraction boundary is unclear
- Requirements are still in flux
- Maintenance resources are limited

In such cases, duplication may be cheaper than premature generalization.

10.9.6 Pro Tip: Packages Are Products

Treat every package as a small product with users, expectations, and lifecycle costs. If you are not prepared to support it, document it, and evolve it responsibly, it should remain application code. Extraction is a commitment, not a cleanup step.

10.10 Anatomy of a Modern React Native Package

Creating a reusable React Native package today carries expectations that did not exist when the ecosystem was younger. Early libraries often succeeded with minimal documentation, loosely defined APIs, and limited guarantees about long-term maintenance. In a modern ecosystem shaped by large teams, long-lived code bases, and frequent platform evolution, those standards are no longer sufficient.

A React Native package is not simply shared code. It is a contract between the author and an unknown set of consumers, each operating under different constraints, timelines, and expectations. Understanding the anatomy of a modern package therefore requires thinking beyond implementation details and focusing on design discipline.

10.10.1 Packages As Contracts, Not Utilities

Application code is written for a known audience. Its assumptions, shortcuts, and implicit conventions are shaped by shared team context. Packages, by contrast, must assume *no shared context*. Every assumption must be explicit, every constraint intentional.

This shift fundamentally changes how code must be designed. A package API should communicate not only *what it does*, but *what it guarantees* and *what it refuses to do*. Ambiguity that is acceptable in application code becomes a liability when externalized.

As a result, successful packages tend to be smaller and more conservative than application modules. Their power comes not from flexibility, but from predictability.

10.10.2 TypeScript As an Architectural Boundary

In modern React Native development, TypeScript is no longer merely a developer convenience. For packages, it functions as an architectural boundary.

Types encode intent. They define legal inputs, valid states, and expected outputs in a way that documentation alone cannot. A well-typed package makes misuse difficult and correct usage obvious, even to developers encountering it for the first time.

From a maintenance perspective, strong typing also reduces future risk. When APIs evolve, types provide immediate feedback to consumers, enabling safer upgrades and clearer migration paths. In this sense, TypeScript is not an implementation choice—it is part of the package's public interface.

10.10.3 Scope Discipline and Responsibility Containment

One of the most reliable predictors of a package's longevity is how narrowly it defines its responsibility. Packages that attempt to solve multiple loosely related problems tend to accumulate configuration options, edge cases, and conditional behavior. Over time, this complexity becomes difficult to reason about or evolve safely.

By contrast, packages that define a single, coherent responsibility are easier to document, easier to test, and easier to replace. They invite composition rather than dependency.

This discipline often requires resisting the temptation to generalize prematurely. What appears to be reuse potential inside one application may, when abstracted, turn out to be context-dependent or unstable. Modern package design favors restraint over ambition.

10.10.4 Platform Awareness Without Platform Leakage

React Native packages frequently need to interact with native platforms. The challenge is not avoiding platform-specific behavior, but managing it responsibly.

A well-designed package acknowledges platform differences explicitly and exposes them deliberately when they matter. At the same time, it avoids leaking incidental platform complexity into the consumer's code. Consumers should not need to understand native internals unless they are making an explicit choice to do so.

This balance preserves both simplicity and control. It allows packages to remain useful across platforms without pretending that platform differences do not exist.

10.10.5 Designing for Change, Not Permanence

React Native itself continues to evolve, and packages must evolve alongside it. Packages that assume stability in internal framework behavior tend to age poorly. Those that isolate assumptions, minimize reliance on unstable internals, and adapt incrementally tend to survive architectural shifts with less disruption.

From a design perspective, this means favoring explicit integration points, avoiding undocumented behavior, and treating compatibility as an ongoing responsibility rather than a one-time achievement.

The goal is not to prevent change, but to make change survivable.

10.10.6 Documentation As Part of the Product

In reusable packages, documentation is not supplementary; it is part of the public API. It sets expectations, defines constraints, and establishes trust.

Clear documentation explains not only how to use a package, but when *not* to use it. It surfaces trade-offs, limitations, and intended scope. Over time, this clarity reduces support burden and discourages misuse.

Packages with poor documentation often fail not because they are technically flawed, but because consumers cannot form accurate mental models of their behavior.

10.10.7 Versioning As Communication

Version numbers are not merely administrative details; they are signals. Predictable versioning communicates stability, caution, and respect for consumers' time.

Breaking changes are inevitable, but in a healthy package, they are rare, well-justified, and clearly documented. Consumers should never be surprised by the cost of upgrading a dependency.

From an ecosystem perspective, disciplined versioning is one of the strongest trust-building mechanisms a package author has.

10.10.8 Note: Package Design Is Social Design

A package is a conversation with future developers you will never meet. Clear boundaries, conservative scope, strong typing, and honest documentation are ways of being respectful in that conversation. Packages that are easy to understand, easy to upgrade, and easy to replace are the ones that endure.

10.11 Staying Current in a Fast-Moving Ecosystem

The React Native ecosystem evolves continuously. New libraries emerge, architectural changes are introduced, platform policies shift, and previously popular tools are deprecated. For many developers, this constant motion creates pressure to keep up with everything—a goal that is neither realistic nor productive.

Staying current does not mean tracking every new release or adopting every new tool. It means developing the ability to distinguish *signal* from *noise* and responding to meaningful change deliberately rather than reactively.

10.11.1 The Cost of Chasing Novelty

One of the most common failure modes in fast-moving ecosystems is novelty-driven adoption. New tools are introduced with compelling narratives, polished demos, and early enthusiasm. In the short term, this can feel energizing. Over time, it often leads to fragmentation, inconsistent patterns, and upgrade fatigue.

Professional teams recognize that novelty carries cost. Every new dependency introduces learning overhead, integration risk, and future maintenance responsibility. Without discipline, the pursuit of newness becomes a form of technical debt.

The goal, therefore, is not to avoid change, but to approach it with intention.

10.11.2 Reliable Signals in the React Native Ecosystem

Not all information sources are equally valuable. Over time, experienced developers learn to prioritize signals that reflect structural change rather than surface-level excitement.

Strong signals tend to include

- Official release notes and migration guides
- Deprecation warnings and policy updates
- Architectural discussions that persist across versions
- Changes that affect core APIs or platform constraints

These signals indicate shifts that will eventually affect most applications, regardless of which libraries are used.

10.11.3 Weak Signals and Ecosystem Noise

By contrast, some sources provide limited long-term value. Blog posts focused on short-term productivity gains, isolated benchmarks, or narrowly scoped comparisons often fail to generalize beyond specific contexts.

Social amplification can also distort perception. Tools that generate excitement may appear more important than they are, while quieter but more foundational changes go unnoticed.

Learning to discount this noise is an essential ecosystem skill.

10.11.4 Building a Sustainable Update Habit

Rather than attempting to monitor everything continuously, effective teams establish rhythms for ecosystem awareness.

Common strategies include

- Periodic review of framework and platform updates
- Scheduled dependency audits
- Designated ownership for ecosystem tracking
- Deliberate adoption windows rather than continuous churn

These practices reduce cognitive load while ensuring that important changes are addressed in a timely manner.

10.11.5 Adapting Without Overreacting

Not every change requires immediate action. In many cases, the correct response is observation rather than adoption. Letting tools mature, ecosystems stabilize, and patterns emerge often leads to better decisions.

At the same time, ignoring meaningful change entirely can lead to painful catch-up work later. The balance lies in responding to *structural shifts* while remaining cautious about transient trends.

10.11.6 Note: Optimize for Awareness, Not Urgency

Staying current is about awareness, not speed. You do not need to adopt every new tool to remain effective. You need to understand which changes matter and why. In long-lived code bases, restraint is often the most valuable skill.

10.12 Popular React Native Packages (March 2026 Snapshot)

The React Native ecosystem evolves continuously, and any list of "popular" packages reflects a moment in time rather than a permanent recommendation. This section provides a **representative snapshot of widely used packages as of January 2026**, grouped by responsibility. The goal is orientation, not endorsement.

Readers should interpret this list as a grounding reference and evaluate any package using the principles discussed earlier in this chapter—particularly those in the "Evaluating Library Quality and Long-Term Risk" section.

10.12.1 Navigation and Application Structure

These libraries define screen hierarchy, routing, and navigation flow. They are among the most structurally significant dependencies in a React Native application.

- **@react-navigation/native**
- **@react-navigation/stack**
- **@react-navigation/bottom-tabs**
- **expo-router**

10.12.2 State Management and Server State

Used to manage shared client state, asynchronous data, and side effects across the application.

- **Redux Toolkit**
- **Zustand**
- **Jotai**
- **TanStack Query**

10.12.3 Animations and Gestures

These libraries operate close to the JavaScript–native boundary and strongly influence perceived performance and responsiveness.

- **react-native-reanimated**
- **react-native-gesture-handler**
- **moti**

10.12.4 Device and Native Capability Access

Provide JavaScript abstractions over native device features and system APIs.

- **expo-camera**
- **expo-media-library**
- **react-native-device-info**
- **react-native-permissions**
- **react-native-mmkv**

10.12.5 Networking and Data Communication

Handle HTTP communication, request lifecycles, caching, and retries.

- **axios**
- **fetch**
- **Apollo Client**
- **TanStack Query** *(also used for server state)*

10.12.6 Storage and Persistence

Used for local, synchronous, or asynchronous data persistence.

- **@react-native-async-storage/async-storage**
- **react-native-mmkv**

10.12.7 Developer Tooling and Diagnostics

Primarily affect developer experience, debugging, and inspection rather than user-facing behavior.

- **Reactotron**
- **TypeScript**
- **ESLint**

10.13 Summary

- React Native operates as a **platform**, with libraries and services defining much of its production behavior.
- The ecosystem is **layered**: core runtime, in-app libraries, and external services evolve at different speeds.
- **Dependencies are architectural decisions** and must be evaluated in proportion to their long-term impact.
- Popularity is a weak signal; **maintenance health, architectural alignment, and stability** matter more.
- Expo offers **productive abstraction** when adopted deliberately and with clear boundaries.
- External services function as **runtime control planes** and should be integrated defensively.
- Feature flags, experimentation, and OTA updates demand **governance and lifecycle discipline**.
- Distribution pipelines are **core architectural concerns**, not mere release mechanics.
- Creating packages introduces **ongoing ownership, compatibility, and trust responsibilities**.
- Staying current means tracking **structural ecosystem change**, not chasing short-term novelty.

CHAPTER 11

Best Practices for Building Large Mobile Applications in React Native

Building a mobile application is easy. Building a mobile application that survives growth, scale, and continuous change is far more difficult. As React Native projects evolve from small prototypes into business-critical platforms, the challenges shift from simply making features work to designing systems that remain stable, maintainable, and performant over time. This chapter is written for that turning point—when architectural discipline becomes as important as development speed.

Building large-scale mobile applications with React Native requires more than knowledge of the framework. It demands thoughtful architecture, consistent coding practices, and delivery processes that can scale across teams and years of product evolution. This chapter brings together practical best practices, proven patterns, and real-world checklists to help you design, build, ship, and maintain large React Native applications with confidence and clarity.

This content is intended for mid-to-senior mobile engineers, React Native developers, technical leads, and software architects who are responsible for complex, long-living code bases. Whether you are shaping architectural decisions, leading teams, or stabilizing an existing product, the guidance in this chapter focuses on enabling informed choices rather than prescribing rigid rules.

A. Nalwaya and A. Paul, *React Native for Mobile Development*, https://doi.org/10.1007/979-8-8688-2977-2_11

It is widely acknowledged in software engineering that an application's success is not determined only by functional reliability, but also by the quality of its user experience.

In the sections that follow, we will explore architecture and boundaries, coding discipline, performance optimization, release strategies, and production reliability. These practices are not about writing more code—they are about writing code that lasts. Whether you are building the next phase of a growing product or modernizing a mature application, this chapter aims to help you move beyond screens and features and begin thinking like a mobile architect.

In this chapter, we will first understand the key challenges involved in building and maintaining large React Native applications, including architectural complexity, team scalability, performance risks, and long-term maintainability.

11.1 Understanding the Challenges of Large React Native Applications

React Native enables teams to move fast—especially in the early stages of a product. A small team can ship features quickly with minimal setup, shared state, and loosely structured code. However, as the application grows, these same patterns often become the source of instability, performance issues, and team friction.

This section explains why scaling React Native applications requires a deliberate shift in mindset, architecture, and engineering discipline.

In small applications, it is common to

- Keep business logic inside components
- Share state globally for convenience
- Define navigation flows inline
- Reuse components without strict boundaries

These shortcuts reduce initial development effort. However, as features multiply and teams grow, the application's complexity increases faster than the team's ability to reason about it.

At scale, the problem is no longer writing code—it is **understanding the impact of change**.

Example: Business Logic Inside Components

```
function CheckoutScreen() {
  const [total, setTotal] = useState(0);

  useEffect(() => {
    fetchCart().then(cart => {
      setTotal(cart.items.reduce((sum, item) => sum + item.price, 0));
    });
  }, []);

  return <Text>Total: {total}</Text>;
}
```

This works well in a small app. In a large application:

- The calculation logic cannot be reused
- Testing becomes difficult
- Any change to pricing rules requires UI changes

Over time, such patterns lead to tightly coupled systems that resist change.

If a piece of logic would still exist without a screen, it does not belong inside a component.

This was just a small example, but if we multiply the code to 1000 files, as applications grow, developers often experience

- Slower feature delivery
- Slower Metro bundler startup times
- Longer Android and iOS build cycles
- Frequent cache invalidation issues

The result is a broken feedback loop—developers wait longer to see the impact of their changes, leading to fewer iterations and reduced code quality.

In this chapter, we will focus on some of these practices.

11.2 Building Large-Scale Application

Based on these challenges, this chapter explores practical strategies to address them through four core pillars. These pillars are not isolated topics, but deeply connected disciplines that together define the foundation of scalable mobile systems. This chapter will introduce you to these practices, explain their importance, and provide guidance on how to apply them. However, true mastery will only come through continuous practice, experimentation, and reflection in real projects.

The goal of this chapter is to make you aware of the right practices so you can move confidently from one topic to another, building a complete understanding over time. These pillars represent the core disciplines of large-scale React Native development, and throughout this chapter, we will explore the concepts, patterns, and decisions that shape successful long-living mobile applications.

- **Defining Clear Architecture and Application Boundaries**: Establishing structure, ownership, and separation of concerns to support long-term scalability
- **Coding Practices and Maintainability at Scale**: Applying disciplined coding standards, reuse strategies, and quality tooling to keep large code bases clean and evolvable
- **Performance Optimization at Scale**: Designing and measuring performance across rendering, networking, images, and offline scenarios
- **Build, Release, and Monitoring in Production**: Automating delivery, enabling safe releases, and maintaining visibility into real-world application behavior

11.2.1 Defining Clear Architecture and Application Boundaries

Large React Native applications do not fail because of missing features—they fail because of unclear architecture. As the team grows, features multiply, and timelines shrink, a poorly defined structure becomes the biggest bottleneck for speed, quality, and stability.

This section explains how to design **clear architectural boundaries** that allow your React Native application to scale across teams, brands, and years of evolution.

Without boundaries

- Business logic leaks into UI components
- API calls are duplicated across screens
- State becomes untraceable
- Bugs become expensive to fix
- New developers take weeks to onboard

With clear boundaries

- Teams can work independently
- Code becomes predictable
- Refactoring becomes safe
- Performance tuning becomes easier
- Long-term maintenance becomes sustainable

Architecture is not about complexity—it is about **clarity**.

We will discuss a few of the points that help us to keep code simple even if the code base increases or the number of team members increases.

Feature-Based vs. Layer-Based Architecture

When a React Native application is small, folder structure feels like a minor decision. Screens go into a `screens` folder, services into services, components into components, and everything seems manageable. However, as the application grows—with multiple teams, dozens of features, and continuous releases—this simple structure slowly becomes a source of confusion, duplication, and coupling. What once felt organized now makes it difficult to understand where a feature truly lives, how its logic flows, and who owns it. This is where architectural structure stops being cosmetic and starts becoming a strategic decision.

Two dominant approaches are used in large applications: layer-based architecture and feature-based architecture. The layer-based approach organizes code by technical responsibility, while the feature-based approach organizes code by business capability. Neither is universally "right" or "wrong"—but choosing the wrong one for a large React Native application can significantly slow development, increase defects, and make refactoring risky. Understanding when and why to use each approach is a foundational step toward building a scalable mobile architecture.

Table 11-1. *Comparison of Layer-Based Architecture vs. Feature-Based Architecture*

Aspect	Layer-Based Architecture	Feature-Based Architecture
Folder Structure	`/components/screens/services/store/utils`	`/features/checkout/features/profile/features/search`
Organization Principle	By technical role	By business feature
Initial Learning Curve	Easy to understand	Requires clear standards
Feature Ownership	Scattered across folders	Fully contained in one folder
Scalability	Weak for large apps	Strong for large apps
Refactoring	Difficult and risky	Easier and safer
Team Collaboration	Ownership becomes unclear	Supports multi-team ownership
Isolation	Low	High
Best Use Case	Small or medium applications	Large, long-term applications
Main Limitation	Breaks when app grows beyond 20–30 screens	Needs strong discipline and conventions

When to Choose Which

Scenario	Recommended
Small MVP	Layer-based
Single team app	Layer-based
Multi-team app	Feature-based
Multi-country/brand	Feature-based
Long-term product	Feature-based

For large React Native applications, feature-based architecture is almost always the better choice.

Separation Between Presentation and Business Logic

In many React Native projects, user interface components slowly become the place where everything happens—rendering, calculations, validations, API calls, and decision-making logic. At first, this feels efficient because everything related to a screen lives in one file. But as features grow and requirements change, these components become harder to read, harder to test, and harder to trust. A small UI change suddenly risks breaking business behavior, and understanding the true rules of the application requires navigating through JSX instead of clear logic.

Separating presentation from business logic is not about adding extra files—it is about protecting the future of the application. The presentation layer should focus only on how data looks and how users interact with it, while the business layer should define what the application does and why it behaves in a certain way. This separation creates clarity, improves testability, enables reuse across platforms, and allows teams to evolve the UI without rewriting core business rules. In large React Native applications, this boundary is not optional—it is essential for long-term stability.

A common mistake is writing logic directly inside React components:

```
const CheckoutScreen = () => {
  const total = cart.reduce(...)
  const discount = total > 500 ? 50 : 0
  const final = total - discount
}
```

This creates

- Hard-to-test logic
- Poor reusability
- UI tightly coupled to rules

You can refactor to this which is a better approach:

```
export function calculateFinalAmount(cart) {
  const total = 500
  const discount = 50
```

```
  return total - discount
}
const CheckoutScreen = () => {
  const final = calculateFinalAmount(cart)
}
```

These are the benefits:

- Business rules are independent.
- UI becomes simple and clean.
- Logic can be reused in the back end or tests.
- Easier debugging.

Monorepo vs. Polyrepo for Large Teams

As React Native applications evolve into full ecosystems—including mobile apps, shared libraries, design systems, back-end SDKs, and tooling—repository structure becomes a strategic decision rather than a technical preference. What once was a single mobile repository now expands into multiple moving parts maintained by different teams. Without a clear repository strategy, dependency conflicts, version mismatches, and broken integrations quickly become everyday problems that slow down development and increase operational risk.

Monorepo and polyrepo are two fundamentally different approaches to organizing this ecosystem. A monorepo keeps all related projects in a single repository with strong internal boundaries, while a polyrepo distributes them across multiple independent repositories. Each model offers unique advantages and trade-offs in terms of ownership, release management, tooling, and collaboration. For large React Native teams, choosing between monorepo and polyrepo is less about convenience and more about how the organization wants to scale its engineering culture.

Aspect	Monorepo	Polyrepo
Structure	Single repository for all projects	Separate repository per project
Code Sharing	Very easy and direct	Requires package publishing
Release Style	Coordinated releases	Independent releases
CI/CD	Complex pipelines	Simpler pipelines
Risk	Requires tooling discipline	Version mismatch risk

For large React Native ecosystems: Monorepo with strong boundaries is usually the best balance.

Use tools like

- Nx
- Turborepo
- pnpm
- Yarn workspaces

Defining Application Layers

As a React Native application grows, the most common source of architectural decay is not missing features or poor performance—it is blurred responsibility. When UI components start handling data transformation, business rules, network calls, and formatting logic all at once, the application loses its internal structure. Developers may still be able to ship features, but understanding the flow of data and behavior becomes increasingly difficult, especially for new team members. Over time, this lack of clarity turns the code base into a collection of tightly coupled files rather than a well-designed system.

Defining clear application layers restores order to this complexity. Each layer exists for a specific purpose and communicates with others through well-defined boundaries. The UI layer focuses on presentation and interaction, the domain layer defines business behavior, the data layer manages communication with external systems, and shared utilities provide common supporting functions. When these layers are properly defined and respected, the application becomes easier to reason about, safer to modify, and far more resilient to long-term change—which is exactly what large React Native products demand.

1. UI Layer

Responsibilities:

- Rendering components
- Handling user interaction
- Calling domain functions

Should NOT contain

- Business rules
- API logic

Example

```
<CheckoutSummary total={total} onPay={payNow} />
```

2. Business/Domain Layer

Responsibilities:

- Business rules
- Calculations
- Validation
- Feature logic

Example

```
export function isEligibleForFreeDelivery(order) {
  return order.amount > 500
}
```

3. API/Data Layer

Responsibilities:

- Network communication
- Response transformation
- Error mapping

Example

```
export const fetchOrders = () =>
  apiClient.get('/orders')
```

4. Shared Utilities Layer

Responsibilities:

- Formatting
- Date helpers
- Validators
- Logging utilities

Example

```
formatCurrency(amount)
```

Layer Rule

A well-architected React Native application should enforce clear and predictable dependency boundaries between layers. One of the most important architectural principles is that dependencies must flow in a single direction.

The dependency direction is

UI → Domain → Data → Network

This sequence represents how layers are allowed to depend on one another.

- The UI layer may depend on the Domain layer.
- The Domain layer may depend on the Data layer.
- The Data layer may depend on the Network layer.

However, the reverse must never happen.

For example:

- The Network layer should never know about UI components.
- The Data layer should not depend on presentation logic.
- The Domain layer should remain independent of framework-specific implementation details.

This rule is often misunderstood as a data flow rule. In reality, it defines **dependency direction**, not runtime data movement.

Data itself can move in both directions:

- User actions and requests typically move downward through the layers.
- Responses, results, and processed data move upward back to the UI.

For example, when a user opens an order history screen:

- The UI layer requests order data from the Domain layer.
- The Domain layer asks the Data layer for the required information.
- The Data layer retrieves data from the Network layer or local storage.
- The result travels back upward until the UI renders the information.

Although data moves both ways, the dependencies remain unidirectional.

Maintaining this separation provides several long-term benefits:

- Reduced coupling between modules
- Better testability
- Easier scalability
- Improved maintainability
- Independent evolution of layers
- Safer refactoring with fewer regressions

Applications that violate dependency direction often become difficult to maintain because infrastructure details leak into business logic or UI layers. Over time, this creates tight coupling and architectural instability.

By enforcing one-way dependency rules, teams can build React Native applications that remain modular, scalable, and easier to evolve as product complexity grows.

Designing a Centralized API Layer

In many React Native applications, network calls begin as small, scattered Axios or fetch requests inside individual screens and hooks. At first, this approach feels fast and flexible. But as the application grows, authentication handling, headers, error mapping, retries, and logging start getting duplicated across multiple places. Small inconsistencies appear, bugs become harder to trace, and any change in API behavior requires touching dozens of files. What was once simple communication slowly becomes one of the most fragile parts of the system.

A centralized API layer transforms network communication into a controlled and predictable system. Instead of letting every feature decide how to talk to the back end, the application defines a single, consistent gateway responsible for request configuration, authentication, error handling, retries, and response transformation. This not only reduces duplication but also creates a foundation for security, observability, and long-term maintainability. In large React Native applications, a centralized API layer is not an optimization—it is a requirement for stability and scale.

This is how typical API Client Setup code looks like:

```
const apiClient = axios.create({
  baseURL: ENV.API_URL,
  timeout: 10000,
})
```

This is how you will create an interceptor and put authentication in it.

```
apiClient.interceptors.request.use(config => {
  config.headers.Authorization = `Bearer ${token}`
  return config
})
```

You can create an interceptor for the following scenarios:

- Centralized auth handling
- Logging
- Error transformation
- Retry logic
- Token expiration handling

We have one more example for handling errors:

```
apiClient.interceptors.response.use(
  response => response,
  error => {
```

```
    if (error.status === 401) logout()
    return Promise.reject(error)
  }
)
```

Error Handling, Retry, and Logging

In small applications, errors are often treated as isolated events—a failed API call, a missing field, or a temporary network issue. Developers handle them locally with simple alerts or console logs and move on. However, in large React Native applications, errors are no longer isolated. They are signals of deeper system behavior, network reliability, user environment, and business impact. Without a consistent strategy for handling, retrying, and logging errors, teams lose visibility into what is really happening in production and are forced to debug problems blindly.

A structured approach to error handling, retry mechanisms, and logging transforms failures into actionable insights. Instead of reacting to errors, the system learns from them. Errors are categorized, retries are applied intelligently, and logs capture meaningful context rather than random messages. This consistency allows teams to detect patterns, prevent recurring issues, and improve user experience over time. In large-scale React Native systems, reliability is not achieved by avoiding errors—it is achieved by designing for them.

A good error strategy answers three questions:

1. What went wrong?
2. Can we retry safely?
3. How do we learn from it?

Instead of passing raw Axios or JavaScript errors to UI, map them into a controlled structure.

```
export function mapApiError(error) {
  return {
    code: error.response?.status || "UNKNOWN",
    message: "Something went wrong",
    retryable: error.code === "ECONNABORTED"
  }
}
```

Some failures are temporary and should be retried automatically.

```
async function retry(fn, retries = 3) {
  try {
    return await fn()
  } catch (e) {
    if (retries === 0) throw e
    return retry(fn, retries - 1)
  }
}
```

Design System and Theming Boundaries

In large React Native applications, visual inconsistency is rarely a design problem—it is usually an architectural one. When colors, spacing, typography, and component styles are defined directly inside features, the UI slowly fragments across screens and teams. A well-defined design system with clear theming boundaries establishes a single source of truth for visual language while allowing flexibility for branding, dark mode, and regional variations. By separating design tokens and UI primitives from feature logic, teams can evolve the product's look and feel without rewriting business code, ensuring both consistency and long-term scalability.

UI must not depend on feature logic. A design system provides

- Buttons
- Typography
- Colors
- Spacing
- And many more atoms

Features consume

```
<Button variant="primary" />
```

Themes

```
theme.colors.primary
theme.spacing.md
```

This enables multi-brand apps, dark/light modes, and consistency in UI.

Design systems are a vast and evolving discipline in their own right, extending far beyond components into design tokens, accessibility, interaction patterns, and governance models. Concepts such as Atomic Design—including atoms, molecules, organisms, templates, and pages—provide powerful mental models for building scalable and consistent UI systems. While this chapter introduces the architectural importance of design system boundaries, readers are strongly encouraged to explore these concepts in greater depth to fully realize their potential.

Enforcing Boundaries

Defining architectural boundaries is only the first step; enforcing them is what truly protects a large React Native application from gradual decay. Without enforcement, even the best-designed architecture slowly erodes under delivery pressure, shortcuts, and team turnover. UI components begin to import API clients directly, business logic leaks into screens, and shared utilities become dumping grounds for unrelated code. Over time, the system may still function, but its structure becomes unclear, fragile, and resistant to change.

Effective boundary enforcement combines tooling, process, and culture. Linting rules, module constraints, and automated checks prevent invalid dependencies at build time, while code review standards reinforce architectural intent at the human level. Just as importantly, teams must treat boundaries as product assets, not optional guidelines. When boundaries are consistently respected, the architecture remains stable, predictable, and scalable—enabling large React Native applications to grow without sacrificing clarity or velocity.

Architecture is useless without enforcement.

Use

- ESLint rules
- Module boundaries
- Folder ownership
- Code review checklists

Example Rule

UI cannot import from the API layer directly.

Real-World Example Structure

Understanding architecture becomes easier when it is seen in practice. The following folder structure represents a real-world, production-ready approach for organizing a large React Native application using feature-based boundaries and shared core layers:

```
/features
  /checkout
    CheckoutScreen.tsx
    checkoutDomain.ts
    checkoutService.ts

/core
  /api
  /config
  /logger

/design-system
  /components
  /themes
```

In this structure, each feature owns its complete flow—from UI to business logic to service interaction—making features easy to understand, test, and evolve independently. The core layer provides shared infrastructure such as API handling, configuration, and logging, while the design system ensures consistent visual language across the entire application.

This structure offers several key advantages. It is scalable, because new features can be added without affecting existing ones. It is readable, because developers can quickly locate where logic belongs. And it supports multi-team development, because ownership is clearly defined at the feature level while shared responsibilities remain centralized.

Good structure does not just organize code—it organizes thinking.

11.3 Coding Practices and Maintainability at Scale

In large React Native applications, maintainability is not a by-product of good developers—it is the result of disciplined coding practices. As teams grow and features evolve, even small inconsistencies in naming, typing, or structure can multiply into significant technical debt. Code that is easy to write but hard to understand becomes a long-term liability. Therefore, coding practices must prioritize clarity, predictability, and long-term evolution over short-term convenience.

Maintainability is about enabling future developers—including your future self—to change the system safely. This requires strong conventions, strict typing, reusable patterns, and automated quality enforcement. The goal is not perfection, but consistency at scale.

11.3.1 Code Organization and Naming

A large code base must read like a well-written book, not like a collection of random notes. Folder structure and naming conventions act as the first layer of documentation.

Good naming answers three questions immediately:

- What is this?
- Why does it exist?
- Where does it belong?

Area	Poor Practice	Recommended Practice	Reason
File Naming	`data.ts`, `utils.ts`	`checkoutDomain.ts`, `formatCurrency.ts`	Names should describe responsibility clearly
Folder Structure	`/screens`, `/services`, `/utils`	`/features/checkout/`	Feature ownership and isolation
Component Naming	`comp.tsx`, `index.tsx`	`CheckoutSummary.tsx`	Improves readability and searchability
Hook Naming	`useData.ts`	`useCheckoutData.ts`	Indicates feature context
Service Naming	`api.ts`	`orderService.ts`	Clear domain responsibility

(continued)

Area	Poor Practice	Recommended Practice	Reason
Type Naming	`IOrder`, `DataType`	`Order`, `CheckoutPayload`	Meaningful domain language
Constant Naming	`VAL1`, `CONST_A`	`MAX_CART_ITEMS`	Self-explanatory intent
Function Naming	`handle()`	`submitOrder()`	Action-oriented clarity

11.3.2 TypeScript

JavaScript offers flexibility and speed, but as code bases grow, that flexibility often turns into unpredictability. As code bases grow, functions start receiving unexpected data shapes, refactors introduce silent breakages, and understanding how data flows across features becomes increasingly difficult. Without explicit contracts, developers must rely on assumptions and runtime testing to validate behavior. This slows down development, increases production bugs, and makes onboarding new team members significantly harder.

TypeScript transforms JavaScript into a self-documented, predictable, and safer system. By enforcing types at compile time, it exposes errors before the application ever runs, turning many production issues into simple development-time fixes. More importantly, TypeScript acts as a shared language between developers, clearly defining how data, APIs, and business rules are expected to behave. In large React Native applications, TypeScript is not just a tooling choice—it is a foundation for scalability, confidence, and long-term maintainability.

TypeScript is not just a safety net—it is a communication tool between developers.

11.3.3 Reusability and DRY Principles

In large React Native applications, duplicated logic is one of the fastest ways to increase bugs, inconsistency, and maintenance cost. The principles of Reusability and DRY (Don't Repeat Yourself) encourage developers to extract common behavior into shared hooks, utilities, and services instead of rewriting similar logic across features. This not only reduces code size, but also ensures that improvements and fixes automatically benefit every part of the application. More importantly, reusable abstractions create a common language within the code base, making the system easier to understand, evolve, and scale over time.

We will now explain a few points that will help us to achieve reusability and the DRY principle:

- **Extract Business Logic into Custom Hooks**: Move logic out of components.

  ```
  export function useCheckout() {
    const [loading, setLoading] = useState(false)
    return { loading }
  }
  const { loading } = useCheckout()
  ```

  Move repeated logic out of components.

  ```
  useCheckout()
  useAuth()
  usePagination()
  ```

- **Create a Dedicated Utility Layer**: Common formatting, validation, and transformation logic should live in utilities.

  ```
  export function formatCurrency(amount: number) {
    return `₹${amount.toFixed(2)}`
  }
  ```

  If the same logic appears twice, it belongs in a utility. Like `formatCurrency(), validateEmail(, parseDate().`

- **Build Shared Service Classes**: All API or storage access should go through services.

  ```
  export const OrderService = {
    fetchOrders() {
      return api.get("/orders")
    }
  }
  ```

- UI should never care how the service works internally.

```
OrderService.fetchOrders()
AuthService.login()
```

This avoids duplicate API logic across features.

11.3.4 Prefer Composition Over Duplication

Duplication often happens when two or more screens look or behave almost the same. Developers copy a component, rename it, and make small changes. Over time, these copies slowly diverge, and fixing a bug or updating a design requires changing multiple files. This increases risk, effort, and inconsistency. Composition avoids this problem by breaking common behavior into smaller reusable parts and assembling them where needed.

Instead of copying layout logic across screens, use the Layout component:

```
<Layout>
  <Header />
  <Content />
</Layout>
```

DRY is not achieved once—it is maintained over time by refactoring duplicates into shared abstractions.

11.3.5 Code Quality Tooling

In large React Native applications, maintaining code quality cannot rely solely on individual discipline or best intentions—it must be enforced through systematic automation. Code quality tooling such as ESLint, Prettier, Husky, and lint-staged serves as an architectural safety net that preserves consistency, readability, and reliability as teams and code bases scale. These tools identify common mistakes, enforce shared standards, and stop low-quality code from entering the repository. By shifting quality control from manual reviews to automated processes, teams reduce review fatigue, improve delivery speed, and ensure that every contribution aligns with a common engineering standard. In scalable systems, tooling is not merely supportive—it is a foundational part of the architecture.

ESLint, Biome, and Prettier

- Enforce consistent coding conventions across the entire code base
- Detect React and TypeScript anti-patterns at an early stage
- Prevent unused variables, unsafe imports, and poor coding practices
- Maintain uniform formatting regardless of individual developer preferences
- Minimize formatting-related discussions during code reviews

Husky and lint-staged

- Automatically run quality checks before each commit
- Block commits that fail linting or formatting rules
- Validate only staged files to keep commit operations fast
- Prevent inconsistent or broken code from entering the repository
- Encourage immediate issue resolution rather than deferred fixes

"Maintainable code is not written for machines—it is written for humans who will change it."

11.4 Performance Optimization at Scale

Performance is not a feature—it is a continuous responsibility. In large React Native applications, performance issues rarely appear as single dramatic failures. Instead, they slowly accumulate as small inefficiencies across components, network calls, images, and state updates. Users may not always articulate these problems, but they feel them: slower screens, delayed interactions, and inconsistent behavior. At scale, even small performance regressions can impact retention, trust, and business outcomes.

Optimizing performance is not about premature micro-optimizations; it is about building awareness into architecture, components, and workflows. A performance-focused mindset treats every render, every network call, and every animation as a cost that must be justified. The goal is not only speed, but consistency across devices, regions, and network conditions.

11.4.1 Avoiding Prop Drilling and Unnecessary Re-renders

Prop drilling creates deeply nested component trees where small changes trigger wide re-render chains. This increases rendering cost and makes components harder to maintain.

Better strategies include

- Context for scoped shared state
- Feature-level state containers
- Component composition instead of long prop chains

Reducing re-renders requires awareness of reference stability and dependency control. Components should only re-render when the data they truly depend on changes.

Optimizing Component Rendering and Memoization

React provides powerful tools to control rendering behavior:

- `React.memo` for pure components
- `useCallback` for stable function references
- `useMemo` for expensive calculations

These should be applied intentionally, not blindly. Memoization is effective when

- Components are rendered frequently
- Props change rarely
- Calculations are expensive

Overusing memoization without understanding can add complexity without real benefit. Performance optimization is about targeted precision, not blanket rules.

11.5 Minimizing JavaScript Costs

With modern React Native architecture and Hermes, significantly improves responsiveness.

11.5.1 Measuring and Profiling Performance

Performance optimization without measurement is guesswork. In large React Native applications, assumptions about what is slow are often wrong. A screen that looks simple may hide expensive re-renders, while a complex flow may perform better than expected. For this reason, performance must always be guided by real data rather than intuition. Measuring and profiling allow teams to understand where time, memory, and resources are actually being consumed.

Profiling should be part of regular development, not only a reaction to user complaints. By continuously observing performance behavior, teams can prevent regressions, validate optimizations, and make informed architectural decisions.

Hermes Performance Tools: Hermes is a JavaScript engine optimized for React Native, designed to improve runtime efficiency and startup performance.

Hermes enables

- Faster application startup times
- Reduced memory footprint
- More efficient JavaScript execution
- Advanced profiling and debugging capabilities

Profiling with Hermes allows teams to detect slow scripts, oversized bundles, and inefficient logic early in the development cycle. This early visibility prevents small inefficiencies from growing into large production problems and helps maintain consistent performance across devices.

Hermes transform performance optimization from reactive troubleshooting into proactive engineering. They give teams the ability to measure, understand, and continuously improve application behavior at scale.

Offline-First Strategies

Large mobile applications cannot assume stable or fast network connectivity. Users move between locations, networks fluctuate, and back-end services may become temporarily unavailable. Designing only for perfect connectivity creates fragile experiences that break when users need reliability the most. An offline-first strategy accepts unreliable networks as the normal operating condition rather than an exception.

An offline-first application prioritizes continuity of experience. Instead of failing when the network is unavailable, it adapts gracefully and keeps the user productive with the best available data.

Caching Policies: Effective caching is the foundation of offline-first design.

Key principles include

- Cache critical data locally to enable basic functionality without network access
- Define clear expiration strategies to prevent serving stale or incorrect data
- Support background synchronization to refresh data when connectivity returns

Caching transforms the application from a network-dependent system into a resilient client.

Graceful Network Failure Handling: Offline-first design is not only about data—it is also about user experience.

Best practices include

- Showing meaningful fallback UI instead of generic error messages
- Allowing partial functionality when full connectivity is not available
- Retrying requests intelligently based on network conditions

Instead of blocking users, the application guides them through degraded but usable experiences.

Offline-first design ensures that users remain engaged and productive even under poor connectivity conditions. It reduces frustration, improves trust, and expands usability across diverse environments and regions.

11.6 Build, Release, and Monitoring in Production

Building a React Native application is only half the journey. The real complexity begins when the application enters production, where real users, real devices, and real network conditions expose every weakness in engineering discipline. At scale, success is no longer defined by how fast features are built, but by how safely they are released, how quickly issues are detected, and how confidently teams can respond to failures. This is why build, release, and monitoring must be treated as first-class architectural concerns, not operational afterthoughts.

A production-ready React Native system must support continuous delivery, safe experimentation, rapid rollback, and deep visibility into application behavior. The following practices form the foundation of reliable large-scale mobile delivery.

11.6.1 Automating Builds with CI/CD

Manual builds do not scale. They are slow, error-prone, and dependent on individual developers. Continuous Integration and Continuous Delivery (CI/CD) pipelines transform builds into predictable, repeatable, and auditable processes.

With CI/CD

- Every code change is automatically built
- Tests are executed consistently
- Artifacts are generated in a controlled environment
- Release candidates are traceable

CI pipelines ensure that broken code is detected early, while CD pipelines ensure that approved builds can be promoted safely across environments such as QA, staging, and production. This removes human dependency from the release process and replaces it with reliable automation.

More importantly, CI/CD establishes confidence. Teams no longer fear releases because every build follows the same proven path. In large React Native organizations, CI/CD is not a productivity tool—it is a stability requirement.

11.6.2 Environment-Based Configuration

As React Native applications move across development, QA, staging, and production environments, hard-coded values quickly become a source of risk and confusion. API endpoints, feature flags, third-party keys, and behavioral toggles must change without requiring code rewrites or unsafe manual edits. Environment-based configuration introduces a clean separation between application logic and deployment context, allowing the same code base to behave differently based on where and how it is running. This approach not only reduces deployment errors, but also enables safer testing, faster releases, and better control over feature exposure in large-scale mobile applications.

Never hard-code values.

```
DEV_API_URL
QA_API_URL
PROD_API_URL
```

Use:

```
ENV.API_URL
ENV.FEATURE_FLAG_X
```

Benefits

- Safe deployments
- Parallel environments
- Faster testing

11.6.3 OTA (Over-the-Air) Updates

OTA updates allow teams to deliver JavaScript and asset changes directly to users without going through app store review cycles. When used correctly, OTA updates dramatically reduce time to fix production issues and improve user experience.

However, OTA must be treated with architectural discipline:

- Only safe changes should be delivered OTA.
- Rollback capability must always exist.
- Version compatibility must be respected.
- Rollouts should be gradual.

OTA is not a shortcut for poor release planning—it is a safety mechanism for production reliability. In large React Native applications, OTA updates become a critical tool for responding to real-world issues while maintaining user trust.

Used responsibly, OTA transforms production from a rigid system into an adaptive one.

11.6.4 Monitoring and Observability

Without monitoring, production is a black box. Teams only learn about issues when users complain, ratings drop, or revenue is affected. Observability changes this by providing continuous insight into application health.

Monitoring should cover

- Crash reporting
- Performance metrics
- Network failures
- Navigation errors
- Business-critical flows

Observability is not only about detecting problems—it is about understanding behavior. Which screens are slow? Which APIs fail most often? Where do users abandon flows?

In large React Native systems, monitoring creates a feedback loop between real usage and engineering decisions. It allows teams to prioritize based on evidence, not assumptions.

A system that cannot be observed cannot be improved.

11.6.5 Feature Toggling and Controlled Rollouts

Feature toggles allow teams to decouple deployment from release. Code can be shipped to production while remaining inactive until explicitly enabled. This enables

- Gradual rollouts
- A/B testing
- Country or user-based activation
- Instant kill switches

Controlled rollouts reduce risk by limiting exposure. Instead of releasing a feature to 100% of users, teams can release to 1%, observe behavior, and then expand gradually. If issues appear, the feature can be disabled without a new build.

This approach turns releases from risky events into controlled experiments.

In large React Native products, feature toggling is not just about experimentation—it is about operational safety.

11.6.6 Production As a Living System

Build, release, and monitoring together transform production from a static destination into a living system. CI/CD provides stability, OTA provides agility, monitoring provides visibility, and feature toggles provide control.

When these elements work together

- Releases become routine, not stressful
- Failures become manageable, not catastrophic
- Innovation becomes safer, not riskier

11.7 Final Thoughts: Thinking Like a Mobile Architect

Building a mobile application is not just an act of engineering—it is an act of vision. Every line of code you write contributes to a system that will be touched by thousands or millions of users, shaped by countless decisions, and challenged by continuous change. Thinking like a mobile architect means recognizing that your work is not limited to features and fixes, but extends to shaping how a product grows, adapts, and survives over time.

A mobile architect chooses intention over impulse and structure over shortcuts. They design with empathy for future developers, respect for business realities, and responsibility for long-term quality. They understand that true craftsmanship lies not in how fast something is built, but in how well it continues to work when the original builders are no longer around.

This journey is not about mastering tools alone—it is about developing judgment. It is about learning when to simplify, when to abstract, and when to say no. It is about protecting the user experience, the team's velocity, and the product's future at the same time. When you begin to think in systems instead of screens, in outcomes instead of tasks, and in longevity instead of delivery, you step into the role of a true mobile architect.

Thank you for taking this journey through React Native architecture, practices, and scale. I hope this book helps you build with confidence, clarity, and courage. Good luck on your path—may your applications be stable, your releases smooth, and your architectural decisions proud ones.

Index

A. Nalwaya and A. Paul, *React Native for Mobile Development*, https://doi.org/10.1007/979-8-8688-2977-2

M

N

O

P, Q

R

U, V, W, X, Y, Z

www.ingramcontent.com/pod-product-compliance
Lightning Source LLC
LaVergne TN
LVHW080018210926
848481LV00011B/3055
* 9 7 9 8 8 6 8 8 2 9 7 6 5 *